ENGLISH FILM APPRECIATION

英语电影赏析

主　编　金国臣
副主编　武晓燕　王明利　赵　璞
编　者　赵浩宇　许元娜　惠莉君
主　审　张继华

清華大学出版社
北　京

内 容 简 介

本书所选取的12部电影涉及教育、家庭、人生励志、生活哲理等各个方面，旨在让学生通过欣赏英文电影了解西方的历史和文化。在每一单元，分别介绍了电影情节、相关的历史文化背景及经典台词，并附有影评，对电影进行精彩透彻的分析。每单元的习题题型多样，帮助学生综合训练听、说、读、写、译等各方面的能力。

图书在版编目（CIP）数据

英语电影赏析 / 金国臣主编. —北京：清华大学出版社，2016（2023.1重印）
ISBN 978-7-302-42307-2

Ⅰ. ①英… Ⅱ. ①金… Ⅲ. ①英语-语言读物②英语-电影影片-鉴赏-世界 Ⅳ. ①H319.4：J

中国版本图书馆CIP数据核字（2015）第287035号

责任编辑：钱屹芝
封面设计：平 原
责任校对：王凤芝
责任印制：朱雨萌
出版发行：清华大学出版社
网　　址：http:// www. tup. com. cn，http:// www. wqbook. com
地　　址：北京清华大学学研大厦A座　　**邮　　编：**100084
社 总 机：010-83470000　　**邮　　购：**010-62786544
投稿与读者服务：010-62776969, c-service@tup.tsinghua.edu.cn
质量反馈：010-62772015, zhiliang@tup.tsinghua.edu.cn
印 装 者：三河市铭诚印务有限公司
经　　销：全国新华书店
开　　本：185mm × 260mm（附光盘1张）　　**印　　张：**18　　**字　　数：**323千字
版　　次：2016年 7 月第 1 版　　**印　　次：**2023 年 1月第 9 次印刷
定　　价：65.00元

产品编号：063271-03

《英语电影赏析》编委会

主　编　金国臣

副主编　武晓燕　王明利　赵　璞

编　者　赵浩宇　许元娜　惠莉君

主　审　张继华

前 言

在21世纪，全球日益趋向全方位、多渠道、大规模的国际交流与合作，英语语言应用能力已成为时代发展对现代人的基本素质要求之一。随着我国经济的进一步发展，社会对大学毕业生的英语素质要求也在不断提高。为了应对这一变化趋势，教育部下发了《大学英语课程教学要求》，为我们在新形势下进行大学英语教学提供了重要的指导原则。目前，伴随着互联网和多媒体技术的高速发展，多媒体教学在全球逐步开展；有关多媒体环境下英语课堂教学模式的探索及研究在我国高校已经如火如荼地开展起来，并已显示出空前的活力。那么，如何在多媒体教学环境下的今天有效地提高大学生英语听、说能力以及跨文化交际能力已成为广大英语教师面临的一个重大课题。为了破解这一难题，经过努力与探索，我们推出了一种全新的、依托于多媒体课堂教学的英语电影赏析课程。在大学英语教学中增设的英语电影赏析课，旨在培养学生的语言能力，增强学生学习的兴趣，对其进行文化熏陶，提高其艺术鉴赏水平。

众所周知，电影诞生已有百余年的历史，在它的成长过程中，文学、戏剧、音乐、美术、摄影等艺术形式为其提供了丰富的营养，使其有力地影响着人们的精神生活，因此英语电影赏析课程作为一种直观、形象、生动的教学方式越来越受到师生们的青睐。实践表明，英语电影赏析课程的开设，不仅有利于提高英语课堂的综合效果，而且全方位地打破了传统的教学理念和教学思想，实现了教学互动、真实再现、资源丰富、信息处理便捷等优势下的课堂环境，也改变了教与学、师生之间的关系，促进自主性学习与研究性学习，有利于培养创新型人才。英文电影赏析作为大学英语教学的一种辅助手段，以其生动的语言、鲜活的画面为学生提供了轻松自然的英语学习环境。它不仅能激发学生的学习热情，丰富学生的英美文化知识，更能够促进学生英语听、说能力的提高。

基于此种考虑，我们编写了《英语电影赏析》这本书，充分运用当今最新的计算机网络技术及多媒体技术进行讲授，将单调、乏味的课堂知识形象地体现在声音、图像、影视、动画中，使得真正基于交流、讨论的这种全新的教学方法成为可能，极大地增强了学生的教学参与意识，学生的外语综合能力得到了进一步提高。

本书由12单元构成，共收录了12部经典电影。这12部影片涵盖教育、家庭、婚姻、人生励志、生活哲理等多个主题，能增长学生的见识，提高学生的文化素养。每单元由3部分组成：Part Ⅰ：Preview the movie；Part Ⅱ：View the movie；Part Ⅲ：Review the movie；本书由金国臣主编，武晓燕、王明利、赵璞、惠莉君、王剧、赵梓媛撰写，金国臣撰写了第3～5章；武晓燕撰写了第1～2章；王明利撰写了第6～8章；赵璞撰写了第9～10章；惠莉君撰写了第11章；王剧、赵梓媛撰写了第12章；周远航负责本书12部影片若干视频片段的截取、编辑及光盘刻录。本书由张继华教授审稿。由于我们水平有限，力量不足，书中一定有很多不足之处，敬请广大同仁多多指正。

编　者

2016年1月15日

Contents

Unit 1 Forrest Gump《阿甘正传》

I Preview the movie

1. Background

Directed by	Robert Zemeckis
Based on	Forrest Gump By Winston Groom
Stars	Tom Hanks Robin Wright Gary Sinise Mykelti Williamson Sally Field
Distributed by	Paramount Pictures
Box office	$677,945,399

2. Plot

Born in Greenbow, Alabama, Forrest Gump's IQ is only 75. His mother always tries to make him feel no different from anybody else. Jenny is a motherless girl, whose father is an alcoholic. Forrest and Jenny are best friends like peas and carrots.

Forrest gains a lot during his life. He runs very fast, so he enters the college, and later he joins the football team in the college. Years later, with his college degree, he is recruited in the army. In the army, he meets Bubba, another important friend in his life. Bubba is always talking about shrimps. During the Vietnam War, Forrest saves many lives of his fellow soldiers. But he loses his good friend, Bubba. One of the soldiers he has saved is Lieutenant Dan, who loses both of his legs. He believes that his destiny is dying on the battlefield rather than surviving the war. During the treatment in the hospital, Forrest finds that he is very good at playing table tennis. And later he is in the All-American Ping-pong Team. In 1971, with President Nixon, the Team visited China. Coming back from China, Forrest makes a lot of money from doing advertisement for a table tennis paddle brand. With the sum of money, he starts his shrimp business in honor of Bubba. Lieutenant Dan, as he has promised, comes to help Forrest as his first mate. Fortunately, their boat survives a severe hurricane, and they become millionaires.

Forrest always loves Jenny, just like what he says: "I am not a smart man, but I know what love is." Coming in and going out of Forrest's life many times, Jenny dreams of becoming a famous singer. One day, Forrest receives a letter from Jenny and is going to see her ... that's where the film starts ...

II View the movie

Clip 1 Forrest's childhood

Words and Expressions:

intend to	打算
brace	托架，支撑物

Task 1 **Watch the video clip and fill in the missing words.**

Mrs. Gump:

What are y'all **1**__________? Haven't you ever seen a little boy with **2**__________ on his legs before? Don't ever let anybody tell you that **3**__________, Forrest. If God **4**__________ everybody to be the same, he'd have given us all braces on our legs.

...

Mrs. Gump:

Remember what I told you, Forrest. **5**__________. Did you hear what I said, Forrest? You are the same as everybody else. You are no different.

Task 2 **Watch the video clip again and answer the questions.**

a) What do Forrest and his mama live on?

____

b) In the video clip, Mrs. Gump emphasizes that Forrest is no different from others. Do you think Forrest is the same as others? Why?

____

____

Clip 2 Jenny's escape from her father

Words and Expressions:

take a nap　　打盹儿

Task 1 **Mark T (True) or F (False) for the following statements according to the clip.**

a) _______ Jenny's father is a very loving man.

b) _______ Jenny and Forrest have the similar life experiences. Some social problems affect their lives.

Task 2 **Answer the questions from this video clip.**

a) Why does Jenny pray to be a bird?

____

b) What is the consequence of Jenny's praying to God?

____

Clip 3 Forrest's joining the army

Words and Expressions:

neat	整洁的
OCS	美国的军官预备学校
private	列兵（美国士兵中最低军衔）

Task 1 Mark T (True) or F (False) for the following statements according to the clip.

a) _______ Forrest adjusts to the military life very well.

b) _______ Bubba sets a new record for putting the weapons together.

c) _______ Bubba is always talking about crabs.

Task 2 Answer the questions from this video clip.

a) How does Drill Sergeant think of Forrest?

____

b) Do you know which country is the army in and which fight is the army going to indulge in?

____

____

Clip 4 The death of Mrs. Gump

Words and Expressions:

straighten out 使变直

destiny 命运

Task 1 Watch the video clip and fill in the missing words of the dialogue.

Forrest: **1**_________, Mama?

Mrs. Gump: **2**_________, Forrest. Come on in. Sit down over here.

Forrest: Why are you dying, Mama?

Mrs. Gump: **3**___________. **4**___________. Oh, now, don't you be afraid, sweetheart. **5**_________. It's something **6**_________. I didn't know it. But I was destined to be your mama. **7**_________.

Forrest: You did good, Mama.

Mrs. Gump: Well, I happened to believe **8**_________. **9**_________.

Forrest: What's my destiny, Mama?

Mrs. Gump: You're gonna have to **10**_________ for yourself. **11**_________, Forrest. You never know what you are going to get.

Forrest: Mama always had a way of explaining things so I could understand them.

Mrs. Gump: I will miss you, Forrest.

Forrest: She had got the cancer and died on a Tuesday. I bought her a new hat with **12**_________ on it.

Task 2 **Dub the voice of Forrest and Mrs. Gump while the video is played again without the sound.**

Task 3 **Discussion: Do you think everyone has his own destiny or we are all just floating around accidentally on breeze? What's your opinion to "destiny"?**

____

____

____

Clip 5 The meeting of Forrest and Jenny after many years

Task 1 **Answer the following questions according to the dialogue.**

a) What surprises Forrest in Jenny's house?

____

b) What's wrong with the gift that Forrest takes to Jenny?

____

c) What is Jenny's scrapbook for?

____

d) How does the kid get his name?

____

e) What is Forrest worried the most about his son?

____

Task 2 **Discussion: How do you feel when you see the father and son sit together watching TV?**

____

____

____

Clip 6

Task 1 **Take down what Forrest said in front of Jenny's tomb.**

____

____

____

III Review the movie

1. Cultural Notes

1) Ku Klux Klan

Ku Klux Klan is short for 3K Club, which was formed in 1865 in Tennessee, with a Confederate General Nathan Bedford as the leader. The club advocated white superiority. They use violent means to prevent the blacks from gaining any rights after the Civil War.

2) Elvis Aaron Presley

Elvis Aaron Presley was a very popular singer in the mid-1950s. The Rolling Stone Magazine said that he made rock and roll the international language of the pop. He defined the music genre of rock and roll and had an extensive impact on culture. He was a music giant who changed the development of music. His music was under the influence of African-American blues, Christian gospel and so on. His dance moves, clothing and even attitude towards life was followed by music enthusiasts.

3) John Lennon

If you are not familiar with the name John Lennon, you may know the famous rock music band Beetles. And John Lennon is one of its founders. He was an English musician, songwriter, singer and political activist.

In 1952, John Lennon began to like music after entering Quarry Bank primary school. In 1955, he organized a rock band called "Quarrymen" at the school. After the Beetles period, he became a famous solo singer. Many of his famous songs, including *Give Peace a Chance* and *Imagine*, were issued in that period.

But in 1980, John was shot to death by one of his fans out of his apartment in Manhattan. It made people begin to reflect on a social phenomenon that the fans were so crazy to the music and musician beyond the artistic extent. It had opened out the problems of the American society.

4) Ping-pong Diplomacy

In April 1971, at the 31st World Table Tennis Championships held in Japan, the US national table tennis team expressed the idea to visit China.

In response, the Chinese Table Tennis Association invited the US table tennis team to visit China. Premier Zhou Enlai met with the US table tennis delegation headed by Nixon.

Premier Zhou said: "By visiting our country, you have opened the gate of the exchanges between the people of us two nations. We believe that a friendly exchange will win approval and support from both the Chinese and American peoples."

5) Watergate Scandal

It is a political scandal of the Republican administration occurring in Watergate Hotel in 1972 when President Nixon engaged in the president election campaign.

Story comes that Nixon appointed five men to break into the DNC headquarters at the Watergate hotel to wire some bugs for listening secretly to the process about the election in the Democratic Party. The scandal made Nixon a focus in American society and left him with great pressure. It didn't influence Nixon's reappointment in that year, but with pressure, he had to admit it and resigned in 1974, which made Nixon the first president to leave his office because of the scandal in American history.

2. Classical lines from the film

1) Life was like a box of chocolate and you never know what you're gonna get.
人生就像一盒巧克力，你永远不知道下一块品尝到的是什么口味。

2) His back is as crooked as a politician.
他的后背像政客一样弯曲（对政客的讽刺）。

3) There is an awful lot you can tell about a person by their shoes. Where they're going. Where they've been. I bet you could walk all day in shoes like that and not feel a thing.
要想知道一个人很多事情，只要看看他穿的鞋就能知道。他会往哪里走，他去过哪里。我敢说你穿这双鞋走一天也不会感觉到累。

4) Stupid is as stupid does.
傻人做傻事（傻人有傻福）。

5) You are no different than anybody else is.
你和其他人没有任何的不同。

6) We were like peas and carrots.
我们形影不离。

7) Dear God, make me a bird, so I can fly far, far, far away from here.
亲爱的上帝，让我变成一只小鸟吧，这样我就能飞很远，远离这里。

8) Death is just a part of life, something we're all destined to do. I didn't know it. But I was destined to be your mama. I did the best I could.
死亡是生命的一部分，是我们注定要面对的。我过去不知道，但我注定要做你的妈妈，我就尽力去做好。

9) I'm not a smart man, but I know what love is.
我不是很聪明，但我知道什么是爱。

3. Film Review

Forrest Gump was born with an IQ of 75, a bit on the slow side, and he has some muscle problems. Why can he become a football star, a Vietnam battlefield hero, a shrimp boat captain, and finally a millionaire? After watching the film I wonder why he can achieve so much success that many people dream of. Many people may ask about Forrest's success, which is actually one of the themes of this film. We can analyze the film with the following aspects:

3.1 Mrs. Gump playing an important role in Forrest's life

Mrs. Gump is a great mother. Her influence on Forrest is irreplaceable. Just because of Mrs. Gump's loving for life, she tries her best to make Forrest feel no different from others. Though she knew her son's IQ is only 75, she still tries her best to let Forrest enter the famous public school to obtain good education. She always encourages him, which is the main reason for Forrest's success.

Mrs. Gump is an anchor for Forrest. Before leaving for Vietnam when saying goodbye to each other, they sit on the rock outside their house, leaning together, and finally Forrest can't help shedding tears in his mother's arms.

From what Forrest said, we can know the great influence of his mother on him. For example, "Mama always had a way of explaining things so I could understand them easily" as well as "stupid is as stupid does".

Before she went to the last part of her life, Mrs. Gump told Forrest that "I didn't know it, but I was destined to be you mama. I did the best I could. I happen to believe that you make your own destiny. You have to do the best with what God gave you". She told him again that "Life was like a box of chocolates and you never know what you are going to get". What his mother said was meaningful, which helps him guide his life.

So after his long running he may remember his mother's words — you get to put the past behind you before you move on. He says he was tired, but mostly he knew what to do with his mother's words.

3.2 Forrest judging from his own

3.2.1 Insistence

Insistence is an important word in the film. Most of us may be smarter than Forrest, but not all of us can focus on one thing constantly. Usually, we can't do one thing till the last moment, so we fail. Forrest always knows his own shortcomings, so he focuses and finally he succeeds.

Another important part in the film moves us a lot. It is about Forrest's running. After Jenny left him again, Forrest was depressed. So he began to run. He run for three years two months fourteen days and sixteen hours. So we can see that Forrest is a man of insistence.

3.2.2 Sincerity and purity

Forrest treated others kindly. He is just like a friend. He is kind to all the people around him, like Lieutenant Dan and Bubba's mother. Forrest Gump loved them in a great way that he himself didn't think so.

His love to Jenny was selfish and without expectation of reward. He said to Jenny: "I'm not a smart man, but I know what love is. " Forrest Gump was sincere. What he said in front of Jenny's tomb moves us to tears. He said that his son was the most beautiful thing he had ever seen. Forrest Gump pursued his happiness in his own way, simple but pure.

3.2.3 Running

The movie gives Gump magic — "running" ability. To Forrest, nothing is important but running. With this magic ability, he runs over the classmates' discrimination in childhood, the football field in the university, the fire swirling in the quagmire of the Vietnam War, and runs over the entire country.

Everyone has their own talent. To realize your advantage and use it fully, you will make a difference, and achieve your success.

3.2.4 A good listener

Forrest Gump always carefully follows his mother's words. So to some extent, we can say that Forrest is really a good listener. When Jenny told him that "Run, Forrest, run.", then he runs. And he runs all the way. With running, he avoids the attack from others. When his teammate gives him the ball and tells him to run, he runs to end the game. Without others telling him to stop, he keeps running although he already has crossed the finishing line. When drill sergeant commands that "Why did you put that weapon together so quickly, Gump?" He answers with "You told me to do, Drill Sergeant." So, without thinking he makes a new Camp record in assembling the gun. After the Vietnam war, when somebody tells him how to play ping-pong and says that no matter what happens never, ever take your eye off the ball, he follows. So playing ping-pong becomes very natural to him.

In a word, Forrest is a success in many fields. If we watch the movie carefully, we can learn a lot about how to succeed.

4. Extended Reading

Film: *Rain Man*

Rain Man is a 1988 American comedy-drama film which is about a selfish yuppie, Charlie Babbit (Tom Cruise) and his brother Raymond (Dustin Hoffman). Charlie discovers that his late father has left his multimillion-dollar estate to his other son, Raymond, an autistic patient, of whom Charlie was never aware. So Charlie has a delicate plan. He takes Raymond out of the hospital and begins a long journey. Raymond has a super brain and he can remember things accurately, so Charlie plans to earn lots of money with his brother's talent. He pays all the mortgage and even takes his brother to the casino. In the process of their journey, Charlie is moved by his brother and enjoys the family love.

In addition to the two leads, there is another role, Charlie's girlfriend, Susanna. After Charlie's change of attitude to Raymond, Susanna was moved by Charlie and her love for him is deeper. *Rain Man* received many positive reviews after its release.

The film won four Oscar Awards at the 61st Academy Awards (March 1989), including Best Picture, Best Original Screenplay, Best Director, and Best Actor in a Leading Role for Hoffman. Its crew received an additional four nominations. The film also won the Golden Bear at the 39th Berlin International Film Festival.

5. Homework

1) Watch the film *Forrest Gump* again and try to write down you feelings after watching.

2) Think about what the feather means in the film.

Unit 2 Truman Show《楚门的世界》

I Preview the movie

1. Background

Released by	Paramount Pictures (1999)
Director	Peter Weir
Screenplay	Andrew Niccol
Stars	Jim Carrey ... Truman Burbank
	Laura Linney ... Meryl
	Noah Emmerich ... Marlon
	Natascha McElhone ... Lauren/Sylvia
	Ed Harris ... Christof
Awards	Three nominations for Academy Awards in 1999
	Best Director, Best Supporting Role and Best Screenplay
	Golden Globe Award for Best Leading Role

2. Plot

Truman is a 29-year-old insurance salesman who lives in Seaheaven town, which is located on an island near the coast of Florida.

Truman is a very nice person, and gets along well with his neighbours. He finds that there is something strange going on around him every day. Gradually, he learns the cruel truth that his whole life is broadcast 24 hours a day to the rest of the world, and everything around him is fake: the fake wife, fake mother, and fake friends — they are just actors and actresses.

Truman decides to leave the island to find out the truth. He is terribly fearful of water, due to his childhood experience. When he was a child, he saw his father drowning in a storm, which is designed by Christof, the director of the TV show. The way to the outside world is mysteriously blocked — from car to bus. But on the other side, Truman grows increasingly closer to finding out the truth.

II View the movie

Clip 1 Truman's everyday life

Words and Expressions:

fashion mag	时尚杂志
whole kit and caboodle	全部，一起
coma	昏迷
meet your quota	满足你的配额

Task 1 Watch the video clip and fill in the missing words.

Man 1: Dog Fancy, please.

News vendor: Dog Fancy, yep?

Man 1: Thank you very much.

Truman: Get me a paper, will you, Errol? And one of these for my wife. Loves her **1**_____________.

News vendor: That will be all for you, Truman?

Truman: That's **2**_____________.

News vendor: Catch you later.

Passer-by: Good morning.

Truman: OK. Yeah. Hank!

Man 2: Good morning, Truman.

Man 3: Good morning, Truman.

Truman: Hey, how are you guys?

Man 4:	Beautiful day, isn't it?
Truman:	Oh, always.
Man 3:	And how's your lovely wife?
Truman:	Good. Good. How about yours?
Man 3:	Oh, **3**____________.
Man 4:	Good. Good.
Man 3:	Nice talking to you, Truman.
Truman:	You too. You too.
Man 4:	We must go now.
Truman:	Hey. Think about that **4**_________. Huh? OK. That's two for one. That's a good deal. Doppelganger special.
Man 4:	Right.
Truman:	Hey, fellas. You going in? Go ahead. Hey. No. You first, please. I'm not that anxious to get there.
Truman:	Yes, hello. Could I have **5**____________ for Fiji, please? Fiji islands.
Co-worker:	Truman, did you see this?
Truman:	I'm sorry, ma'am; if he's in a coma, he's probably **6**_________. Hello? Yes, Fiji, please. Do you have a listing for Lauren Garland? Nothing listed. OK. Do you have a Sylvia Garland? "S" for Sylvia. Nothing. Okay, thank you.
Truman:	Lawrence.
Lawrence:	Hi, Burbank. I've got a **7**_________ in Wells Park I need you to close.
Truman:	Wells Park? On Harbour Island?
Lawrence:	You know another one?
Truman:	Well, I can't do it. I have an appointment. Dentist, uh ... yeah.
Lawrence:	You're going to lose a lot more than your teeth if you don't meet your quota. Look, Truman, they're making **8**_________ at the end of this month.
Truman:	Cutbacks?
Lawrence:	Yeah. And you need this. Besides, a half hour across the bay, a little sea air, will do you good.

Task 2 **Mark T (True) or F (False) for the following statements according to the clip.**

a) _______ Truman buys the Dog Fancy because his wife loves it.

b) _______ Truman doesn't like going to the Wells Park probably because he is afraid of water.

Clip 2 A Talk about the reappearance of Truman's father

Words and Expressions:

insane 疯的，疯狂的

Task 1 **Watch the video clip and fill in the missing words.**

Truman's mother: It doesn't sound **1**__________, Truman. I see him ten times a week in 100 different faces. I almost **2**______________ in the salon last Thursday.

Truman: It was Dad, I swear. Dressed like a homeless man. And you know what else was strange? A businessman and a woman with a little dog came out of nowhere and **3**______________.

Truman's mother: Well, it's about time they **4**______________ before we become just like the rest of the country.

Truman: They never found Dad's body. Maybe somehow ...

Truman's mother: Oh, God!

Truman: I'm telling you if it wasn't him, it was his twin! Did Dad have a brother?

Truman's mother: Truman, you know perfectly well that your father was an only child, just like you. Now Sweetie, you're just feeling bad because of what happened. **5**______________. But I've never blamed you, Truman. And I don't blame you now.

Task 2 **Answer the questions from this video clip.**

a) What did Truman think is the reason for his father's death before?

____

b) Do you believe what Truman's mother said? And what do you think is the purpose of her words?

____

Clip 3 Truman's first love

Words and Expressions:

commit this to memory	记住
copy off	抄袭

Task 1 **Mark T (True) or F (False) for the following statements according to the clip.**

a) _______ Truman is preparing for the exam when he meets Lauren.

b) _______ Truman is not the type Lauren likes.

c) _______ Lauren is taken away by his father.

d) _______ The man will take Lauren to Fiji.

Task 2 **Answer the questions from this video clip.**

a) Why does Lauren say that she is not allowed to talk to Truman?

____

b) Do you think Truman really gets something from Lauren's words?

____

Clip 4 Trying to escape from the island

Words and Expressions:

spontaneous 自发的，自然的

eat into 侵蚀，消耗

Task 1 Watch the video clip and fill in the missing words of the dialogue.

Truman: Let's go now. I'm ready to go now. Why wait?

Meryl: What?

Truman: **1**____________. **2**____________. Right?

Meryl: Truman, what are you doing? Truman.

Truman: Where shall we go? Where shall we go?

Meryl: Truman, where are we going?

Truman: I don't really know. I guess I'm being **3**_________. Somebody help me! I'm being spontaneous! Forget Fiji. We can't drive to Fiji, can we?

Meryl: No.

Truman: What about Atlantic City?

Meryl: No, you hate to **4**_________.

Truman: That's right, I do, don't I?

Meryl: So why do you want to go there?

Truman: Because I never have. That's why people go places, isn't it?

Meryl: Truman, Truman, I think I'm going to **5**_________.

Truman: Me too. **6**____________. Beautifully synchronized, don't you agree?

Meryl: You're blaming me for the traffic?

Truman: Should I?

Meryl: Truman, let's go home.

Truman: You're right. We could be stuck here for hours. It could be like this all the way to Atlantic City. Let's go back. I'm sorry. I don't know what got into me.

Meryl: Can you please slow down?

Truman: Yes, I can.

Meryl: Truman, Truman, that's our turn-off.

Truman: I changed my mind. What's New Orleans like this time of year? Mardis Gras! Look, Meryl. Same road, no cars. It's magic.

Meryl: You let me out, Truman, **7**____________. If you want to destroy yourself, you do it on your own.

Truman: I think I'd like a little company.

Meryl: Oh, Truman. You knew this would happen. You know you can't drive over water. Let's go home where you'll feel safe.

Truman: Give me your hand.

Meryl: Sweetie.

Truman: You drive!

Meryl: Truman! We shouldn't be doing this, Truman, we're breaking the law! Oh, my!

Truman: You can do it!

Meryl: Please don't! Please!

Truman: You can make it!

Meryl: Oh, Truman! We're over! We're over the bridge! We're over the bridge! We're over the bridge! We're over the bridge!

Truman: We're over!

Meryl: Truman, Truman, what about that sign?

Truman: **8**____________. We'll be fine.

Meryl: They are exaggerating? Do you believe that? Oh my! On my! Truman, we're on fire!

Truman: It's OK.

Meryl:	We're on fire!
Truman:	It's OK. It's just smoke. You okay?
Meryl:	Yes!
Truman:	Wanna do it again?
Meryl:	No! Truman, stop! Oh, God. So what we're going to do for money when we get to New Orleans?
Truman:	I have my Seahaven bank card.
Meryl:	So what we're just gonna **9**____________, is that it? You know I'll have to call your mother when we get there. She's going to be worried sick. I don't know how she is going to take this.
Truman:	What now?
Meryl:	Truman, looks like **10**____________.
Policeman:	Back up. Back up. Leak at the plant. Get to shut down.
Truman:	Is there any way around?
Policeman:	The whole area is being evacuated.
Meryl:	Is there anything I can do?
Policeman:	No, ma'am. Thank you for your help. You're welcome, Truman.
Truman:	Truman!

Task 2 **Answer the following questions according to the dialogue.**

a) Why is Truman shocked when he hears the man call his name at the end of the movie clip?

____

____

____

Clip 5 Interviewing Christof

on pins and needles	如坐针毡
catalyst	催化剂，刺激因素
infiltrate	渗入，渗透

Task 1 Answer the following questions according to the dialogue.

a) Why does it mention the Great Wall of China?

____

b) What's the catalyst for the recent dramatic events on the show? And how does Christof plan to solve it?

____

____

c) What is the viewers' attitude towards the show?

____

d) What benefits does the TV show bring?

____

Task 2 Discussion: Do you think Truman's life is wonderful or miserable? How do you think about a life without privacy?

____

____

____

____

Clip 6 Truman's fighting for freedom

Task 1 **Watch the clip and retell the story in your own words.**

____

____

____

Clip 7 Truman's farewell to Christof

deceit	欺骗
in case	以防

Task 1 **Dub the voice for Truman and Christof while the video is played without the sound.**

____

____

III Review the movie

1. Cultural Notes

1) Utopia

In Thomas More's book *Utopia*, Parallel can be drawn. The book *Utopia* describes an island with only one entrance and one exit and only people who lived in this island knew how to leave the island safely and unharmed. This situation is just similar to *The Truman Show* because there are limited ways into the world that Truman knows. Truman does not belong to this utopia in which he has been living, and his childhood experience of seeing his father drowning in the storm makes him frightened to leave the island by sea.

2) **Religious analogy**

Benson Y. Parkinson of the Association for Mormon Letters noted that Christof represented Jesus as an "off-Christ" ("Christ-off") or Antichrist, comparing the Hollywood producer to Lucifer. The conversation between Truman and Marlon at the bridge can be compared to one between Moses and God in the Book of *Exodus*.

2. Classical lines from the film

1) Truman: Good morning, and in case I don't see you, good afternoon, good evening, and good night!
楚门：早上好。假如再也见不到你，就再祝你下午好，晚上好，晚安！

2) Sylvia: Look at what you've done to him!
Christof: I have given Truman the chance to lead a normal life. The world, the place you live in, is the sick place.
西尔维亚：看看你都对他做了什么！
克里斯托弗：我给了楚门过正常生活的机会。而你所生活的世界，是一个病态的世界。

3) Network Executive: For God's sake, Chris! The whole world is watching. We can't let him die in front of a live audience!
Christof: He was born in front of a live audience.
网络执行官：看在上帝的面上！全世界都看着呢。我们不能让他当众死亡！
克里斯托弗：但他当众出生。

4) Truman Burbank: Was nothing real?
Christof: You were real. That's what made you so good to watch ...
楚门·伯班克：一切都是假的？
克里斯托弗：你是真的，所以大家才爱看你的节目 ... ...

3. Film Review

The film *Truman Show*, is a comedy by Jim Carrey, who is really a comic talent. In this film, there are several main characters. They are so different that they make the film fantastic. So first, we will analyze the main characters of this film. And then we will further understand some symbolism and the theme of this film.

3.1 Character analysis

3.1.1 Truman Burbank

It's the name of the hero in the film. We can understand the name Truman as "true" plus "man". Firstly, he is not a totally true man. He lives a life without privacy. His everyday life is watched by the whole world 24 hours a day. Secondly, he can be a true man. If he is willing to leave the island and pursue a real life, then he can be a true man. Thirdly, he is the only true man. In the TV show, he is the only totally innocent man who doesn't know what's happening. All the others are just actors and actresses.

Burbank is Truman's last name. Actually it is the name of a city in the US. It's a beautiful city and many famous film factories locate here, such as the Warner's Brothers Film Factory, DreamWorks, etc.

3.1.2 Lauren (Sylvia)

She is Truman's first love and Truman still loves her even after his marriage. She stands for real. She is the only one who tells the truth to Truman. Even though she is dispelled from the TV show, she still concerns about Truman in the real world.

3.1.3 Christof

He is the creator and director of the TV show. It is not Truman who needs his creator. It is the creator who needs his creation. Without Truman, Christof is nothing. He is the creator of the perfect world. He creates the Seaheaven Island, which is actually a giant television studio. To some extent, he is Truman's father, because he was watching when Truman took his first steps, and he knows Truman even better than Truman himself.

4. Symbolism

(1) The island Truman lives on is like the Garden of Eden. The Seaheaven Island is a "perfect" place to live in. People living on this island have no fear and they have no choice for their own life, just like in the Garden of Eden. The creator, Christof, is like the God and he controls everything. Just like Adam and Eve, if you want to be free from this place, you have to pay a price. So Truman tries to escape from the island by every means, even at the expense of his life.

(2) Sylvia symbolizes Satan in the Eden. Like Satan, she persuades Truman to leave this "Eden". She is looked on as an evil by the "God" — the creator.

(3) The darkness in the exit of this huge "studio" symbolizes the following:

a) It symbolizes Truman's unknowness of the outside world;

b) It symbolizes Truman's fear for the outside world waiting for him;

c) It symbolizes the director's fear that Truman will leave him and ruin all his effort;

d) It symbolizes Truman's future in the outside world;

e) It symbolizes the cruelty of the real world.

5. Humanism

a) When Truman was born, he was chosen by the creator, who totally controlled his life. This is against humanism. The creator deprived of Truman's right of choosing his own way of life. Truman was not a free citizen from his birth.

b) The creator of this show robbed Truman of his right for free love, which is also inhumane. Truman did not love the girl arranged for him; while at that time he was not brave enough to fight against the destiny controlled by the creator, and thus he lost his true love.

c) From his birth, Truman's life is watched by million's of people for 24 hours every day, which is against his privacy right as a citizen.

d) When Truman was a child, he was very curious about the outside world. He wanted to explore the world. While the director tried every way to stop him, even "killed" his father, which made him afraid of water and did not leave this island for the whole 30 years. He also suffered a sense of guilt thinking that he killed his father. To Truman, this is very cruel and also against humanism.

e) When Truman began to suspect his life and decided to find the truth, everyone tried to confuse him and stop him, including his wife, his mother, his best friend and his "dead" beloved father. All of them were just lying to him. Every individual has the right to know the truth of his own life. What the people in the show did to him is inhumane.

f) At last, Truman was determined to leave the "island". The creator tried his best to make Truman stay there even at the expense of Truman's life. At this time, we can see that the director is almost crazy. He wanted to deprive Truman of his right of living, which is totally against humanism.

6. Extended Reading

Film: *The Thirteenth Floor*

Computer scientist Hannon Fuller has discovered something extremely important yet strange. He plans to tell the secret to his colleague, Douglas Hall. He knows that someone is after him, so the old man leaves a letter in his computer generated parallel world that's just like the 1930's with seemingly real people with real emotions. Fuller is murdered in our real world the same night, so his colleague Douglas Hall is a suspect. Douglas discovers a bloody shirt in his bathroom and he cannot remember what he was doing the night Fuller was murdered. He logs into the system in order to find the letter, but has to confront the unexpected situation. The truth is much tougher than he could ever imagine ...

7. Homework

1) Watch the film *Truman Show* again and try to write down you feelings after watching the film.

2) Write a film review of the film *Truman Show*.

Unit 3 The Pursuit of Happyness 《当幸福来敲门》

I Preview the movie

1. Background

Directed by	Gabriele Muccino
Distributed by	Columbia Pictures
Release dates	December 15, 2006 (United States)
	January 12, 2007 (United Kingdom)
Running time	117 minutes
Country	United States
Genre	Biography Drama

2. Plot

The Pursuit of Happyness is directed by Gabriele Muccino in 2006. It is based on the true story of Chris Gardner. The hero of the film is a salesman who sells bone-density scanners but eventually turns a stockbroker. It portrays the story of a homeless father with a 5-year-old son pursuing his happiness. In *The pursuit of happiness*, he faces many obstacles, but he never gives up. Finally he succeeds.

Chris Gardner works hard, but he fails to change the unsatisfactory situation at first. His wife, Linda, cannot put up with the pressure of taking two double shifts for four months to support the whole family and leaves him, leaving her 5-year-old son, Christopher, to him. He becomes a single father to survive the hardship of life. At one time, Chris has only 21 dollars and cannot pay the rent, so they are thrusted out of the apartment. Chris finally gets the chance to be an intern at Dean Witter Company. However, there is no salary during the six-month internship, and only one person out of twenty has access to the ultimate success. But Chris understands that this is his last chance, and it is the only way that leads to a happy life. He is frustrated with poverty, but with regard to his son's future and his own beliefs, Chris believes that only if he works hard enough, happiness will come tomorrow!

II View the movie

Clip 1 Hardship of life

Words and Expressions:

hang on	坚持，等一下
feed the meter	缴（停车）费

Task 1 Watch the video clip and fill in the blank.

Chris: Man, I got two questions for you: **1**_____________? **2**_____________?

Man: I'm a stockbroker.

Chris: Stockbroker. Oh, goodness. Had to go to college to be a stockbroker, huh?

Man: You don't have to. Have to be good with numbers and good with people. That's it.

Chris: Hey, you take care. I'll let you **3**_____________ for the weekend. But I need it back for Monday.

Man: **4**_____________.

Chris: I still remember that moment. They all looked so damn happy to me. Why couldn't I look like that?

Chris: I'm gonna try to get home by 6. I'm gonna stop by a brokerage firm after work.

Linda: For what?

Chris: I wanna see about a job there.

Linda: Yeah? What job?

Chris: You know, when I ... when I was a kid, I could go through a math book in a week. So I'm gonna go see about what job they got down there.

Linda: What job?

Chris: Stockbroker.

Linda: Stockbroker?

Chris: Yeah.

Linda: Not an astronaut?

Chris: Don't talk to me like that, Linda. I'm gonna go down and see about this, and I'm gonna do it during the day.

Linda: You should probably do your sales calls.

Chris: I don't need you to tell me about my sales calls, Linda. I got three of them before the damn office is even open.

Linda: Do you remember that **5**_____________? Probably not. We're already two months behind. Next, next week we'll owe three months. I've been **6**_____________ for four months now, Chris. Just, just sell what's in your contract. Get us out of that business.

Chris: Linda, that is what I am trying to do. This is what I'm trying to do for my family, for you and for Christopher.

Task 2 Watch the video clip again and answer the questions.

a) Why does Chris ask the man the two questions?

____

b) Why does Linda respond to Chris in such a way?

____

____

Clip 2 Chris' escape from paying the taxi driver

Words and Expressions:

intern 实习生

Task 1 **Mark T (True) or F (False) for the following statements according to the clip.**

a) _______ Chris is on the same way to the Noe Valley as Mr. Twistle.

b) _______ Finally, Chris finishes playing the cube.

c) _______ When they arrive at the destination, it's Chris' treat.

Task 2 **Answer the questions from this video clip.**

a) What's Chris's purpose of sharing a ride with Mr. Twistle?

____

b) How do you think about Chris's escape from paying the taxi driver?

____

Clip 3 Chris' caught up by the police

Words and Expressions:

verify 证实

Task 1 **Watch the video clip and fill in the missing words.**

Policeman: Chris Gardner?

Chris: Yeah. What happened?

Policeman: **1**_____________.

Chris: Does it have to be **2**_____________?

Policeman: You gotta pay each **3**_____________. Otherwise, you're staying.

Chris: This is all I got.

Policeman: You verify at 9:30 tomorrow morning.

Chris: What?

Policeman: You gotta stay until this thing clears.

Chris: No. No, I, I can't, I can't spend the night here. I have to pick up my son.

Policeman: You verify at 9:30 tomorrow morning.

Chris: Sir, I have a job interview at Dean Witter at **4**_________ tomorrow morning. I cannot stay ...

Policeman: 9:30 tomorrow morning.

Chris: What am I supposed to do with my son? What am I supposed to do with my son?

Woman: Is there anyone else who can ...

Chris: I take care of him.

Policeman: Maybe we can go and have **5**_____________.

Chris: All right. Can I have my phone call, please?

Task 2 Answer the questions from this video clip.

a) Why does the landlord suggest Chris go to the Mission Inn Motel two blocks away?

____

b) Why does the landlord allow Chris to live in the apartment one more week?

____

c) What is the reason for Chris' being caught up?

____

Clip 4 Chris' interview

Words and Expressions:

come up with 想出，提出

Task 1 Watch the video clip and fill in the missing words of the dialogue.

Secretary: Chris Gardner.

Chris: Chris Gardner. How are you? Good morning. Chris Gardner. Chris Gardner, good to see you again. Chris Gardner. Pleasure.

Chris: I've been sitting there for the last half-hour **1**____________ ... that would explain my being here dressed like this. And I wanted to come up with a story that would **2**____________ ... that I'm sure you all admire here, like earnestness or diligence. Team-playing, something. And I couldn't think of anything. So the truth is ... I was arrested for **3**____________.

Jay: Parking tickets?

Chris: And I ran all the way here from the Polk Station, the police station.

Interviewer: What were you doing before you were arrested?

Chris: I was painting my apartment.

Interviewer: Is it dry now?

Chris: I hope so.

Interviewer: Jay says **4**____________.

Jay: He's been waiting outside the front of the building, with some 40-pound gizmo for over a month.

Interviewer: He said you're smart.

Chris: Well, I like to think so.

Interviewer: And you want to learn this business?

Chris: Yes, sir. I wanna learn.

Interviewer: Have you already started learning on your own?

Chris: Absolutely.

Interviewer: Jay?

Jay: Yes, sir.

Interviewer: How many times have you seen Chris?

Jay: I don't know. **5**____________, apparently.

Interviewer: Was he ever dressed like this?

Jay: No. No. **6**____________.

Interviewer: First in your class in school? High school?

Chris: Yes, sir.

Interviewer: How many in the class?

Chris: Twelve. It was a small town.

Interviewer: I'll say.

Chris: But I was also first in my radar class ... in the Navy, and that was a class of 20. Can I say something? I'm the type of person ... if you ask me a question, and I don't know the ... I'm gonna tell you that I don't know. But **7**____________. I know how to find the answer, and I will find the answer. Is that fair enough?

Interviewer: Chris. What would you say if a guy walked in for an interview without a shirt on, and I hired him? What would you say?

Chris: He **8**____________.

Task 2 **Discussion: As we all know that a job interview is very important for a good job, so how do you think of Chris' humorous answer to the executive? And how will you prepare for a job interview in the future?**

____

____

____

____

____

____

Clip 5 Chris' internship at Dean Witter

Words and Expressions:

in essence 实际上

pop out 突然冒出来

Task 1 Watch the video clip and fill in the missing words of the dialogue.

Chris: This part of my life is called "Internship".

Frakesh: The 1200 building is Medley Industrial and Sanko Oil. The building across the street is Lee-Ray Shipping. In a couple weeks, you'll get **1**_____________ of employees from every Fortune 500 company **2**_____________. You will be pooling from 60 Fortune companies. You will mainly be **3**_____________ clients. But if you have to have lunch with them, have breakfast with them, if you even have to baby-sit for them, you will do whatever it takes to **4**_____________ We need you to **5**_____________ to one of our many financial plans. **6**_____________, you reel them in. We'll cook the fish. Some of you guys are here because you know somebody. Some of you guys are here because you think you're somebody. There's one guy in here who's gonna be somebody. That person's gonna be the guy who can **7**_____________. You, you, help me hand these out. This is going to be your bible. You'll eat with it. You'll drink with it.

Clip 6 Chris' success

Task 1 Answer the questions from this video clip.

a) What's the consequence of Chris' internship?

____

b) Why does Chris come to see his son first after he was received by the firm?

____

Task 2 **Discussion: Chris calls this part of his life "happiness". How do you define your "happiness"?**

____

____

____

____

III Review the movie

1. Cultural Notes

1) Declaration of Independence

The Declaration of Independence is the usual name of a statement adopted by the Continental Congress on July 4, 1776, which announced that the thirteen American colonies, then at war with Great Britain, regarded themselves as thirteen newly independent sovereign states, and no longer a part of the British Empire. Instead, they formed a new nation — the United States of America. John Adams was a leader in pushing for independence, which was unanimously approved on July 2. A committee of five had already drafted the formal declaration, to be ready when Congress voted on independence. The term "Declaration of Independence" is not used in the document itself.

Adams persuaded the committee to select Thomas Jefferson to compose the original draft of the document, which Congress would edit to produce the final version. The Declaration was ultimately a formal explanation of why Congress had voted on July 2 to declare independence from Great Britain, more than a year after the outbreak of the American Revolutionary War. The national birthday, Independence Day, is celebrated on July 4, although Adams wanted July 2.

2) American Dream

The American Dream is a national ethos of the United States, a set of ideals in which freedom includes the opportunity for prosperity and success, and an upward social mobility for the family and children, achieved through hard work in a society with few barriers. In the definition of the

American Dream by James Truslow Adams in 1931, "life should be better and richer and fuller for everyone, with opportunity for each according to ability or achievement" regardless of social class or circumstances of birth.

The American Dream is rooted in the Declaration of Independence, which proclaims that "all men are created equal" with the right to "Life, Liberty and the pursuit of Happiness."

2. Classical lines from the film

1) Don't ever let somebody tell you that you can't do something, not even me.
不要让别人告诉你你不能做什么，甚至我也不可以。

2) You got a dream. You gotta protect it.
你有自己的梦想，就要守护它。

3) People can't do something themselves. They wanna tell you that you can't do it. If you want something, go get it.
人们做不了的事情，就会告诉你，你也做不了。如果你想要什么，就去追求。

4) I'm the type of person. If you ask me a question, and I don't know the answer, I'm gonna to tell you that I don't know. But I bet you what: I know how to find the answer, and I'll find the answer.
我是这样的人，如果你问的问题我不知道答案，我会直接告诉你“我不知道”。但我向你保证：我知道如何寻找答案，而且我一定会找出答案的。

5) There is an I in "happiness". There is no Y(why) in "happiness". It's an I.
“幸福”的英文拼法，中间是I不是Y。幸福当中没有为什么，幸福当中只有我。

3. Film Review

The *Pursuit of Happyness* is a fine film that portrays the experiences of a single father. Will Smith's performance as a single dad is excellent and moving. There's very little self-congratulation about the film, and much that is dark. It shows the connections between the American dream and its nightmare shadow.

The movie is set in San Francisco in 1980s, and it is based on a true story of Chris Gardener. Chris is smart, but he doesn't have an opportunity to realize and use his potential. In the film, Chris' whole life is divided into six parts:

Part one: Riding the bus

In 1981, Chris and Linda spent all their money buying bone density scanners, but later they found that they were not that accepted among doctors, because they were expensive and almost useless. He tried his best to sell the equipment, but he can't earn enough money to support the family. So he experienced the hardship of life.

Part two: Being stupid

In this part, when applying for a job as an internship in a investment company, he left the bone density scanner with a hippie girl singing besides the street, but the girl took it away. Chris didn't get it back.

Part three: Running

He ran after the girl who had stolen the bone density scanner, and finally, he took it back. Another running situation is his escaping from the taxi driver. The third running situation is as follows. When Chris was sent to the prison for failing to pay the taxes, the next morning, he ran to the Dean Witter company for a interview with painted stains on his clothes.

Part four: Internship

Finally Chris got the job as a intern for six months without salary. And he had to take care of Christopher at the same time. It was really a hard time for him. Fortunately, he took back one bone density scanner from the old man, and after fixing it, he sold it to a doctor so as to support the family.

Part five: Paying taxes

In this part, there was a big hit to him. The government took $600 from his bank account for his failure to pay the parking tickets, leaving only $21.33, so he was broke again. During that period, he and his son had to live in the subway bathroom, the public spaces, shelters, and so on. They had to live on the dole. Though there were many barriers, he carried on seeking for the happiness.

Part six: Happiness

This little part is called happiness. Chris was finally successful, and he became a successful stockbroker.

From this story, we know that if we have a dream, we have to protect it. No pains, no gains. Only if we work hard, we will have a chance to succeed.

4. Extended Reading

Film: *A Beautiful Mind*

A Beautiful Mind is a 2001 American biographical drama film based on the life of John Nash, a Nobel Laureate in Economics. The film is directed by Ron Howard, and was inspired by a bestselling, Pulitzer Prize-nominated 1998 book of the same name by Sylvia Nasar. The story begins in the early years of a young prodigy named John Nash, who developed paranoid schizophrenia and endures delusional episodes. He didn't overcome the illness till his old age. But with his wife's support and love, he can lead a normal and happy life.

The film won four Academy Awards, for Best Picture, Best Director, Best Adapted Screenplay and Best Supporting Actress. It was also nominated for the Best Actor, Best Film Editing, Best Makeup, and Best Original Score.

The film was well received by critics, but also has been criticized for its inaccurate portrayal of some aspects of Nash's real life, especially about his other family and a son born out of marriage. However, according to the filmmakers, it was an art but not meant to be a literal representation.

5. Homework

1) Watch the film *The Pursuit of Happyness* again and try to write down your feelings after watching.

Unit 4 The Shawshank Redemption 《肖申克的救赎》

I Preview the movie

1. Background

Directed by	Frank Darabont (德拉邦特)
Screenplay by	Frank Darabont
Based on	Rita Hayworth and Shawshank Redemption by Stephen King
Stars	Tim Robbins
	Morgan Freeman
Distributed by	Columbia Pictures
	Warner Bros. (Home Media)
Release date	1994
Box office	$28,241,469

2. Plot

Young banker Andy Dufresne is mistakenly charged with murdering his wife and her lover and imprisoned in the Shawshank jail. In prison, Andy and Red become bosom friends. Andy brings a lot of benefits for his friends. For having a banking experience, he filters the money for the warden of the prison and the chief guard in an illegal way. Meanwhile, he records the evidence of their guilt.

During the duration of his prison life, Andy has been secretly planning for prison escape. It is in a night of thundering and lighting that he successfully gets the freedom. Andy crawls through the hole he dugs, 500 yards in a narrow pipe. After the prison break, Andy withdraws a large sum of money from several banks and mails the evidence of warden's corruption to a newspaper office. Then Andy goes to Mexico, the place he has been dreaming to get to. In the end, Red and Andy are happily reunited on the beach.

II View the movie

Clip 1 Andy getting the roof-repair work with his inmates

Words and Expressions:

tar	以焦油或沥青覆盖或涂抹
wind up	最终落得；（以……）告终
magnanimous	宽宏大量的
hunker	盘坐
curry favor	巴结；讨好
cons	反对者

Task 1 Watch the video clip and fill in the missing words.

Red: And that's how it came to pass, that on the second-to-last day of the job, the **1**_________ that tarred the plate factory roof in the spring of 49 wound up sitting in a row at 10:00 in the morning, drinking icy-cold Bohemian style of beer, **2**_________ of the hardest screw that ever walked a turn at Shawshank State Prison.

Hadley: Drink up while it's cold, ladies.

Red: The colossal prick even **3**_________ to sound magnanimous.

Red: We sat and drank with the sun on our shoulders, and felt like free men. We could have been tarring the roof of one of our own houses. We were the **4**___________.

Red: As for Andy, he spent that break hunkered in the shade, a strange little smile on his face, watching us drink his beer.

Heywood: Hey. Want a cold one, Andy.

Andy: No, thanks. I gave up drinking.

Red: You could argue he'd done it to curry favor with the guards. Or maybe make a few friends among us cons. Me? I think he did it just to **5**_________ again ... if only for a short while.

Task 2 **Watch the video clip again and answer the questions.**

a) What does Andy do for his inmates and himself?

____

b) Do you think Andy is the same as other convicts? Why?

____

____

Clip 2 Brook's ending

Words and Expressions:

bonus	意外收获；红利
kick up any fuss	在意；滋事

Task 1 **Mark T (True) or F (False) for the following statements according to the clip.**

a) _______Brook loses his faith for life due to old age.

b) _______Brook kills himself in the end.

Task 2 **Answer the questions from this video clip.**

a) Why does Brook want to get a gun and rob?

____

b) How do you understand the word "institutionalized" in the movie?

____

Clip 3 Andy helping warden laundering money

Words and Expressions:

fingers in a lot of pies	到处管闲事
scam	诡计，阴谋，骗局
kickback	回扣
honeypot	装蜜的罐子；极有吸引力的事物
wind up	最终落得
conjure	用魔术变出；捏造

Task 1 Watch the video clip and fill in the missing words.

Red: He's got his fingers in a lot of pies, from what I hear.

Andy: What you hear isn't half of it. He's got scams you haven't dreamed of. I kickbacks on his kickbacks. There's a river of dirty money flowing through this place.

Red: Can be a problem having all that money. Cause sooner or later you're gotta have to explain where it came from.

Andy: That's where I come in. I **1**_____________ ... stocks, securities, tax-free municipals ... I send that money out into the real world. And when it comes back.

Red: Clean as a virgin's honeypot?

Andy: Cleaner. By the time Norton retires, I will have made him a millionaire.

Red: If they ever catch on him, he's gonna wind up here **2**_____________.

Andy: Oh Red, I thought you had a little more faith in me than that.

Red: I know you're good, but all that paper leaves a trail. Now anybody gets curious, FBI, IRS, whatever. It's going to lead to somebody.

Andy: Sure it is. But not to me, and certainly not to the warden.

Red: All right, who?

Andy: Randall Stevens.

Red: Who?

Andy: The "silent" silent partner. He's the guilty one, your Honor. The man with the bank accounts. It's where the filtering process starts. They trace anything, so it's gonna lead to him.

Red: But who is he?

Andy: He's a **3**____________. Second cousin to Harvey the Rabbit. (off Red's look) I conjured him out of thin air. He doesn't exist ... except on paper.

Task 2 **Dub the voice for Andy and Red while the video is played again without the sound.**

Clip 4 Andy's fancy for Zihuatanejo

Task 1 **Mark T (True) or F (False) for the following statements according to the clip.**

a) ______Andy dreams of going to Zihuatanejo.

b) ______Red will adjust to the life outside by what he says in the movie.

c) ______Red thinks Andy's dream will come true someday.

Task 2 **Discussion: What's your opinion towards "get busy living or get busy dying"?**

____

____

____

____

Clip 5 Andy's escape from the Shawshank

Task 1 Answer the following questions according to Red's statement.

a) How long does it take Andy to make it to his plan?

____

b) What surprises Red on Andy?

____

Task 2 Discussion: According to Andy's successful escape, what is the Shawshank-style "prison drama" in your mind?

____

____

____

Clip 6 Red getting parole after 40-years imprisonment

Task 1 Watch the video clip and fill in the missing words.

There's not a day goes by I don't feel regret. Not because I'm in here, or because you think I should. I look back on the way I was then. Then a young, stupid kid **1**____________. I want to talk to him. I want to try and talk some sense to him, tell him the way things are. But I can't. That kid's long gone and this old man is all that's left. I got to live with that. Rehabilitated? It's just a bullshit word. So you go on and **2**____________, sonny, and stop wasting my time. Because to tell you the truth, I don't give a shit.

Task 2 **Translate the underlined sentences into Chinese.**

a) ______________________________

b) ______________________________

Clip 7 Two freemen's reunion

Task 1 **Watch the video clip and write down what Red said.**

____

____

____

III Review the movie

1. Cultural Notes

1) Sears & Roebuck

Born during the latter part of the 19th century, Sears & Roebuck Company is one of the most trusted economic institutions in US history and eventually grew to be the 7th largest corporation in the world during the 20th century.

2) Rita Hayworth

Rita Hayworth (1918–1987), an American actress and dancer, is one of classic Hollywood beautiful leading ladies. She achieved fame during the 1940s as one of the era's top stars, and was perhaps best known for her performance in the 1946 film *Gilda*. She is listed by the American Film Institute as one of the 100 Greatest Stars of All Time.

3) **Hank Williams**

Hank Williams (1923–1953) was an American singer-songwriter and musician. Regarded as one of the most significant and influential singers and songwriters of the 20th Century, Williams recorded 35 singles (five released posthumously) that would place in the Top 10 of the Billboard Country & Western Best Sellers chart, including 11 that ranked number one. Despite his short life, Williams has had a major influence on twentieth-century popular music, and especially country music.

4) **Wolfgang Amadeus Mozart**

Mozart (1756–1791) was a prolific and influential composer of the Classical era. He composed over 600 works, many acknowledged as pinnacles of symphonic, concertante, chamber, operatic, and choral music. He is among the most enduringly popular classical composers, and his influence on subsequent Western art music is profound. Ludwig van Beethoven composed his own early works in the shadow of Mozart.

5) **Robert Lee Frost**

Robert Lee Frost (1874–1963) is one of the most popular and critically respected American poets of the twentieth century, highly spoken of for his realistic depictions of rural life and his command of American colloquial speech. Frost was honored frequently during his lifetime, receiving four Pulitzer Prizes for Poetry.

2. Classical lines from the film

1) Hope is a good thing, maybe the best of things, and no good thing ever dies.
希望是美好的，也许是人间至善，而美好的事物永不消逝。

2) I guess it comes down to a simple choice: get busy living or get busy dying.
我想生命可以归结为一种简单的选择：要么忙于生存，要么赶着去死。

3) It takes a strong man to save himself, and a great man to save another.
坚强的人救赎自己；伟大的人拯救他人。

4) These walls are kind of funny like that. First, you hate them. Then you get used to them. Enough time passed, then you depend on them. That's institutionalized.
监狱里的高墙着实有趣。刚入狱的时候，你痛恨周围的高墙；慢慢地你习惯了活在其中；最终你会发现自己不得不依靠它而生存。这就是体制化。

5) Prison life consists of routine, and then more routine.
坐牢是一段段例行公事，忙完一段又接一段。

6) Fear can hold you prisoner. Hope can set you free. A strong man can save himself. A great man can save another.
懦怯囚禁人的灵魂，希望可以感受自由。强者自救，圣者度人。

7) Some birds aren't meant to be caged. That's all. Their feathers are just too bright.
有的鸟是不会被关住的，因为它们的羽毛太美丽了！

3. Film Review

1) Hope

In the film, a conflict is portrayed between the strong yearnings for hope in a typically hopeless place and the greed to take it away. The irony manifests itself in expressing a message of hope to the most hopeless people in one place, and indicting conviction to those who destroy it. In a hopeless environment, such as prison, maintaining hope is, in particular, significant. Dufresne, for the first time, came to Red for help with a rock hammer, saying, "I understand you're a man who knows how to get things". Although Red obtained the hammer for him, he thought it was hopeless to escape because it would take six hundred years for a man to tunnel through the wall with it. Initially, Dufresne used the hammer to carve his initials into the cell wall and immediately found that the wall was made of soft stones. He realized that he could tunnel through the wall and escape with the hammer. His hopeless situation appeared hopeful. Dufresne immediately seeks out Red to obtain a poster of Rita Hayworth for him. The poster was used to hide his hope of tunneling out of the prison.

By helping the captain of the guards through a financial dilemma, Dufresne indirectly earns respect and popularity among the inmates. The captain permitted the men to have three beers in return for Dufresne's assistance in finding a way to hide his income without paying tax. The beer relieved the men of their hopeless prison environment, but they recognized it was only temporary. Even though temporary, such "relief" may be the only hope that many prisoners experience or hold on to.

"In jail a man has nothing but time. Some build things like little matchstick houses. Andy, he built a library." This proves that he is also the owner of his environment which deprives him of leading any kind of a privileged life. The library helps many of Andy's inmates pass their high school equivalency test. Andy helped all of the guards with no taxes paid and the wardens with the paper work for their dirty money. As a result, he enjoyed special treatment. This is the reason that the sisters left him alone. Andy was pretty smart, and he kept hope alive. Every inmate was living a regular prison life. However, through his cell wall, he was digging a hole to freedom. This hole brightened his hope. Whether he was cruelly punished by the warden or he encountered the sisters, he always had something to spirit up.

2) Friendship

Andy adds Red up. He is a veteran of the penal system, and their growing friendship over 20 years develops into the tenor of the film. Andy was a man of few words and he said no more for the first few years in prison. He eventually befriended Red with a reputation for helping prisoners get what they wanted. Red was already at Shawshank for 20 years by the time Andy arrived. He was pessimistic about the hopeless prison life and accepted it as his fate. He ever said to Andy that he had been institutionalized and thought that he could not survive as a free man. As close friends, Red and Andy respected each other. Even though he always felt hopeless, Red admired Andy's belief in hope. He learned a lot about himself from his friendship with Andy as it grew, from many risks taken by Andy, which resulted in positive results despite the setbacks with physical abuse and some time in solitary confinement. As Andy's best friend, he helped Andy during the busy tax season and thus reaped the benefits of the help. Red was an attentive listener to Andy and the other inmates, and he was also an effective communicator expressing empathy and concern. Toward the end of the movie, he succeeded in the development of the self-expression skill when he was able to passionately speak up for himself in front of the board of officials who eventually approved his claim of being a "changed man". He was fearless when he made it clear to the Parole Board that he didn't care about his release and even questioned the Board's definition of rehabilitation. His testimony led to an approval of his freedom. He, already as a civilian, took another risk by honoring his promise to Andy, which resulted in the two reuniting in Mexico.

3) Wisdom

Andy also had a deep empathy with people. He gave an empathetic ear to others' feelings and was willing to help anyone around him. When he first arrived at Shawshank, he was taciturn man and he talked to nobody but Red. Fortunately, Andy was chosen for a coveted job outside prison, while inmates had to tar the prison roof. While engaging in the coveted job, Andy overheard Captain Hadley, the main guard, talking about his inheritance he would enter on. Although dangerously, Andy told the guard that he could save his money using a legal loophole of tax law. After a rather intense conversation, Captain Hadley agreed to accept Andy's assistance in return for a few cold beers for his co-workers.

As a successful and cultured man, Andy believed that the Shawshank prison library was of great importance and decided to raise funds for its growth. Through weekly letters and tireless efforts, he secured adequate funds to allow the library to thrive.

Andy showed his social skill when he inspired Red to get paroled rather than to waste his chances by repeating the same answers at each board meeting. Given the similarity between Red and Brooks, who could not handle issues in life outside of the prison well, Andy felt that Red would be the perfect companion for his life in Mexico. Their understandings of the difficult life inside and outside of prison would provide both of them with valuable support in coping with any hardships in life. By managing his relationship with Red, Andy revealed his ability to push people in the desired direction.

4. Extended Reading

Film: *Schindler's List*

Schindler's List (1993) is Steven Spielberg's unexpected award-winning masterpiece — a profoundly shocking, unsparing, fact-based, three-hour long epic of the nightmarish Holocaust. Its documentary authenticity vividly recreates a dark, frightening period during World War II, when Jews in Nazi-occupied Krakow were first dispossessed of their businesses and homes, then placed in ghettos and forced labor camps in Plaszow, and finally resettled in concentration camps for execution. The violence and brutality of their treatment in a series of matter-of-fact incidents was indelibly and brilliantly orchestrated. Oskar Schindler was an enterprising, womanizing Nazi Sudeten-German industrialist, opportunist and war profiteer, who first exploited the cheap labor of Jewish workers in a successful enamelware factory, and eventually rescued more than one thousand of them from certain extinction in labor/death camps.

5. Homework

1) Watch the film and write an article after watching.

2) Think about what redemption means in the film.

Unit 5 Brave Heart《勇敢的心》

I Preview the movie

1. Background

Directed by	Mel Gibson
Screenplay by	Randall Wallace
Stars	Mel Gibson
	Sophie Marceau
Distributed by	Paramount Pictures, Inc.
Release date	1995
Box office	$210,409,945

2. Plot

William Wallace is the national hero who fights for Scottish freedom in the 13th century. At the outset of the story, Wallace intends to live a peaceful life with his wife Murron. After Murron is murdered, Wallace slits the murderer's throat. From then on, Wallace determined to revolt against Edward's tyranny. But hero is always lonely and painful. As the Edward's emissary, Princess Isabelle pretends to make peace with Wallace. Unbelievable as it may be, they fall in love with each other and the princess gets pregnant in the end. Credulity drives him to be caught in a trap set by the elder Bruce and the nobles and escorted to the English. In the court, the executioner charges Wallace with treason. Finally, Wallace is sentenced to death. Until the last moment, Wallace still refused to submit to Edward I. He is tortured and executed by beheading.

II View the movie

Clip 1 Wallace's exhilarating speech

Words and Expressions:

defiance	蔑视；反抗
tyranny	暴行；专横
trade	交换

Task 1 Watch the video clip and fill in the missing words.

William Wallace: I am William Wallace, and I see a whole army of my countrymen here in defiance of tyranny. You have come to fight as free men, and free men you are! What will you do with that freedom? Will you fight?

Soldiers: No! No!

Veteran soldier: Against that? No, we will run, and we will live.

William Wallace: Aye. **1**______________. At least a while. And dying in your beds many years from now, **2**______________ from this day to that for one chance, just one chance to come back here and tell our enemies that they may take our lives, but they'll never take our freedom.

Task 2 Imitate Wallace's speech in the movie.

Clip 2 Princess Isabelle's negotiation with Wallace

Words and Expressions:

estate	财产	chest	大箱子
truce	休战	barn	谷仓
notion	观念；看法		

Task 1 Watch the video clip and fill in the missing words.

William: You ask your king to his face. Ask him.You see if his eyes can convince you of the truth.

Princess Isabella: Hamilton ... Leave us.

Hamilton: My lady ...

Princess Isabella: Leave us. Now. Let us talk plainly. You invade England. But you cannot complete the conquest. So far from your shelter and supply. The king desires peace.

William Wallace: Longshanks desires peace?

Princess Isabelle: He declares it to me, I swear it. He proposes that **1**____________. In return he grants you title, estates, and this chest of gold which I am to pay to you personally.

William Wallace: A lordship and titles ... gold ... that I should become Judas.

Princess Isabelle: Peace is made in such ways.

William Wallace: **2**____________. The last time Longshanks spoke of peace, I was a boy. And many Scottish nobles, who would not be slaves, were lured by him under a flag of truce to a barn, where **3**____________. I was very young, but I remember Longshank's notion of peace.

Princess Isabella: I understand you have suffered. I know ... about your woman.

William Wallace: She was my wife. We married in secret. Because I would not share her with an English lord. They killed her ... to get to me. I have never spoken of it. I don't know why I tell you now, except ... I see her strength in you. One day, you'll be a queen ... And you must open your eyes. You tell your king that William Wallace **4**____________ and nor will any Scot while I live.

Task 2 **Portray heroes as you can and do a wonderful role play with your partner.**

Clip 3 Robert's remorseful feeling after Wallace troop being defeated by Longshank's

Words and Expressions:

alliance	结盟
prevail	占优势
throw ... off	抛弃；摆脱
tear apart	扯开；使心碎

Task 1 **Mark T (True) or F (False) for the following statements according to the clip.**

a) ________ Robert follows his father's advice to have alliance with England.

b) ________ Robert does not regret for his wrong action.

Task 2 **Watch the video clip again and answer the questions.**

a) What does it mean to Robert after Wallace was defeated on the battlefield?

____

b) What will probably Robert do next?

____

Clip 4 Longshank's conspiracy coming to nothing by Isabella's second warning

Words and Expressions:

dispatch	派遣	hostage	人质
jeopardy	危险（境地）	ally	使联盟
supplies	补给；粮食		

Task 1 Watch the video clip and fill in the missing words.

Longshanks: If what Lord Hamilton tells me is correct, he warmed to our future queen. He would trust her. So we'll dispatch her with the notion that she comes in peace.

Hamilton: My lord, the princess **1**_____________ or her life be put in jeopardy.

Longshanks: Oh, my son would be most distressed by that. Uh, but in truth, if **2**_____________, we would soon find the king of France a useful ally against the Scots! You see, asking, you must find the goods in any situation.

Assassin: It's William Wallace, Sure. He's giving up his sword. Be ready.

William: My lady ... I received your message. This is ... the second time you've warned me of danger. Why?

Isabella: There will be a new shipment of supplies coming north next month ... foods and weapons. They will ...

William: No, stop. Why do you help me? Why do you help me?

Isabella: **3**_____________.

Clip 5 Robert breaking with his father after his father's betrayal

Words and Expressions:

bastard	杂种
deceive	欺骗

Robert: Father! You rotting bastard! Why? Why?

Leper: Longshanks acquired Wallace. So did our nobles. That was the price of your crown.

Robert: Die! I want you to die!

Leper: Soon enough I'll be dead. And you'll be king.

Robert: I don't want anything from you. You're not a man! And you're not my father.

Leper: You're my son, and you've always known my mind.

Robert: You deceived me.

Leper: You let yourself be deceived. In your heart, you always knew what had to happen here. At last, you know what it means to hate. Now you're ready to be a king.

Robert: My hate ... will die with you.

Task 1 Dub the voice with your partner.

Task 2 Discussion: Analyze the characters of Robert and his father.

Clip 6 Wallace getting nabbed

Words and Expressions:

taint	污点；玷污	treason	叛国（罪）
allegiance	忠诚；拥护	confess	承认；供认
purify	给……赎罪		

Task 1 Watch the video clip and fill in the missing words.

Executioner: William Wallace, you stand in taint of high **1**__________.

William: Against whom?

Executioner: Against your King. Have you anything to say?

William: Never in my whole life ... did I swear **2**__________ to him.

Executioner: It matters not. He is your King. Confess, and you may receive a quick death. Deny, and you must be **3**__________ by pain. Do you confess? Do you confess? Then on the morrow, you shall receive your **4**__________.

Clip 7 Isabella persuading Wallace swearing allegiance to the king

Words and Expressions:

dull	减轻	numb	使麻木
wail	哀号	torture	使痛苦

William: My lady.

Isabella: Sire ... I come to beg you ... to confess all and swear allegiance to the king that he might show you mercy.

William: Will he show mercy to my country?

Isabella: Mercy is to die quickly, perhaps even live in a tower. In time, who knows what can happen? If you can only live ...

William: If I swear to him, then all that I am is dead already.

Isabella: You will die. It will be awful.

William: a) Every man dies. Not every man really lives.

Isabella: Drink this. It will dull your pain.

William: No. It will numb my wits. I must have them all. For b) if I'm senseless, or if I wail, then Longshanks will have broken me.

Isabella: I can't bear the thought of your torture. Take it.

William: All right.

Task 1 Translate the underlined sentences into Chinese.

a) ______________________________

b) ______________________________

Clip 8 Isabella praying for absolving Wallace

Isabella: I have come to beg for the life of William Wallace.

Prince: You're quite taken with him, aren't you?

Isabella: I respect him. At worst, he was a worthy enemy. Show mercy, O thou great king, and win the respect of your own people. Even now ... you are incapable of mercy. And you ... To you, that word is as unfamiliar as love.

Prince: Before he lost his powers of speech, he told me his one comfort was that he would live to know Wallace was dead.

Isabella: ______________________________.

Task 1 **Watch the video clip and take down what Isabella said in the last turn.**

____

____

____

____

III Review the movie

1. Cultural Notes

1) Edward I

Edward I (17 June 1239 – 7 July 1307), also known as Edward Longshanks and the Hammer of the Scots, was King of England from 1272 to 1307, the first son of Henry Ⅲ. Edward I was a tall man for his era, hence the nickname "Longshanks". According to some English chroniclers, Edward I was a great king. He set up a parliamentary system, conquered Wales and Ireland, and also loved his wife deeply. But the atrocities that appear in the film do not seem to have been exaggerated, since, for example, the executions of Robert I's three brothers actually took place, as did the execution and quartering of Wallace, all of which suggests that his cruel behaviour in Scotland is not overstated in the film.

2) William Wallace

William Wallace (1270 – 23 August 1305) was a Scottish landowner who became one of the main leaders during the Wars of Scottish Independence. Wallace defeated an English army at the Battle of Stirling Bridge in September 1297. He was appointed Guardian of Scotland and served until his defeat at the Battle of Falkirk in July 1298. In August 1305, Wallace was captured in Robroyston and handed over to King Edward I of England, who had him hanged, drawn, and quartered for high treason and crimes against English civilians.

2. Classical lines from the film

1) Fight, and you may die. Run, and you'll live. At least a while. And dying in your beds many years from now. Would you be willing to trade all the days from this day to that for one chance ... just one chance ...
作战，你也许会死；逃走，你会活下来，至少暂时是这样，然而多年以后，你会终老而死。你们是否愿意用一切来换今天一个机会……就这么一个机会……

2) You tell your king, that William Wallace will not be ruled. Nor will any Scot while I'm alive.
你回去告诉你的国王，威廉姆·华莱士绝不会屈服。苏格兰人民也绝不会屈服。

3) Every man dies. Not every man really lives.
每个人都会死，但不是每个人都真正活过。

3. Film Review

1) Hero and Love

The story of William Wallace unfolded in leading the Scots into a struggle for freedom from England's brutal regime, through which the epic qualities — tragic romance and unbounded heroism were revealed. In the early episode, Wallace was sent abroad to be educated. Afterwards, he returned and fell in love with a beautiful woman named Murron. In order to get round an English law allowing a nobleman to rape a Scottish bride on her wedding night, Wallace and Murron got married in secret. But brutally, Murron was murdered by an Englishman. With a vengeance, Wallace slit the murderer's throat. From then on, the story developed into the episode full of political treachery and unrelenting battles. Later on, Wallace had a second romance with Princess Isabelle, Longshank's daughter-in-law, who got pregnant in the end. She confided to Wallace all the secrets she kept as an emissary to the Scots. It is sarcastic love. But hero's love always ends with lament. Before execution, Isabella persuaded Wallace to drink some kind of stuff to dull his pain. However, Wallace refused to do so, saying "No. It will numb my wits. I must have them all. For if I'm senseless, or if I wail, then Longshanks will have broken me." It is the true portrayal of heroism. Fighting till the end, Wallace had never given in to the king despite being half hanged and racked. Facing death unflinchingly, the fighter shouted instead, "freedom!" as he was about to be beheaded.

2) Loyalty and Treachery

What most strikes us in the film is the legendary Scots warrior, William Wallace who led his Scotsmen into uprisings against the English oppressor. In the film the director succeeded in portraying the hero, a Scots Spartacus. In the year of about 1300, Scotland was under the English crown — Edward I, who was a cruel, fiendish and brutal tyrant. As a young boy, William Wallace witnessed Edward's treachery. He pretended to negotiate with the rebellious Scotsmen but murdered them all. Many years later, Wallace grew up. He became a leader of revolt against Edward I. His troops were the most glorious in the history of Scotland. When we watched the film, we were touched by Wallace's strong will and unyielding struggle for freedom and independence. He devoted his life to the independence of Scotland. His bravery and courage was completely showed in the execution in Bannockburn.

The film reveals the spiteful Scotland aristocracy who betrayed Wallace. Scotland's nobles, including Robert Ⅶ de Bruce who is most likely to become the king of Scotland, swore to stand alongside Wallace and dispatched armed forces to fight with him. However, in the battle of Falkirk, the Scotland aristocracy deserted Wallace by withdrawing their cavalry, which caused the total destruction of Wallace's army. Surprised, Wallace found that it was Robert Ⅶ the Bruce who pretended to be caught by an English knight. However, in the end, Robert Ⅶ the Bruce was reluctant to be an accomplice and helped Wallace escape from the siege. Robert Ⅵ the Bruce discerned his son's ambivalence and helped to bring about another negotiation with Edward. Unfortunately, Wallace ended up being captured and sentenced to death.

The portrayal of Robert Ⅵ the Bruce, as a father, is impressive. In all scenes he set himself an example of Machiavellianism as well as of paternal love, as he guided his son along the difficult road to the throne of Scotland, which had been his own great ambition. Ethically, he is more than blamed; he strikes us with his skill, intrigue and machination. However, his paternal love faded away after his son was desperate to leave.

Finally, Robert Ⅶ the Bruce stood on the side of his people who bravely revolted against the English regime. In the battlefield of Bannock, he called on his Scotsmen to fight for freedom and independence, and won the battle. In the end, Scotland gained independence under Robert's leadership. And Robert the Bruce became the new king of Scotland.

3) Brave and Cunning

A hero is a persona who can make remarkable accomplishments and be remembered and admired for bravery, strength, and goodness, and a person who possesses the quality of extraordinary valor and fortitude. Every epic movie must have a hero, who represents a lofty and heroic quality. William Wallace in *Brave Heart* is an incarnation of a real legendary hero.

Before the battle of Stirling, Wallace rode ahead of hundreds of Scots and inspired them to march forward. "If they fail to go forward," he says, "one day they will look back with regret and be willing to give everything to reclaim that chance to fight for freedom." William Wallace was a prominent commander in the battlefield. He invented unique tactics and weapons, defeating the English troops. The English army rained hundreds of arrows at the Scots, who returned fire by throwing spears. The English army's morale began to slump.

Wallace was ignorant about what politics was. As a result, he was defeated by Edward I in the battle of Falkirk because he believed in Scotland nobles who would sacrifice their profits for their own motherland and supported him with their armed forces. But what interested the nobles was how many lands and what profits they could get in the war against the English, rather than their homeland. They betrayed him. Again when his comrades-in-arms and friends persuaded him not to negotiate with Scotland nobles, he didn't listened to their warnings and insisted going to do what he thought right on his own will. Consequently, he was captured. It was his weakness in his personality that cost him his life. In a sense, William Wallace was a tragic figure in *Brave Heart*. However, Wallace was still a powerful and passionate man, and would be remembered as a Scots Spartacus, and deserve all the credits given by his country.

In *Brave Heart*, King Edward I (Longshanks) was no doubt a cunning, sly, and cold-blooded villain. At the beginning, he disdained the rebellion led by William Wallace, regarding them as merely a gang of bandits. But the revolt spread throughout Scotland and Wallace's army conquered many shires which used to be under the control of the English regime. However, a chain of bad news didn't panic him. His vision of the war showed us what a real politician was. He had a clear idea that his son was incompetent to be heir to the throne, nor had the ability to command the army fighting back. Therefore, Edward I utilized his beautiful daughter-in-law to negotiate with Wallace, which could buy him time to call up troops to suppress the rebellion. His plot succeeded in driving a wedge between Wallace and Scotland nobles. Consequently, Wallace was deserted and arrested due to the nobles' betrayal. His head was hung on London Bridge, and his arms and legs was traveled around Britain as a warning. Finally, Wallace's remains were thrown over the Scotland to scare the Scots not to revolt. But, Longshanks failed. His cruel and violent ruling could only frighten the coward. After Wallace died, Robert, inspired by Wallace's spirit, continued to call on the Scotsmen to fight against the English crown. It was Robert the Bruce who carried on Wallace's cause and won the freedom and independence of Scotland finally.

4. Extended Reading

Film: *Far and Away*

Far and Away (1991), the title of the movie, is also the distance between dreams and reality. The detachability of the dreams offers the story's possibility and credibility.

Joseph (Tom Cruise) and Shannon (Nicole Kidman) were two Irish young people. One was the son of a poor tenant who could not afford the tenancy. He had his house burnt as a result and died away fortuneless. The other was the daughter of a rich landlord who gained a lot of wealth through years' accumulation. The tenant happened to be paying for the landlord's field, so Joseph met Shannon when he entered her father's mansion to take his revenge for his father's death. He failed, having more time to stay with the noble maid. Two hearts were both pursuing for freedom and independence. Joseph always bore in mind his father's last words: "A man is worthless and soulless until he has had his own land." He was tolerant of miseries but reluctant to leave his home for a new life. Shannon was well-educated and open-minded and eager to seek for a new life in the New World but unready to face obstacles and setbacks. Once they united accidentally and set for America, their dreams seemed approachable ...

5. Homework

1) Watch the film *Brave Heart* again and try to write down your feelings after watching.

2) Think about what freedom means in the film.

Unit 6 Mona Lisa Smile 《蒙娜丽莎的微笑》

I Preview the movie

1. Background

Directed by	Mike Newell
Screenplay by	Lawrence Konner and Mark Rosenthal
Based on	the Mona Lisa, the famous painting by Leonardo da Vinci, and the song of the same name, originally performed by Nat King Cole, which was covered by Seal for the movie
Stars	Julia Roberts, Kirsten Dunst, Julia Stiles and Maggie Gyllenhaal
Distributed by	Revolution Studios and Columbia Pictures
Release date	2003
Box office	$141,337,989

2. Plot

Mona Lisa Smile is an inspirational film that explores life through marriage, feminism and education led by a liberal-minded teacher, Katherine Watson from Oakland State, who finds a job in the art history department at an all-girl's college, called Wellesley, in the fall of 1953. Her impression of Wellesley quickly fizzled after her first day of class where she was baptized and humiliated by smug students in front of a supervisor. However, Katherine, determined not to surrender under pressure, departs from the syllabus in order to regain the upper hand. She challenged the girls' idea of what is composed of art and prompted them to explore their potential for change, rather than accept the traditional views of an institution where education was viewed merely as a stopgap before marrying a man. However, her teaching was considered unorthodox; over time Katherine earned their esteem.

II View the movie

Clip 1 : The First Class at Wellesley

Words and Expressions:

impulse	冲动
sophisticated	复杂的，精致的，深奥微妙的
archeologist	考古学家
herd	兽群
suggested supplements	课后辅导材料

Task 1 **Mark T (True) or F (False) for the following statements according to the clip.**

a) _______ Katherine is bad treated at the beginning of the first class.

b) _______ Girls are snobbery in the first class.

c) _______ Katherine finishes her first class with confidence.

Task 2 **Answer the questions from this video clip.**

a) How do girls behave at the first class?

____

b) What does Katherine's feeling after dismissing the first class?

____

____

Clip 2 The second class

Words and Expressions:

syllabus	教学大纲	grotesque	怪诞的
aggressive	富于侵略性	erotic	色情的
rotted	腐烂的	much less	更不用说
brilliant	精彩绝伦的	screw you	去你的

Betty: What is that?

Katherine Waston: You tell me. Carcass by Soutine,1925.

Susan Delacorte: It's not on the syllabus.

Katherine Waston: No, it's not. Is it any good? Come on, ladies. There's no wrong answer. There's also no textbook telling you what to think. It's not that easy, is it?

Betty: All right. No. It's not good. In fact, I wouldn't even call it art. It's grotesque.

Connie: Is there a rule against grotesque?

Giselle: I think there's something aggressive about it ... and erotic.

Betty: To you, everything is erotic ...

Giselle: Everything is erotic.

Katherine Waston: Girls.

Susan Delacorte: Aren't there standards?

Betty: Of course. Otherwise a tacky velvet painting could be equated to a Rembrandt.

Connie: My uncle Ferdie has two tacky velvet paintings. He loves those clowns.

Betty: There are standards, technique, composition, color, even subject. So if you're suggesting that rotted side of meat is art ... much less good art, then what are we going to learn?

Katherine Waston: Just that. You have outlined our new syllabus, Betty. Thank you. What is art? What makes it good or bad?And who decides? Next slide, please. Twenty-five years ago someone thought this was brilliant.

Connie: I can see that. Who?

Katherine Waston: My mother. I painted it for her birthday. Next slide. This is my mom.

Betty: Is it art?

Susan Delacorte: It's a snapshot.

Katherine Waston: If I told you Ansel Adams had taken it, would that make a difference?

Betty: Art isn't art until someone says it is.

Katherine Waston: It's art!

Betty: The right people.

Katherine Waston: Who are they?

Giselle: Betty Warren! So we're lucky we have one right here.

Betty: Screw you.

Katherine Waston: Could you go back to the Soutine, please? Just look at it again. Look beyond the paint. Let us try to open our minds to a new idea. All right, back to chapter three. Has anyone read it? Okay.

Task 1 Dub the voice for the roles in the movie according to the clip.

Task 2 Answer the questions from this video clip.

a) What change does Katherine make in the second class?

____

b) Does the change make an effect? Why?

____

____

Task 3 **Discussion: what standards does one judge a good art?**

Clip 3 President's warning

Task 1 **Watch the video clip and fill in the missing words.**

President Jocelyn Carr: I've been getting some **1**_________ about your teaching methods, Katherine. They're a little **2**_________ ... for Wellesley. We are **3**_________, Katherine.

Katherine Waston: Yes, I noticed.

President Jocelyn Carr: So if you'd like to stay here ...

Katherine Waston: Is that a question?

President Jocelyn Carr: More a **4**_________.

Katherine Waston: About my staying here?

President Jocelyn Carr: You'll have your **5**_________ in May. Until then ... a little less modern art.

Task 2 **Answer the questions from this video clip.**

a) Does president think Katherine is qualified?

____

b) What does president warn Katherine?

____

Clip 4 Betty's persuasion to Joan

Words and Expressions:

gab	空谈；瞎扯
Yale	耶鲁大学

Joan: Beautiful! You've got everything you've ever dreamed of.

Betty: You will too.

Joan: I've got a secret to tell you. You swear you won't gab to anyone? I got accepted early to Yale Law School.

Betty: To what?! Why?! You don't want to be a lawyer.

Joan: Maybe I do.

Betty: You won't a) switch cold creams without asking me, but you applied to school?

Joan: b) On a lark. We never thought I'd get in.

Betty: Who's "we"?

Joan: Miss Watson. She practically filled out my application for me.

Betty: You've got to be kidding me! What right does she have? You're getting married!

Joan: First of all, there's no ring on this finger. Second, I can do both. I can.

Betty: How does Tommy feel about this?

Joan: He doesn't know. No one does.

Betty: Not even her?

Joan: No.

Task 1 **Dub the voice for the roles in the movie according to the clip.**

Task 2 **According to the context, guess the correct meaning from the underlined phrases.**

a) You won't switch cold creams without asking me, but you applied to school?

A. 泼冷水 B. 改变计划 C. 肆意妄为 D. 食言

b) On a lark. We never thought I'd get in.

A. 令人高兴的是 B. 意想不到的是 C. 令人惊讶的是 D. 令人困惑的是

Task 3 **Answer the questions from this video clip.**

a) What is Betty angry for?

____

Clip 5 Clash between Katherine and Betty

Words and Expressions:

a sight for sore eyes	受欢迎的人
turn their heads	漠视
subversive	颠覆分子
consequence	后果

Task 1 Watch the video clip and fill in the missing words.

Connie: You're a sight for sore eyes.

Betty: I would've been here sooner, silly me. I thought class was in the classroom.

Katherine Waston: Glad you could join us, Mrs. Jones. We thought we'd lost you.

Connie: There's a sort of an unwritten rule for married girls.

Katherine Waston: Don't bother Since your wedding, you've missed six classes, a paper and your midterm.

Betty: Well, thank God, I didn't miss the paint-by-numbers lecture. I was on my honeymoon and then I had to set up house. What does she expect?

Katherine Waston: **1**_________.

Connie: Most of the faculty turn their heads when the married students miss a class or two.

Katherine Waston: Then why not get married as freshmen? That way you could graduate without actually ever **2**_________ on campus.

Betty: Don't **3**_________ our traditions just because you're **4**_________.

Katherine Waston: Don't **5**_________ this class just because you're married.

Betty: Don't disrespect me just because you're not.

Katherine Waston: Come to class, do the work, or I'll **6**_________ you.

Betty: If you fail me, there will be **7**_________.

Katherine Waston: Are you **8** _________ me ?

Betty: I'm educating you.

Katherine Waston: That's my job.

Task 2 Answer the questions from this video clip.

a) How do you examine the character of Betty?

____

b) How do you examine Katherine from the perspective of teaching?

____

Clip 6 Joan's choice

Words and Expressions:

Philadelphia	费城
seal	决定
bake one's cake and eat it	两者兼得
petrify	使惊呆
spur-of-the-moment	头脑一热
elope	私奔

Katherine Waston: Come in Seven law schools within 45 minutes of Philadelphia. You can study and get dinner on the table by 5:00.

Joan: It's too late.

Katherine Waston: No. Some accept late admissions. I was upset at first. I can tell you now. When Tommy told me that he got accepted to Penn, I thought: "Oh, god, her fate is sealed. She works so hard. How can she throw it all away?" I realized you won't have to. You could bake your cake and eat it, too. It's just wonderful.

Joan: We're married. We eloped over the weekend. It turned out he was petrified of a big ceremony ... so we did a sort of spur-of-the-moment thing. Very romantic. Look.

Katherine Waston: It's beautiful.

Joan: It was my choice. Not to go. He would have supported it.

Katherine Waston: But you don't have to choose.

Joan: No, I have to. I want a home. I want a family. It's not something I'll sacrifice.

Katherine Waston: No one's asking you to sacrifice that, Joan. I just want you to understand that you can do both.

Joan: Do you think I'll wake up one morning and regret not being a lawyer?

Katherine Waston: Yes, I'm afraid that you will.

Joan: Not as much as I'd regret not having a family. Not being there to raise them. I know exactly what I'm doing, and it doesn't make me any less smart. This must seem terrible to you.

Katherine Waston: I didn't say that. I ...

Joan: Sure you did. You always do. You stand in class and tell us to look beyond the image, but you don't. To you, a housewife is someone who sold her soul for a center hall colonial. She has no depth, no intellect, no interests. You're the one who said I could do anything I wanted. This is what I want.

Katherine Waston: Congratulations. Be happy.

Task 1 Translate the underlined sentences into Chinese.

a) ______________________________

____

b) ______________________________

____

____

Task 2 Mark T (True) or F (False) for the following statements according to the clip.

a) _______ Joan has made a compromise to life.

b) _______ Joan is not a smart girl.

c) _______ Joan's choice indicates that girls at Wellesley learn to think independently.

Clip 7 Katherine showing her attitude to love

Task 1 Mark T (True) or F (False) for the following statements according to the clip.

a) _______ Katherine will forgive Bill's dishonesty.

b) _______ Katherine aims to help people find her way at Wellesley.

Task 2 Answer the questions from this video clip.

a) What is Katherine's attitude towards love?

____

b) Why does Bill say it is impossible to be honest with Katherine?

____

Clip 8 Betty's agony

Task 1 Answer the questions from this video clip.

a) What's Betty's agony?

____

b) What will Betty do next?

____

III Review the movie

1. Cultural Notes

1) Wellesley College

Wellesley College is a private women's liberal-arts college in the town of Wellesley, Massachusetts, the United States, west of Boston. Founded in 1870, Wellesley is one of the original Seven Sisters Colleges and consistently ranks among the top five liberal arts colleges in the United States. Wellesley, founded by Pauline and Henry Fowle Durant, believes in educational opportunity for women. Wellesley was founded with the intention to prepare women for "... great conflicts, for vast reforms in social life".

2) Bohemian

Bohemian, a word in this film, denotes "a socially unconventional person, especially one who is involved in the arts".

3) Electra complex

In Neo-Freudian psychology, the Electra complex, as proposed by Carl Gustav Jung, is a girl's psychosexual competition with her mother for possession of her father. In the course of her psychosexual development, the complex is the girl's phallic stage.

4) Vincent van Gogh

Vincent van Gogh (30 March 1853 – 29 July 1890) was a major Post-Impressionist painter. As a Dutch artist, his work had a far-reaching influence on the 20th-century art. His output includes self portraits, landscapes, still lives, portraits and paintings of cypresses, wheat fields and sunflowers. Van Gogh drew as a child but did not paint until his late twenties, completing many of his best-known works during the last two years of his life.

2. Classical lines from the film

1) Then I'd miss the meeting. Sorry, guys. We take a rain check?
那我会错过会议的。抱歉，朋友们。我们延期好吗？

2) You're a sight for sore eyes.
你真让我们望眼欲穿。

3.) Then why not get married as freshmen?
为什么不大学一年级就结婚？

4) That way you could graduate without actually ever stepping foot on campus.
那样的话你可以不用到学校上课就能毕业。

5) Don't disregard our traditions just because you're subversive.
不要因为你是个颠覆分子，就可以无视我们的传统。

6) Don't disrespect this class just because you're married.
不要因为你结婚了，就不重视这堂课。

7) Don't disrespect me just because you're not.
不要因为你没结婚，就不尊重我。

8) Come to class. Do the work, or I'll fail you.
按时上课，做作业，要不然给你不及格。

9) If you fail me, there will be consequences.
如果你让我不及格，后果自负。

10) Well, not every relationship is meant for marriage.
不是每次恋爱最后都以结婚告终的。

11) They've been on-again, off-again for the past few years.
过去几年他们一直分分合合。

12) Don't wash your dirty laundry in public.
家丑不可外扬。

3. Film Review

1) Patriarchy and Feminism

Traditional and conservative ideology about women still dominated the society at Wellesley where girls were taught how to serve their husbands with their heart and soul, rather than seek an education or career. The girls had been preached that, if they pursue their own careers, they could not be able to be home in time to get dinner cooked for their husbands. They did not have a clear idea of what they really want. Betty and Katherine are, respectively, representatives of Patriarchy and Feminism.

Betty, an upper-crust girl, who was strong in her belief in what her mother had instilled in her, challenged Katherine from the beginning. She believed that a woman's role in life was to be a good wife, mother and homemaker. There was nothing wrong with the belief. However, if the society and college take it as the main goal or even the only goal for girls, they could lose their identity in the conventionality. Betty was immersed in illusion to be a qualified housewife though she was not so happy with it. She still believed that she could be a devoted wife even if it seemed impossible until Betty finally learned that she had been seen as another woman rather than a wife. She remembered everything her mother told her, and took her belief very seriously. Betty's marriage ended in haste, revealing that conservative ideology becomes a barrier to individual freedom. Betty was apathetic, forbidding, vicious and blunt, showing that she lost the freedom of soul and stubbornly adhered to the outworn rules and ideas.

Katherine, a modernist instructor, who intended to make a difference, — pursue freedom and liberty, was called "subversive" at Wellesley college. What Katherine did is to help the students find their identity, a hard task. She was thrilled at the vision of cultivation some brightest women. However, after her first day in the college, her visional image of Wellesley quickly faded away. In the dark, she licked her wounds and fled from the established practice. Katherine exposed the students to the modern artist not permitted by the school board. However, the students did not show respect for the alien form of art at first. Over time, her independent and unorthodox personality earned their understandings and esteem.

By carefully designing the course, she taught girls how to comprehend the spirit of exploration and innovation. For example, students were encouraged to reflect on the technique of painting in multiple perspectives during teaching. They learnt how to appreciate Vincent van Gogh's work, *sunflower*. By exploring the works' connotation, she enlightened students to combine art and life, through which they could look into themselves and found their self-worth. She knew how much Joan wanted to be admitted to Yale, and believed that Joan had the best chance of all the students. She filled out the application form for Joan. When Joan give up the admission to Yale, Katherine felt upset. However, she still talked Joan around.

By marrying Paul, she showed her students that she was no different than they were, and it was normal to stress marriage over career. Katherine also fell in love with Professor Bill, despite the fact that he had an affair with a student. Katherine said to him: "No students. I'm serious. I don't want to teach a class wondering why a girl is wearing my perfume ... I need your word." Her words showed that she took her love seriously. However, Katherine quickly learned that Bill had been lying to her about his past, and she terminated their short-term affair. Different from Nancy, she could boldly pursue her love with passion. In contrast, greatly influenced by feudal ideas, Nancy adhered to the traditional concept of marriage, and became the victim of patriarchy. The youth doesn't mean rebellion but fit in with the shackling system.

2) Female consciousness from weak to strong

The film challenges the traditional objectives of woman's education which develops girls into a good mother and a good wife. The teacher, Watson, tried to tell young women that there were other possibilities in life worthwhile to fight for. She suggested that girls could do well in both higher education and a family at the same time. Katherine sees teaching at Wellesley as an opportunity to enlighten the girls' minds, and encourages them to explore all the possibilities that life has offered besides marriage and family. She attempts to liberate her students from a very conservative ideology.

Katherine had a conversation with Joan outside of Wellesley College after Joan got C in the exam. She gave Joan another chance to revise her paper and persuaded her into applying for law school in Yale. She tried to convince Joan that she could balance having education and doing dinner, after Joan decided to give up education. Joan thought that to be a housewife was not a bad option. In the end, Joan resolutely decided to get married and became a housewife. The important thing is that she made her decision on her own will without any pressure from others. Joan realizes her dream: she can choose to be what she desires to. She becomes the master of her life. Joan's "retreat" is not a compromise but a huge step forward, which implies that girls at Wellesley have begun to think and choose independently.

Unlike Joan's marriage, there is no premarital romance between Betty and Spencer, as the basis of their marriage. Only while they were getting married, her mother gave her a piece of advice on how to deal with family relationship, "a good wife lets her husband think that everything's his idea, even when it's not". We see a husband's authority over his wife and the wife's resistance to it. Betty, who showed respect for tradition, followed her parents' advice. She has plenty of fantasies about perfect marriage, but she neglects that all illusions have no love as solid foundation. Betty, who gave in to her destiny, made a plea for help from her mother when her marriage was about to break down, only receiving the reply—"don't wash dirty laundry in public". She pointed at the portrait of *Mona Lisa* and queried her mother—"You see, she has been being smiling, but is she really happy? She looks happy. However, a lot of affairs are not what we superficially see of it". Betty is never a master of her own life. She was an obedient girl, giving in to her family, society, and female's predetermined future. By opening up Betty's mind, Katherine has made a change to her life. She was lectured that they have equal rights and opportunities in the society as men have. In the end, Betty filed for divorce and started a new life. Betty also decided to continue her study in Yale and took law as her major.

Katharine's attitudes towards love and life deeply influenced the students around her. The United States got involved in the World War Ⅱ, which profoundly affected the American's life, and Katharine is no exception. Her sweetheart since childhood left for battlefield. When the war was over, she married someone else. Then Katherine decided to continue her study. Katharine told her students about her past experiences frankly at the party. They felt sorry for what she had experienced. However, Katherine didn't think it so bad. She told them that love was not necessarily for marriage. Nancy, a teacher of the school, whose lover married another person similarly after war had never said goodbye to shadows of grey. She even didn't dare to admit that her lover had left her. Katherine's independent and open-minded attitudes towards love and marriage won respect from those students who had ever despised her as Old Miss.

4. Extended Reading

Film: *Dead Poets Society*

The movie tells about the story of a group of rich students at the Welton Academy, which is a famous preparatory school in Vermont. They come to the school to accept the best education so that they can make their dreams come true. In others' eyes, these students are successful and will have a wonderful future. However, it is obvious that they just do what their parents or their teachers have told them and their future has been arranged. They have dreams but not true ones. So what the movie shows to us is that a passionate and unconventional teacher, Mr Keating, inspires his students to fight against the conventional social system to pursue what they really want. Finally, these students begin to know what the real dream is and what the real happiness is asweuas what the real meaning of life is.

5. Homework

1) Watch the film again and write an article after watching.

2) Think about what feminist ideas mean in the film.

Unit 7 Princess Diaries《公主日记》

I Preview the movie

1. Background

Directed by	Garry Marshall
Based on	The Princess Diaries By Meg Cabot
Stars	Julie Andrews Anne Hathaway Heather Matarazzo Héctor Elizondo
Distributed by	Buena Vista Pictures
Box office	$165,335,153

2. Plot

Mia Thermopolis is a 15-year-old girl who lives with her artist mother Helen and her cat Fat Louie in San Francisco. She is somewhat clumsy and unpopular, and her only real friends are Lilly Moscovitz and Lilly's brother Michael, who has a crush on Mia secretly.

Just before her 16th birthday, Mia meets her paternal grandmother, Clarisse, from Genovia, a small European kingdom, and is stunned to learn that Clarisse is in fact the Queen and that she herself is actually the princess and heir to the Genovian throne. Mia refuses to take the throne at first but is finally persuaded to take "princess lessons" first and reconsider her decision before the upcoming Genovian Independence Day ball. During these days, Mia is given a makeover from hairdresser Paolo who then breaks his confidentiality agreement, causing a press frenzy, and a sudden surge in popularity at school for Mia. However, that's not the worst. At a state dinner, Mia embarrasses herself with her clumsiness. In order to release Mia's expended pressure, the Queen allows Mia to take her out in Mia's late 60s Ford Mustang convertible for the day to an amusement arcade but Mia runs her car into a cable car. Luckily and surprisingly Queen Clarisse saves the day by appointing the attending police officer and tram driver to the "Genovian Order of the Rose", which leaves a deep impression on Mia.

Mia accepts Josh Bryant's invitation to a beach party happily, but only to find the truth hurtful. Josh only wants to get his fame by publicly kissing her, and meanwhile Josh's ex-girlfriend, Lana, tricks her into changing clothes in a tent, pulling it away as she is semi-nude just as the paparazzi arrive. Momentarily, Mia is thrown to the forefront of public opinion. Too much humility makes her feel that she is nowhere near ready to be a true princess.

Having experienced so much, Mia finally decides to run away before the ball. She cannot defeat the terror at the thought of publicity announcing her decision. When she packs up luggage, she finds a letter from her late father. His touching words make her change her mind, and she makes her way to the ball. But, the weather isn't as good as expected. Mia's car breaks down in the rain. It seems that she will miss the ball. Suddenly, there is a car coming towards her ...

II View the movie

Clip 1 First meeting with grandma

Words and Expressions:

shut up	闭嘴	beg one's pardon	请求某人原谅
Your Majesty	陛下	heir	继承人
rewind and freeze	倒过去，暂停一下	royal	王室的

Task 1 Watch the video clip and fill in the missing words.

Mia: Why **1**__________ would you pick me to be your princess?

Clarisse: Since your father died, you are the natural heir to the throne of Genovia. That's our law. I'm royal by marriage. You are royal **2**__________. You can rule.

Mia: Rule? Oh, no. Oh, no. No, no, no. Now you have really got the wrong girl. I never lead anybody not at Brownies, not at Camp Fire Girls ... Queen Clarisse, **3**____________, and I'm good at it.

Clarisse: Amelia, I had other expectations also. In my wildest dreams **4**____________. But you are the legal heir, the only heir to the Genovian throne and we will accept the challenge of helping you become the princess that you are. Oh, I can give you books. You will study **5**____________. I can teach you to walk, talk, sit, stand, eat, dress like a princess. Given time, I think you'll find the palace in Genovia a very pleasant place to live.

Mia: Live in Genovia?

Clarisse: It's a wonderful country. Amelia, really.

Mia: Whoa, whoa, just — **6**____________. I'm no princess. I'm still waiting for normal body parts to arrive. I refuse to move to and rule a country and — do you want another reason? I don't want to be a princess!

Task 2 Watch the video clip again and answer the questions.

a) Why does Clarisse pick Mia to be the princess?

____

b) In the video clip, Mia thinks that she isn't qualified to be the princess. Why does she think so? Does she have any other reasons?

____

____

Clip 2 The exposure to Mia's identity

Words and Expressions:

can we quote you	我们能引用你的话吗?	ring off the hook	电话响个不停
on one's way	在去 … … 的路上	get to the bottom of this	找出真相
so to speak	可以说	I outed you.	我出卖了你。
bargain	协议	cope with	应付

Task 1 **Mark T (True) or F (False) for the following statements according to the clip.**

a) _______ Lily reveals to the press that Mia is a princess.

b) _______ Mia thinks that she can bear huge pressure from the public because she looks at the big picture for her family.

Task 2 **Answer the questions from this video clip.**

a) Why does Clarisse mention security plans for Mia's safety?

____

b) What's the opinion of Helen in this scene?

____

Clip 3 One-day tour in Los Angeles

Words and Expressions:

blaze up	燃烧起来	expire	期满
put sb on hold	让 … … 在线等	diplomatic immunity	外交豁免权
bestow upon sb the honor	授予某人荣誉	All in a day's work.	日常工作，不足为奇。

Task 1 **Watch Clip 3 and fill in the missing words of the dialogue.**

Clarisse: I do believe **1**____________.

Mia: Uh, uh, uh.

Clarisse: Maybe you can just sneak gently through?

Mia: OK. OK. I'll try.

Clarisse: Good! Right, now, **2**____________.

Mia: I got it!

Clarisse: Yes. You've got it!

Mia: I got it!

Clarisse: You've got it! Uhh!

Mia: Oh! I haven't got it!

Clarisse: Uh-oh! Mia! Brake! Brake! Look out! Down here.

Mia: Uh!

Nun1: 911, I need to report an accident.

People on the trolly. You didn't hear the bell!?

Nun1: They **3**____________.

Nun2: Oh, for the love of god!

Bruce: Put down destruction of **4**____________.

Arthur: I will, I will. And **5**____________, driving without a license, accompanied by an adult whose license expired 45 years ago.

Clarisse: I've been trying to tell you, officer. Licenses don't expire in Genovia. Not for the queen. Don't I have **6**____________?

Arthur: You do. But her, we have to take downtown.

Mia: What?

Arthur: I'm sorry, miss.

Clarisse: It's all right, officer. I understand I ... I understand perfectly.

Mia: You do?

Clarisse: Mia, no town, no city, no country can **7**__________ if its officers and its transportation engineers don't follow **8**______________. Why, I would be proud to have **9**_____________ in Genovia.

Arthur: Aw, shucks, ma'am.

Bruce: Ma'am, **10**_____________.

Task 2 **Dub the voice for Clarisse, Mia and policeman while the video is played again without the sound.**

Clip 4 The beach party

Words and Expressions:

ruin	毁坏
There's no one. I'd rather be here with than you.	我只想和你在这里。

Task 1 **Mark T (True) or F (False) for the following statements according to the clip.**

a) _______ Mia finally goes to Lily's TV show on Saturday night.

b) _______ Mia's first kiss is unfortunately ruined by paparazzi.

c) _______ Michael deceives Mia and informs the media that Mia is on the beach party.

Task 2 **Discussion: As we all know, life in the spotlight is visible. Recently the media have exposed celebrities' private life one after another. People begin to concern about their safety of privacy. On the other hand, some people find that the media can also play the role of supervision and assume the sacred duty of justice. So what's your opinion towards "media"? Which side do you support?**

____

____

____

____

Clip 5 The letter from Mia's father

Words and Expressions:

pardon me	原谅我	pass on one's wisdom	传承智慧
but rather	反而	absence	缺乏

Task 1 **Watch the clip and take down the letter from Phillipe.**

____

____

____

____

Clip 6 At the Genovian Independence Day ball

Task 1 Answer the following questions according to the dialogue.

a) Why does Mia change her mind?

____

b) What does Mia want to do if she were the princess of Genovia?

____

c) Who does Clarisse recognize that has the same spirit as Mia?

____

Task 2 Discussion: Fear is a kind of emotions. It can keep us from pursuing the things in life that really matter — like following dreams, and developing and taking care of important relationships. Take your own experience as an example and tell us how to get rid of fear.

____

____

____

____

III Review the movie

1. Cultural Notes

1) Catch a Falling Star

Catch a Falling Star is a song composed by Paul Vance and Lee Pockriss and its melody is based on a theme from Brahms' Academic Festival Overture. This song was released in 1957 by Perry Como and became a massive hit. It was Como's last hit, reaching No. 1 on the Billboard "Most Played by Jockeys" chart and it was the first single to receive a gold record certification in 1958. Later in 1959, it won Como the Grammy Award for Best Vocal Performance, Male.

2) Ford Mustang

The Ford Mustang is a car concept of the Ford Motor Company. The name was adopted in memory of the World War Ⅱ P-51 Mustang fighter plane. Since the first generation in 1964, the Mustang has gone through several transformations to its current sixth generation. The Mustang made its first public appearance on a racetrack as pace car for the 1964 Indianapolis 500. Since then it has been popular and successful in various kinds of races, such as drag racing, sports car racing and stock car racing. The 1965 Mustang won the Tiffany Gold Medal for excellence in American design, the first automobile ever to do so. And it was on the Car and Driver Ten Best list in 1983, 1987, 1988, 2005, 2006, and 2011. The Mustang has appeared in many films, such as *Goldfinger*, *Bullitt* and *Diamonds Are Forever*.

3) Fabergé

The House of Fabergé is a jewellery firm founded by Gustav Faberge in 1842 in St. Petersburg, Imperial Russia. Gustav was followed by his son Peter Carl Fabergé, until the firm was nationalized by the Bolsheviks in 1918. The accented name "Fabergé" suggests an explicit French character which was closely associated with luxury goods, appealing to the Russian nobility's francophilia. The firm has been famous for designing elaborate jewel-encrusted Fabergé eggs for the Russian Tsars and a range of other works of high quality and sophisticated details. In 1937, the brand name "Fabergé" was sold and then re-sold in 1964 to cosmetics company Rayette Inc., which changed its name to Rayette-Fabergé Inc. As the name was resold more times, Fabergé companies (such as Fabergé Inc.) launched clothing lines, the cologne Brut (which became the best-selling cologne at the time), the perfume Babe, hair products, and undertook film production.

4) Hermès

Hermès, or Hermès International S.A., Hermes of Paris, is a French manufacturer founded in 1837. Since the 1950s its logo has been a Duc carriage with horse. Hermès has 14 product divisions covering leather, scarves, ties, men's wear, women's fashion, perfume, watches, stationery, footwear, gloves, enamel, decorative arts, tableware, and jewellery. The company keeps tight control over the design and manufacture of its vast inventory and is very attached to its old-fashioned business mode, rejecting mass production, assembly lines, and mechanization. Hermès goods are almost entirely made by hand in France in middle-sized workshops, with an emphasis on quality manufacturing. Indeed, Hermes claims most items are fabricated from beginning to end by one person only, which is supposed to be a guarantee of the quality and uniqueness of Hermès products.

5) Woodstock Rock Festival

The Woodstock Festival, or the Woodstock Music & Art Fair, or simply Woodstock, was a music festival, billed as "An Aquarian Exposition: 3 Days of Peace & Music". It was held at Max Yasgur's 600-acre dairy farm in the Catskills near the hamlet of White Lake in the town of Bethel, New York, from August 15 to 18, 1969. During the weekend, 32 acts performed outdoors before an audience of 400,000 young people. It is widely regarded as a pivotal moment in popular music history. Rolling Stone listed it as one of the 50 Moments that Changed the History of Rock and Roll. The festival is also widely considered to be the definitive nexus for the larger counterculture generation. The event was captured in the 1970 documentary movie *Woodstock*, an accompanying soundtrack album, and Joni Mitchell's song *Woodstock*, which commemorated the event and became a major hit for Crosby, Stills, Nash & Young.

6) Jeopardy!

Jeopardy! is an American television game show created by Merv Griffin in 1964. The show features a quiz competition in a unique form of Q&A, encompassing various fields, such as history, literature, art, popular culture, technology, sports, geography, languages, etc. Contrary to the common quizzes, contestants are presented with general knowledge clues in the form of answers, and must phrase their responses in the form of questions. There are three contestants each time and they need to compete in three rounds: *Jeopardy!*, Double Jeopardy!, and Final Jeopardy! Before the start of the round, the host will regularly remind contestants of topics or place emphasis on category themes. The show has not only gained popularity in the US but has also gained a worldwide following in many other countries with some regional adaptations.

2. Classical lines from the film

1) Courage is not the absence of fear but rather the judgment that something else is more important than fear. The brave may not live forever but the cautious do not live at all.
勇者并非无所畏惧，而是能判断出还有比恐惧更重要的东西。愚勇不可取，但故步自封则一点机会也没有。

2) To be a princess, you have to believe that you are a princess. You've got to walk the way you think a princess would walk. So, you gotta think tall. You gotta smile and wave, and just have fun.
要想成为公主，你得相信自己就是一个公主。你应该像你所想象中的公主那般为人处世。所以，你得高瞻远瞩，从容不迫，笑对人生。

3) My expectation in life is to be invisible and I am good at it.
我希望在生活中默默无闻，而且我也很擅长这样。

4) I am still waiting for normal body parts to arrive.
我还等着正常的生长发育呢。

5) Because you saw me when I was invisible.
因为你在我默默无闻的时候也能看见我。

6) My thoughts, and thoughts of other people who are much smarter than me, can be heard, and just maybe, those thoughts could be turned into actions.
我的想法以及比我更聪明的人的想法能为人所知晓，而且也许那些想法还有可能付诸现实。

7) I'm really not good at speech-making.
我真的不善言辞。

8) I present you with this diary to fill the pages with your special thoughts, special thoughts of your wonderful life.
我送你这本日记本让你记下你精彩的一生。

3. Film Review

The *Princess Diaries* is a modern day fairy tale which is adored by 10-year-old girls who think they're 14 going on 18, thanks to a comic gem of a performance by these best actors and director.

Shot on the same soundstage that was used for Mary Poppins, the Disney comedy catapulted Julie Andrews to international stardom. The *Princess Diaries* is an enjoyable fairy tale that its picture is not that different from Andrews's 1964 Oscar-winning picture. This time, the very graceful Andrews starts as a European Queen, endowed with the task of transforming her shy and awkward granddaughter, who's unaware of her royal blood, into a real-life princess.

Compared with Garry Marshal's previous work, the new comedy is even softer and more old-fashioned than his commercial hits, *Pretty Woman* and *Runaway Bride*. Although marketed as an all-family film, *Princess Diaries* is mostly targeted at young, impressionable girls, who're likely to be swept away by the bubbly romantic feel of a movie. The picture's merits — feel of good nature, happy ending, and a terrific debut by Anne Hathaway, should make this G-rated wish-fulfillment, female empowerment fairy tale a box-office hit.

The heroine of Meg Cabot's young-adult novel is a timid 15-year old San Franciscan, Mia Thermopolis (Hathaway), who's thrown for a loop when, out of the blue, she learns of her being the heir apparent to the crown of Genovia, a tiny European kingdom (not unlike Monaco, and its late actress-princess, Grace Kelly). She's lovely and funny at the same time — not as easy as it looks. Moms, meanwhile, will be delighted in recalling their adolescent anxieties and first — first kiss, first car and first cup of tea with the queen of Genovia.

That's also where the picture's crown jewel comes in. When Mia is summoned to have a cup of tea with her formidable grandmother, Queen Clarisse Renaldi (Andrews), who at that moment informs her that she's about to begin a series of "princess lessons" under her strict supervision.

The two women, who couldn't have been more different, instantly clash. Initially, Mia has no intention of dropping her normal life to become the ruler of a far-off, obscure country. However, Clarisse insists that it's not a matter of choice. It's her duty. Although Mia is a stubbornly-minded girl, Clarisse is determined to do a complete makeover of Mia, a sparkling-diamond-in-the-rough, so that she can assume that her granddaughter is competent for royal position.

Most of the narrative depicts how social life is turned upside down in front of Mia. Her most difficult decision is whether to stay with her loving mother, or leave everything behind and accept royal responsibilities. In a series of crises, Mia said, "I don't want to run my own country. I just want to pass the tenth grade!"

Recalling Pygmalion (and, of course, its musical and film version, *My Fair Lady*), and countless other ugly duckling's sagas, *Princess Diaries* is structured as a comic journey, in which a rough girl who lacks manners is introduced into the upper-class etiquette. Mia and the audience go through the requisite motions of how to walk and talk like a lady, eat with finesse, dress more suavely, dance gracefully, and so on.

Pandering to older viewers, the film also contains intimations of latent romantic yearnings between Clarisse and Joseph, the queen's head of security, assigned to protect Mia. Older viewers may even shed a tear in the scene, in which the clumsy Mia learns how to gracefully glide across the floor while following Joseph's leading. After Mia leaves the room, Joseph beckons Clarisse to join him in a dance. Joseph and particularly Clarisse, are so naturally elegant, that even when they're hamming it up, as they do here, they're still charming.

In the meanwhile, Mia also encounters problems on interpersonal relationships. At first, Mia's school friends are all disturbed by her sudden celerity and subsequent transformation. Her best friend, Lilly Moskowitz, who runs a local radio program, is not only shocked by Mia's overnight fame, but also is afraid of losing their intimate bonds. What's more, the school's ex-popular and charming girl, Lana, changes to be Mia's enemy, for she wants to get back her popularity and boyfriend from Mia.

The most striking element of *Princess Diaries* is its centrist ideology, the way it compromises seemingly divergent values: royalty vs. working-class, blue-blood privileges vs. more normal growing pains. The whole narrative is based on a series of dichotomies, not just of values, but of girlfriends and boyfriends. Hence, not neglecting the love interest, Mia is placed between two different boys, ending up with the one who's outside her milieu, again indicating the film's reconciliatory nature.

As always, Marshall's philosophy is that a movie should have "something" for everyone.

He's still polarizing good and bad, rich and poor, in the same simplistic way he had done in his second outing, back in 1984. In this movie, we can get knowledge of being yourself and bettering yourself; we can know who your real friends are; we can learn living up to your own expectations. And maybe that sounds corny in the present, but I know a lot of adults who could learn lessons from these.

4. Extended Reading

Film: *Pretty Woman*

Pretty Woman, directed by Garry Marshall, is an American romantic comedy film released in 1990. The story centers on the unlucky Hollywood prostitute Vivian Ward (Julia Roberts) who is hired by Edward Lewis (Richard Gere), a wealthy businessman, to be his escort for several business and social functions. While Edward holds a no-nonsense approach to life, Vivian has an energetic spirit which challenges and appeals to Edward. Thus soon they are learning from each other and falling in love with each other.

In fact, the film was supposed to be a dark cautionary tale showing the class and sex work in Los Angeles, but was commonly regarded as a romantic comedy with a large budget. This film became one of the most successful money-makers of 1990. And it is also one of the most popular films of all time, with the highest number of ticket sales in the US ever for a romantic comedy.

5. Homework

1) Watch the film *Princess Diaries* again and write down your own feelings about the film.

2) The film also leaves us a deep impression about Mia and Lilly's friendship. Write down your opinion about friendship.

Unit 8 The Devil Wears Prada《穿普拉达的女王》

I Preview the movie

1. Background

Directed by	David Frankel
Based on	The Devil Wears Prada by Lauren Weisberger
Stars	Meryl Streep Anne Hathaway Emily Blunt Stanley Tucci
Distributed by	20th Century Fox
Box office	$326,551,094

2. Plot

Andrea just graduates from Northwestern University. She dreams of being an aspiring journalist to report serious social news in popular newspapers. Although Andrea has no style or sense of fashion, she, by mistake, becomes an assistant of a fashion magazine, whose job is regarded as "a million girls would kill for". However, her boss, Miranda Priestly, who is famous as an irony maiden, always sets difficult, even impossible missions for her staff. Under the huge pressure, Andrea decides to put up with Miranda's bizarre and humiliating treatment for one year in hopes of getting a job as a reporter or writer somewhere else.

At first, Andrea thinks that she cannot get on well with these empty-minded girls in Runway, especially Miranda's senior assistant Emily Charlton. They are all curious about fashion that seems totally far away from her world, and work disappoints her all the time. Finally, Andrea has to turn to Nigel (the art director) for help, who loans her designer clothes; she gradually learns her responsibilities and begins to dress more stylishly to show her effort and commitment to the position. When everything seems to fall into place, problems arise in her relationship with her boyfriend Nate. She has to face the problem about how to balance her work with love. And at the same time, an attractive young writer, Christian Thompson, appears in her life and sways her heart.

After several well-completed tasks, Andrea gains the trust from Miranda so that she is allowed to be the one to bring the treasured "Book". To her surprise, later Andrea is even required to attend the fall fashion show in Paris instead of Emily. But all the things change in Paris. When Andrea finds out the plan to replace Miranda with Jacqueline (editor of French Runway) as editor of Runway, and sees the way Miranda treats Nigel, she realizes this life is not what she really wants, and finally makes a surprising decision ...

II View the movie

Clip 1 Lines on interview

Words and Expressions:

Human Resources	人力资源部	hear of	听说
have no style or sense of fashion	没有时尚品位		
expose	揭露	fit	适合
get the exclusive on somebody	得到某人的独家		

Task 1 **Watch the video clip and fill in the missing words.**

Miranda: Who are you?

Andrea: Uh, my name is Andy Sachs. I recently **1**__________ Northwestern University.

Miranda: And what are you doing here?

Andrea: Well, I think I could **2**____________. And um ... Yeah, I came to New York to be a journalist, and **3**____________, and then finally got a call from Elias Clarke, and met with Sherry up at Human Resources and basically, it's this or Auto Universe.

Miranda: So you don't read *Runway*?

Andrea: Uh. No.

Miranda: And before today, you had never **4**__________?

Andrea: Uh, no.

Miranda: And you **5**____________.

Andrea: Well, um, I think that depends on what you're ...

Miranda: No, no. That wasn't a question.

Andrea: Um, I was **6**____________. I also won a national competition for college journalists with my series on the janitors' union, which exposed the exploitation of ...

Miranda: That's all.

Andrea: Yeah, you know, okay. You're right. I don't fit in here. **7**____________. But I'm smart. I learn fast and I will work very hard.

Task 2 **Watch the video clip again and answer the questions.**

a) Why does Andrea want to be an assistant in *Runway*?

____

b) What reason is it that causes Miranda to choose Andrea to be her assistant?

____

____

Clip 2 Andrea realizing her problems

Words and Expressions:

pick on	作弄某人	kill oneself doing	竭尽全力
live your life in	生活在其中	a shining beacon of hope	闪耀的希望灯塔
under the covers	在被窝里	deign to	被迫去做

Task 1 Mark T (True) or F (False) for the following statements according to the clip.

a) ______ Nigel comforts Andrea with warm words.

b) ______ Nigel used to pretend to go to soccer with his brothers but he really wanted to go sewing class and reading *Runway*.

Task 2 Answer the questions from this video clip.

a) What kind of way does Andrea want to be treated by Miranda?

____

b) What does Nigel think of *Runway* in his heart?

____

Clip 3 Andrea taking the place of Emily

Words and Expressions:

freak out	行为反常	swear to	对……发誓
a pathetic excuse	破借口	deserve	值得

Task 1 Watch Clip 3 and fill in the missing words of the dialogue.

Emily: I don't care if she was gonna fire you or beat you with a red-hot poker. You should have said no.

Andrea: Emily, I didn't have a choice. You know how she is.

Emily: Please. **1**______________.

(The doctor walks in.)

Emily: Thanks. Do you know what really just gets me about this whole thing? Is that, you know, you're the one who said that **2**______________. And you don't really care about fashion. You just wanna be a journalist. Oh, what a pile of bollocks!

Andrea: Emily, I know you're mad, **3**______________.

Emily: Face it, Andy, you **4**__________ the day you put on that first pair of Jimmy Choo's. I saw it. And do you know what really just kills me about this whole thing? Is the clothes that you're gonna get. **5**______________. You eat carbs, for Christ's sake! God! It's so unfair.

Andrea: Emily ...

Emily: Just go.

Andrea: Emily, I ...

Emily: I said, go.

Task 2 Answer the questions from this video clip.

a) Does Emily worry about Andrea initially? Why?

____

b) What is it that really kills Emily about this whole thing?

____

Clip 4 Andrea breaking up with Nate

Words and Expressions:

pole dancing	钢管舞	own up (to)	承认
Peace Corns	和平护卫队	make fun of	取笑

Task 1 **Mark T (True) or F (False) for the following statements according to the clip.**

a) ______ Nate is mad because Andrea works late and misses his birthday party.

b) ______ Andrea cannot bear Nate and puts forward the idea to break up with him.

Task 2 **Discussion: It is said that it isn't easy to manage a career while keeping a good relationship with your beloved one. So in daily life, how can people juggle their relationships and career?**

____

____

____

Clip 5 Resignation

Words and Expressions:

jump at	急于接受	be impressed by	留下深刻印象
get ahead	出人头地	Don't be ridiculous.	别逗了；别胡说

Task 1 **Answer the following questions according to the dialogue.**

a) Why does Jacqueline give up being the editor of *American Runway*?

____

b) What makes Irv change his mind?

____

c) What kind of features does Miranda see in Andrea that are like herself?

____

d) Why does Andrea quit the job of the fashion magazine? What urges her to make such a big decision?

____

Task 2 **Discussion: How do you feel when Miranda sacrifices Nigel's opportunity to save her job? Does everyone want the life she lives?**

____

____

____

____

Clip 6 The interview at *New York Mirror*

Task 1 **Dub the voice for Andrea and Greg while the video is played again without the sound.**

Words and Expressions:

blip	突然而暂时的变化；突然而暂时的中断	screw up	搞砸
call over to	打电话给	leave word	留言

III Review the movie

1. Cultural Notes

1) Prada

Prada S.P.A. is an Italian luxury fashion house, founded by Mario Prada in 1913. It has products of various kinds, such as clothing, cosmetics, fashion accessories, jewelry, perfumes, spirits, cell phone, watches, wines, etc. With its headquarters located in Milan, Italy, it has over 250 boutiques all around the world. During the one-century development, Prada has been working hard on the pursuit of innovation while maintaining the classic elements, making it a fashion leader and a top luxury brand.

2) Roberto Cavalli

Born on November 15th, 1940, Roberto Cavalli is an Italian fashion designer from Florence. In his design, he always emphasizes the wildness and desire of women and is known for exotic prints and for creating the sand-blasted look for jeans. He is also famous for travelling around the world by jet and holding grand banquets, of which the guests are either rich or famous, covered with the works of Roberto Cavalli from head to toe.

3) D&G

D&G is an Italian luxury industry fashion house, founded in 1985 in Legnano by Italian designers Domenico Dolce and Stefano Gabbana.

4) Karl Otto Lagerfeldt

Karl Lagerfeld is a German fashion designer, artist, and photographer based in Paris. He is the head designer and creative director of the fashion house Chanel as well as the Italian house Fendi and his own label fashion house. Over the decades, he has collaborated on a variety of fashion and art-related projects. He is well recognized around the world for his trademark, white hair, black glasses, and high starched collars.

5) Banana Republic

Banana Republic is a clothing and accessories retailer owned by American multinational corporation Gap Inc. It was founded in 1978 by Mel and Patricia Ziegler with a safari theme; in 1983, Gap purchased the company and gave it a more upscale image. Banana Republic has over 600 stores located internationally.

6) Chicago

Chicago is a musical with music by John Kander, lyrics by Fred Ebb and a book by Ebb and Bob Fosse. Set in Prohibition-era Chicago, the musical is based on a 1926 play of the same name by reporter Maurine Dallas Watkins about actual criminals and crimes she reported on. The story is a satire on corruption in the administration of criminal justice and the concept of the "celebrity criminal".

The original Broadway production opened in 1975 at the 46th Street Theatre and ran for 936 performances until 1977. Bob Fosse choreographed the original production, and his style is strongly identified with the show. Following a West End debut in 1979 which ran for 600 performances, *Chicago* was revived on Broadway in 1996, and a year later in the West End.

The Broadway revival holds the record as the longest-running musical revival and the longest-running American musical in Broadway history, and is the second longest-running show in Broadway history, behind only *The Phantom of the Opera*, having played its 7,486th performance on November 23, 2014, surpassing *Cats*. The West End revival ran for nearly 15 years, becoming the longest-running American musical in West End history, and it has enjoyed several tours and international productions. The Academy Award-winning 2002 film version of the musical was directed by Rob Marshall and starred Renée Zellweger, Catherine Zeta-Jones, Richard Gere, John C. Reilly, and Queen Latifah.

7) Harry Potter

Harry Potter is a series of seven fantasy novels written by the British author J. K. Rowling. The series chronicles the adventures of a young wizard, Harry Potter, the titular character, and his friends Ronald Weasley and Hermione Granger, all of whom are students at Hogwarts School of Witchcraft and Wizardry. The main story are Harry's quest to overcome the Dark wizard Lord Voldemort, who aims to become immortal, conquering the wizarding world, subjugating non-magical people, and destroying all thosc who stand in his way, especially Harry Potter.

Since the release of the first novel, *Harry Potter and the Philosopher's Stone* on 30 June 1997, the books have gained immense popularity, critical acclaim, and commercial success worldwide.

The series has also had some share of criticism, including concern about the increasingly dark tone as the series progressed. As of July 2013, the books had sold between 400 and 450 million copies, making them one of the best-selling book series in history, and had been translated into 73 languages. The last four books consecutively set records as the fastest-selling books in history, with the final installment selling approximately 11 million copies in the United States within the first twenty-four hours of its release.

2. Classical lines from the film

1) Let me know when your whole life goes up in smoke. That means it's time for a promotion.
当你的生活化为乌有的时候告诉我一声。这就意味着你该升职了。

2) An accessory is merely a piece of iconography ... used to express individual identity.
配饰代表了一个人的形象，展示着一个人的个性。

3) Everybody wants this. Everybody wants to be us.
人人都想要这种生活，人人都想成为我们这样。

4) Fashion is not about utility.
时尚无关于实用。

5) That's really what this multibillion-dollar industry is all about anyway, isn't it? Inner beauty.
这就是数十亿资产的价值所在，对吧？内在美。

6) We need to find someone who can survive here.
我们需要能在这儿生存的人。

7) A million girls would kill for that job.
你不知道有多少女孩想得到这份工作呢。

8) You have no style or sense of fashion.
你一点时尚品位都没有。

3. Film Review

Andrea Sachs is a girl who graduated from North Western University and wants to be a journalist in New York. She has sent a lot of letters out, and finally gets the interview from *Runway*, a fashion magazine. To her surprise, this chance makes her become a co-assistant to the icy editor-in-chief of *Runway* fashion magazine, Miranda Priestly. Although a million girls will kill for this job, Andrea has no interest in it. She thinks fashion has nothing to do with her. All that she needs to do is just to stick to it for a year and then she can get a job at any magazine she wants. At *Runway*, Andrea is laughed at, because of her rustic outset, by her colleagues, especially Emily Charlton, Miranda's first assistant.

Andrea has a tough time adapting to *Runway*'s working style. She works for Miranda days and nights, and always has to be prepared for her calling. What she can do is preparing her breakfast, hanging her clothes and serving her. Even Andrea's father asks her to quit the job. The only thought that supports Andrea is her dream. She tries hard to do it. However, even if she does something right, it is unacknowledged. Miranda never says thank you to her; but if she does something wrong, Miranda will become vicious. It seems unfair to Andrea, so she turns to Nigel for help.

Nigel is the art director of *Runway*. He points out that Andrea is not trying. She's whining. Then she changes her attitudes towards the job and becomes fashionable to adapt to *Runway*. There is no doubt that she is an excellent girl and makes progress little by little. Eventually, she surpasses Emily and wins Miranda's approval in her efforts. However, she realizes that she pursues her dream in the opposite direction by losing her boyfriend and college friends. Thus she makes a decision to leave Miranda, *Runway*, and fashion behind.

I'm deeply impressed by many plots of this movie. After watching this movie, many people show their dislike to Miranda, who is powerful, strict and merciless. She is vicious to Andrea and sacrifices Nigel in order to keep her own job. It seems that she has devoted her whole life to *Runway* and fashion. Once she explains to Andrea that the blue sweater is not just blue but actually cerulean which represents millions of dollars and countless jobs, and that it is ridiculous that while Andrea has made a choice to leave the fashion industry. In fact she's just wearing a sweater that was selected for her by the people of fashion industry. Miranda's words win great respect for her. While Miranda respects fashion as her life, her success and achievements in career are at the expense of harming family harmony. To be her husband, one has to be tolerant of such difficulties or their marriage is doomed to failure. However, she accepts it and never complains. In this aspect, we need to and have to admire and respect her sacrifices.

As to Andrea, she endures the eccentric requests of her boss with her strong faith and becomes able to accomplish tough requests little by little. At the same time, she changes her plain looking by wearing fashionable clothes and makes up with cosmetic top grade brands. It is true that Andrea is just like a Cinderella turning to be a beautiful one. But it is also true that she is getting far away from her dream under the influence of the people around. And she is also hurting the feeling of her beloved boyfriend. At first, Andrea just regards it as her responsibilities to dress more stylishly, showing her effort and commitment to the position. However, gradually she loses herself in life. Her boyfriend is angered by her because she refuses to admit that she has already become one of *Runway* girls.

Luckily, Andrea's story is not a sad one. When Andrea gets her dreamy job at *New York Mirror*, we know that she is not the one at *Runway* anymore. Dressed casually but with a bit more style, she's confident and knows what she really wants. At last, she comes across Miranda in the street. The two heroines exchange looks and finally we know that no matter what kind of life we live, we can pursue our respective dreams without hesitation.

Likewise, Emily Blunt, as Miranda's first assistant, does a wonderful job as an insecure, over compensating slave to someone else's expectation. Her portrayal provides the requisite foil to our heroine's wide-eyed innocence on the target. Emily's performance is commendable, but it leaves the audience nothing to like her character. The dilemma here is that the film presents her in such a way that we have this nagging feeling about this character.

The one true bright spot of the film is Stanley Tucci, as Nigel, who seems to infuse a refreshing dimension and humanity to this character which is not written in the book. Nigel is the man that desperately devotes himself to *Runway* and Miranda. Even though Miranda keeps her job at his expense, he never complains. The charisma from this character makes Stanley continues to amaze.

In fact it is only we ourselves that can make our own decisions about how to live. We shouldn't change ourselves just because of other people's attitudes. Nowadays, many people lose themselves in the world of temptation. They lose their dreams and compromise to reality. Some people regard their jobs as their whole life. Instead of working to live, they live to work, spending most of time in running their business instead of their friendship and kinship. Indeed, it's a behavior of putting the cart before the horse. The truth is working can never replace their families. One day, they may lose their jobs, but they should never leave their love, friends and families. This is what is reflected in this movie.

4. Extended Reading

Film: *Coco Before Chanel*

Coco Before Chanel is a French film directed by Anne Fontaine in 1990. It tells about the early life of the famous French fashion designer Coco Chanel. This role is played by French actor Audrey Tautou.

The young Gabrielle Chanel is an orphanage whose father abandoned her and her sister. When she grows up, she finds a job in a provincial bar. She is both a seamstress for the performers and a singer, earning the nickname "Coco" from the song she sings nightly with her sister. A liaison with the charismatic Baron Balsan (Belgian actor Benoit Poelvoorde) gives her an entry into French high society; from then on she begins to design popular hats for ladies.

When Coco meets the English businessman Arthur Capel (American Alessandro Nivola) who has been betrothed to a woman in England, she, without any awareness, falls in love with him. Capel appreciates Coco's talent on fashion and helps her start the business. However, as Coco's business flourishes and life is going well, Capel dies in a car accident ...

By now, *Coco Before Chanel* has been nominated for four BAFTA Awards, three European Film Awards, six César Awards and the Academy Award for Best Costume Design. It is a successful biopic.

5. Homework

1) Watch the film *The Devil Wears Prada* again and write down your own feelings about it.

2) As it is known to all, women are playing more and more important roles in our society. Some are tough, strong and ...

Unit 9 The Social Network 《社交网络》

I Preview the movie

1. Background

Directed by	David Fincher
Based on	The Accidental Billionaires by Ben Mezrich
Stars	Jesse Eisenberg Andrew Garfield Justin Timberlake Armie Hammer
Distributed by	Columbia Pictures
Box office	$224.9 million

2. Plot

At the age of 19, Mark Zuckerberg, a Harvard University student, is dumped by his girlfriend. He then writes an insulting entry about her on his blog and sets up a website called Facemash which allows site visitors to rate girls by their attractiveness. The great amount of clicking on Facemash makes Harvard's computer network crashes. Zuckerberg is given six months of academic probation. However, Zuckerberg is so popular that he attracts the attention of twin brothers — Cameron and Tyler Winklevoss and their business partner Divya. They invite him to work on Harvard Connection, a social network for Harvard students who would like to date someone.

After meeting with Winklevoss twins, Zuckerberg accepts their plans with delight. He then asks his friend Eduardo to work on a social network website that he calls The Facebook, available to Ivy League students only. Eduardo becomes the CFO of The Facebook and provides $1,000 in seed funding to help Zuckerberg build the website. When The Facebook quickly becomes popular, the Winklevoss twins and Divya believe that Zuckerberg steals their idea and turns to Harvard President for help, but it ends up with ignorance. At the lecture, Eduardo and Zuckerberg meet Christy who asks them to "Facebook me". This phrase impresses both of them and lets them realize their success.

With an increasing popularity of The Facebook, Zuckerberg decides to extend it to other universities in the United States. So Christy arranges them to meet Napster founder Sean Park who has already been interested in their project. Sean's words leave a deep impression on Zuckerberg but Eduardo thinks him ridiculous. After hearing Sean's suggestion, Mark moves the company to Palo Alto, with Eduardo remaining in New York.

Later, the Winklevoss twins discover that Facebook has expanded to the UK and decide to sue the company for stealing the intellectual property. In the meanwhile, Eduardo objects to Sean making business decisions for company and freezes the company's bank account in the resulting dispute. Because of the frozen account, Mark feels dissatisfied with him and sets a trap with Sean that the new investment deal allows Eduardo's share of Facebook to be diluted from 34% to 0.03%, while maintaining the ownership percentage of all other parties. At the same time, his name is removed from the masthead as co-founder. The relationship between two best friends at last breaks up ...

II View the movie

Clip 1 Setting up Facemash

Words and Expressions:

perfect timing	时间刚刚好	key ingredient	关键因素
split up	分手	at any given time	在任何给定的时间
match up	相配	traffic	流量

Task 1 Watch the video clip and fill in the missing words.

Wardo: Hey, **1**____________?

Mark: **2**__________. Eduardo's here and he's going to **3**____________.

Wardo: Hey, Mark.

Mark: Wardo.

Wardo: You and Erica **4**__________?

Mark: How did you know that?

Wardo: **5**____________.

Mark: Yeah.

Wardo: Are you all right?

Mark: I need you.

Wardo: I'm here for you.

Mark: No, I need the algorithm you use to rank chess players.

Wardo: Are you OK?

Mark: **6**____________.

Wardo: You mean other students.

Mark: Yeah.

Wardo: You think this is such a good idea?

Mark: I need the algorithm.

Wardo: Mark ...

Mark: I need the algorithm.

Wardo: Give each girl a base rating of 1400. **7**____________ Girl A has a rating R-a and Girl B has a rating R-b.

Mark: When any two girls are **8**__________, there's an expectation of which will win based on their current rating, right?

Wardo: Yeah. **9**____________.

Mark: Let's write it.

Task 2 **Watch the video clip again and answer the questions.**

a) Why does Mark want to set up Facemash?

____

b) Which key ingredient does Mark think Eduardo is going to have?

____

____

Clip 2 The discussion with Winklevoss twins

Words and Expressions:

check out	核实	kind of a no-brainer	小儿科
recognize	识别	taste	品味
prestigious	知名的	take it in the shins	打开天窗说亮话

Task 1 **Mark T (True) or F (False) for the following statements according to the clip.**

a) _______ Mark invented an app for an MP3 player in high school and sold it to Microsoft.

b) _______ Mark agrees to join the team to be a programmer and build Harvard Connection without any hesitation.

Task 2 **Answer the questions from this video clip.**

a) How is Harvard Connection different from MySpace or Friendster?

____

b) Why do Winklevoss twins and Divya find Mark for help?

____

Clip 3 The foundation of The Facebook

Words and Expressions:

come up with 想出

tell you something that you're not gonna believe 告诉你件难以置信的事

hang on 等候 punch 潘趣酒

I'm totally psyched about this. 这太让人兴奋了。

term 条件

one's line of questioning 盘问 off the record 不宜公开

Task 1 Watch Clip 3 and fill in the missing words of the dialogue.

Wardo: Mark! **1**_____________.

Mark: I think I've **2**_____________.

Wardo: Hang on. **3**_____________.

Mark: What?

Wardo: I **4**_________ by the Phoenix.

Mark: **5**_____________?

Wardo: No.

Wardo: I mean, it's just the **6**_____________, but they slid the invitation under my door tonight. I go to my first punch party tomorrow.

Mark: So ... You got punched by the Phoenix.

Wardo:	Yeah, but, you know, probably it was just **7**____________. It was just a diversity thing. Just ride that horse until ... What did you wanna talk about? Mark?
Mark:	Yeah.
Wardo:	You said you'd come up with something.
Mark:	Yeah, I think I've come up with something. Come outside and let's talk.
Wardo:	**8**____________.
Mark:	I can't stare to that loop of Niagara Falls, which **9**____________ with the Caribbean.

Task 2 **Answer the questions from this video clip.**

a) What does Eduardo say to Mark that makes him surprised?

____

b) Why do people like to come to Facemash in a stampede?

____

Clip 4 A dinner with Sean

Words and Expressions:

in royalties 版税

make a name for yourself 一举成名

paranoid 偏执狂

target for ……的目标

trip somebody up 使某人犯错

Private behavior is a relic of a time gone by 根本没有私人空间

delusional 妄想

get around to 抽出时间做……

on campus 在校内

That's a good analogy. 这比喻恰到好处。

up close 差不多

have a dog in this fight 掺和进来

Task 1 **Mark T (True) or F (False) for the following statements according to the clip.**

a) ________ In court, Sean brought down the record companies with Napster.

b) ________ Sean agrees that it's time to start making money from The Facebook.

Task 2 **Dub the voice for Sean, Mark, Eduardo and other people while the video is played again without the sound.**

Clip 5 The Winklevoss twins' striking back

Words and Expressions:

That's awesome. 太棒了!

Take the bitter with the better. 要过好日子，总要吃苦。

knock off 停止

Showing up on Monday for a race that was run on Sunday. 后知后觉

Task 1 **Mark T (True) or F (False) for the following statements according to the clip.**

a) ________ Mr Kenwright's daughter goes to the school in the States.

b) ________ The Winklevoss twins lost to Dutch today by less than a second.

Task 2 **Answer the questions from this video clip.**

a) Why does Tyler say he doesn't mind they lost the race today?

____

b) What kind of measures have Winklevoss twins and Divya has already taken to warn Mark?

____

Clip 6 Out of Facebook

Words and Expressions:

be wired in	参与	screw up	搞砸
set somebody up	陷害某人	masthead	报头
parade	游行	plant	栽赃

Task 1 Watch Clip 3 and fill in the missing words of the dialogue.

Mark: You signed the papers.

Wardo: **1**____________.

Mark: You're gonna blame me because you were the business head of the company, **2**____________?

Wardo: It's gonna be like I'm not a part of Facebook.

Sean: It won't be like you're not a part of Facebook. You're not a part of Facebook.

Wardo: My name's **3**____________.

Sean: You might wanna check again.

Wardo: **4**____________?

Sean: You think **5**____________ pretending you were running this company?

Wardo: Sorry, my Prada's at the cleaner's! Along with my hoodie and my fuck-you flip-flops, you pretentious douche bag!

Sean: Security's here. You'll be leaving now.

Wardo: I'm not signing those papers.

Sean: We will get the signature.

Wardo: Tell me this isn't about me getting into the Phoenix. You ... You did it. I knew you did it. **6**____________!

Mark: I didn't plant that story about the chicken.

Sean: What's he talking about?

Wardo: **7**____________..

Sean: Seriously. What the hell's the chicken?

Wardo: And I'll bet what you hated the most is that they identified me as a co-founder of Facebook, which I am. You'd better lawyer up, asshole. **8**____________. I'm coming back for everything.

Sean: Get him out of here.

Wardo: It's okay. I'm going.

Sean: Hang on. Almost forgot. Here's your $19,000. **9**____________, though. I drew it on the account you froze.

Wardo: I like standing next to you, Sean. It makes me look so tough.

Task 2 **Discussion: Someone said: "Don't start a company with your best friends." How do you feel when you have watched this movie?**

____

____

____

III Review the movie

1. Cultural Notes

1) Mark Elliot Zuckerberg

Mark Elliot Zuckerberg (born on May 14, 1984) is an American computer programmer and Internet entrepreneur. He is best known as one of five co-founders of the social networking website Facebook. As of April 2013, Zuckerberg is the chairman and chief executive of Facebook, Inc. and his personal wealth, as of July 2014, was estimated to be $33.1 billion. Mark Zuckerrberg receives a one-dollar salary as CEO of Facebook.

2) Facebook

Facebook is an online social networking service headquartered in Menlo Park, California. Its website was launched on February 4, 2004, by Mar Zuckerberg with his college roommates and fellow Harvard University students Eduardo Saverin, Andrew McCollum, Dustin Moskovitz and Chris Hughes. The founders had initially limited the website's membership to Harvard students, but later expanded it to colleges in the Boston area, the Ivy League, and Stanford University. It gradually added support for students at various other universities and later to high-school students. Facebook now allows anyone who claims to be at least 13 years old to become a registered user of the website. Its name comes from a colloquialism for the directory given to it by American university students.

3) Super Bowl

Super Bowl is the annual championship game of the National Football League (NFL), the highest level of professional football in the United States, culminating a season that begins in the late summer of the previous calendar year. Super Bowl was played on January 15, 1967, following the 1966 regular season. The most recent game, Super Bowl XLIX, which was won by the New England Patriots, was played on February 1, 2015, following the 2014 season.

4) Porcellian Club

The Porcelllian Club is a men-only final club at Harvard University, sometimes called the Porc or the P.C. The year of founding is usually given as 1791, when a group began meeting under the name "the Atgonauts", or as 1794, the year of the roast pig dinner at which the club, known first as "the Pig Club" was formally founded. The club's motto, Dum vivimus vivamus (while we live, let us live) is literally Epicurean. The club emblem is the pig and some members bear golden pigs on watch-chains or neckties bearing pig's-head emblems. The club was originally started by a group of 30 students from Massachusetts who wanted to avoid the dining halls and their food by roasting pigs.

The Porcellian Club is the iconic "hosty-totsty" final club, often bracketed with Yale's Skull and Boness, Priceton's Ivy Club, the University of Cambridge's Pitt Club and the University of Oxford's Gridiron Club. A history of Harvard calls the Porcellian Club "the most final of them all". Also, an urban legend's website mentions a belief that "if members of the Porcellian do not earn their first million before they turn 40, the club will give it to them".

5) **Napster**

Napster was the name given to two music-focused online services. It was originally founded as a pioneering peer-to-peer (P2P) file sharing Internet service that emphasized sharing audio files, typically music, encoded in MP3 format. The original company ran into legal difficulties over copyright infringement, ceased operations and was eventually acquired by Roxio. In its second incarnation Napster became an online music store until it was acquired by Rhapsody from Best Buy on December 1, 2011.

6) **Tower Records**

Tower Records was a retail music chain based in Sacramento, California. It currently exists as an international franchise and an online music store. From 1960 until 2006, Tower also operated retail stores in the United States, which closed when Tower Records filed for bankruptcy and liquidation. Tower.com was purchased by a separate entity and was not affected by the retail store closing.

2. Classical lines from the film

1) But I am willing to let bygones be bygones.
但我愿意既往不咎。

2) You don't get to 500 million friends without making a few enemies.
要想成就5亿人的社交王国，得先背叛几个朋友。

3) Did you know there are more people with genius IQs living in China than there are people of any kind living in the United States?
知道吗，中国的天才比全美国的人加起来还多？

4) Dating you is like dating a StairMaster.
和你约会就像在和台阶器材约会。

5) You are probably going to be a very successful computer person, but you're gonna go through life thinking that girls don't like you because you're a nerd.
你也许会成为电脑领域的一个成功人士，但你这辈子都会觉得女生不喜欢你，因为你是个书呆子。

6) You don't think I deserve your attention?
你认为我不配吸引你的注意？

7) You can read the weather. You can predict the price of heating oil.
你能预测天气，就能预测燃油价格。

8) The Internet's not written in pencil. It's written in ink.
在网上，信息不是用铅笔书写的，而是一种烙印，无法抹去。

3. Film Review

The Social Network is directed by David Fincher and written by Aaron Sorkin. It covers a series of triumphs and betrayals, and ends with what feels like darkness closing in on an isolated soul. This movie can be described as a brilliantly entertaining and emotionally wrenching film, telling about the foundation of famous social network — Facebook.

In 2003, a nineteen-year-old Harvard sophomore whose name is Mark Zuckerberg, invents Facebook and eventually creates a five-hundred-million-strong network of "friends". Zuckerberg is so egotistical, work-obsessed, and he can't stay close to anyone. When he finally becomes successful, he breaks up with his only real friend, Eduardo Saverin, who helps him to launch the site at first.

The movie is not a traditional story of a young man corrupted by riches; nor is it harsh reality finally stabbed into the heart of a poor little rich guy. Both themes are there, but the dramatic development of the material pushes beyond our sights. In this movie, you can see Zuckerberg is a many-sided and ambiguous person, and no two viewers will see him in quite the same way. Many people begin to doubt about the movie's accuracy, but Fincher, the director of this movie has selected from known facts and his free interpretation makes it artistic.

This film is adapted from a book, *The Accidental Billionaires*, written by Ben Mezrich in 2009. Ben also went to Harvard, so Harvard lore in his book is laid on a little thick. The eager suburban co-eds trucked in for parties, the rabbity competitiveness and status-seeking among the men, the terrific excitement of being "punched" for one of the all-male "final clubs" (off-campus social sites for the chosen élite) — to outsiders, all this frenzied self-importance seems slightly mad. Yet the filmmakers don't satirize Harvard, and you can see why: they needed to re-create the pressures and the social stratifications that led to Zuckerberg's revolt. When we watch

Zuckerberg and his friends toss beer-bottle caps and share ideas with one another in the dorm. We know that they really are the brightest and perhaps the most obnoxious kids in the country. In the opening scene, Zuckerberg tells his girlfriend — Erica that he could introduce her to important people if he gets into one of the clubs, but his prickly words lead him to act like a jerk. The harder he tries to impress her, the faster he drives her away. Eisenberg creates an emotionally stunted, closed-off young man. It is worth mentioning that Eisenberg portrays details. Eisenberg pauses, stares, then rushes ahead, talking in bristling clumps, like a computer spilling bytes. The self-assurance he gives Zuckerberg is audacious and funny.

As Zuckerberg and his friends keep working on computers, they turn women into objects. They rate girls and remark them upon their appearance. In the end, Facebook becomes gender neutral, but the movie is sparked by a bitterly comic irony: a worldwide social network revolution just began with nothing more urgent than the desire of two middle-class boys to be considered cool at college and meet girls without having to endure the humiliation of campus mixers. By focusing on the moment of creation, Fincher gets something new. From the first scene to the last, it hints at a shift produced by the Information Age, a new social network that affects almost everyone. After all, Facebook, like Zuckerberg, is a label of the new era: a Website can provide a chance for people to keep contact and pay attention to friends' news. Karl Marx suggested that from the beginning of capitalist age, we began to treat one another as commodities. However, The Social Network shows that we now treat one another as packets of information. As interpreted by this film, Mark comes off as a binary personality. As far as he's concerned, either you support him or you object to him. Either you have information that he can use or you don't. Apart from that, he's not interested.

At Harvard, Zuckerberg hacks into the university's computer system and builds Facemash that gets him into trouble with the administration but also brings him to the attention of Tyler and Cameron Winklevoss, who are members of Porcellian Club. Devoted to Harvard crew team, the twins keep practicing their bodies, rowing at dawn on the Charles River time after time; they aim at heading for the Olympics. Yet the Winklevosses want to get into the social-media business.

After talking about their plan on Harvard Connection, Mark decides to join them and be their programmer. However, Mark strings them along while he and Eduardo develop the prototype of Facebook; that's the root of his eventual legal troubles. The movie is started by the two civil suits brought against Zuckerberg after Facebook succeeds — one by the Winklevosses, who claim that he stole an idea that they had developed with their partner, Divya Narendra; the other by Saverin, whom Zuckerberg with Sean set a trap to make him out of the company. The movie is a tightly fitted mosaic of memory fragments. As the lawyers and the disputants keep asking questions at one another across a conference-room table, the film repeatedly goes back to the scenes, first back to Harvard and then to California, where Zuckerberg lands in the summer of 2004, enticed by the siren song of Sean Parker, the co-founder of Napster.

When Zuckerberg gets to Silicon Valley, he is innocent and knows nothing about there. At that time, his life is surrounded by pizza boxes and beer cans, and dressed in gray sweats, flip-flops, and a hoodie. He even looks like a monk. But Sean Parker teaches a lesson to him, and his siren song of words — "A million dollars isn't cool. You know what's cool? A billion dollars", makes Mark believe that he finds someone knows him. And though still dressed on hoodie, everything else seems to change. When all the people believe that Parker is a smart businessman and can see the future success of Facebook, he finally destroys his success by drugs. Justin Timberlake, with his charm and his physical dynamism, and with a wicked visionary gleam in his eye, torques the movie even higher. The colors in Jeff Cronenweth's cinematography changes from Harvard crimson to the electric pink of a San Francisco night club. Yet, no matter how quickly the film moves, Fincher can pause within the fast tempo and let the emotional power of the moment expand. Relying on nothing more than tiny shifts of emphasis and inflection, the director, to an amazing degree, makes us care about the split between the unyielding Zuckerberg and Saverin, who's a decent guy but unimaginative and perhaps a little timid. As Saverin, Andrew Garfield has the emotional fluency — the fear, the indignation, and the hurt feelings — that Eisenberg has to suppress. If The Social Network is a linear accelerator that breathes, Fincher is the one who created the breathing room. Fincher was born in Denver in 1962. He grew up in Oregonand Northern California, skipped college, and he went to work as camera operator at the age of seventeen. A few years later, Fincher moved to George Lucas's Industrial Light & Magic, where he worked on the special effects for *Return of the Jedi* (1983) and *Indiana Jones and the Temple of Doom* (1984). In his late twenties, Fincher had found his own cinematic style in razory, provocative, and beautiful music videos. He directed a lot of music videos for singers like George Michael and Madonna.

Back to this movie we can find that Fincher forces us to make our own judgments. For example, Tyler and Cameron Winklevoss, although they are members Porcellian and row crew for Harvard, their lack is Zuckerberg and Parker's intuitive apprehension of it as a new form of virtual social life. They worship traditions. When they find out Mark steals their idea on network, they go to see the president of Harvard to complain about Zuckerberg. From this moment, all the viewers can feel, in this seemingly unimportant scene, history falling into places, a shift from one kind of capitalism to another. Fincher wants to let Zuckerberg tell the people that a new era is coming and the world develops faster than we think.

It is Zuckerberg's tragedy that he leaves behind his friends as well as his intellectual inferiors. In this movie, Fincher has set him up as a symbolic man of the age, an ambiguous and prickly man. It seems that Mark Zuckerberg only engages in the net world he is creating. But those audiences who think of him as nothing more than a bookish will be responding to only one part of him. He's a revolutionary because he broods on his personal grievances and, as insensitive as he is, reaches the aggrieved element in everyone, the human desire for response. He seems to be a hero — certainly he's Fincher's hero, an artist who sticks to his vision works in codes and is helpless to prevent himself from suffering the most wounding personal loss.

4. Extended Reading

Film: *Pirate of Silicon Valley*

Pirate of Silicon Valley is a 1999 original TNT film about the story between Steve Jobs and Bill Gates. Noah Wyle plays the role of Steve. And Anthony Michael Hall plays the role of Bill. This film is directed by Martyn Burke.

This is a semi-humorous biographical film about the men who made the world of technology what it is today, their struggles during college, the founding of their companies, and the ingenious actions they took to build up the global corporation empires of Apple Computer Corporation and Microsoft Inc.

Pirates of Silicon Valley was nominated Primetime Emmy Awards in 1999, and won American Cinema Editors in 2000 as Best Edited Motion Picture Movie for Commercial Television, it was also nominated Directors Guild of American in that year.

5. Homework

1) Watch the film *The Social Network* again and write down your own feelings about it.

2) What causes Eduardo to leave the company? Has Mark ever been jealous when Eduardo got punched by the Phoenix Club?

Unit 10 Million Dollar Baby 《百万美元宝贝》

I Preview the movie

1. Background

Directed by	Clint Eastwood
Based on	Rope Bourns: Stories from the Corner By F.X. Toole
Stars	Clint Eastwood Hilary Swank Morgan Freeman
Distributed by	Warner Bros. Pictures
Box office	$216.8 million

2. Plot

Margaret "Maggie" Fitzgerald, who likes boxing very much, is a waitress from a Missouri town in the Ozarks. One day she shows up in the Hit Pit, a deserted Los Angeles gym owned and operated by Frankie Dunn, an old, cantankerous trainer and his friend as well as employee Eddie Scrap-Iron Dupris. Maggie asks Frankie to train her, but Frankie refuses, saying that she is "too old" to begin a boxing career at her age and that he has never trained a female boxer.

While hearing so many negative words, Maggie still works out tirelessly each day. Then one night, on her 32th birthday in the gym, she impressed Frankie so much by her persistence that he reluctantly agrees to train her. But he warns her that he will teach her only the basics and then finds a manager for her. Before her first fight, Frankie leaves Maggie with a random manager in his gym, which makes her so depressed. But in the middle of the bout, Frankie replaces that manager and coaches Maggie instead. Under the guidance of Frankie, Maggie fights her way up in the women's amateur boxing division, winning many of her lightweight bouts with first-round knockouts. Earning a reputation for her KOs, Frankie must resort to bribery to get other managers to put their trainee fighters up against her. And then Frankie takes a chance to put Maggie in the junior welterweight class where her nose is beaten broken in her first match. Frankie fixes it momentarily and then Maggie gets back to the fight and wins. After that, Frankie cautiously accepts a fight for Maggie to fight against a top-ranked opponent in the UK, and he bestows a Gaelic nickname "Mo cuishle" on her. Having so much experience in boxing, Frankie is finally willing to arrange a title fight. He secures Maggie a $1 million match in Las Vegas, Nevada against the WBA women's welterweight champion, Billie, "the Blue Bear", a German ex-prostitute who is known as a dirty fighter. Experiencing a hard fight, Maggie is almost wining the fight, but after a round has ended, Billie knocks her out with an illegal sucker punch from behind after the bell has sounded indicating the end of the round. Before Frankie can pull the corner stool out of the way which was inappropriately placed on its side by Frankie's assistant, Maggie lands hard on it, breaking her neck and leaving her a ventilator-dependent quadriplegic.

Frankie seeks multiple doctors' opinions to cure Maggie but only to find it disappointing. When Maggie's family members come to visit her, they arrive accompanied by an attorney after having visited Disneyland and Universal Studios Hollywood; their only concern is to transfer Maggie's assets to them. She orders them to leave, threatening to sell the house and inform the IRS of her mother's welfare fraud if they ever appear again. As the days pass by, Maggie develops bedsores and undergoes an amputation for an infected leg. She asks Frankie a favor: to help her die. Frankie refuses at first but Maggie keeps tourturing herself to seek death. After some forms of intense suffering, Frankie eventually decides to administer a fatal injection of adrenaline to put Maggie's life to an end, and before that Frankie tells Maggie the meaning of the nickname, Mo cuishle: Irish for "my darling, my blood".

II View the movie

Clip 1 Before Frankie agreeing to train Maggie

Words and Expressions:

wear out	穿坏	be in a position	处于某种位置
take sb. on	同 ... ... 较量	knock out	敲空；击倒

Task 1 Watch the video clip and fill in the missing words.

Frankie: You are not **1**_________ right, that's why you are **2**_________. So it's your birthday, ha? How old does that make you?

Maggie: I'm 32, Mr. Dunn. And I'm here celebrating the fact that I spent another year **3**_________ dishes and **4**_________ which is what I've been doing since 13. And according to you, I'll be 37 before I can even throw a **5**_________ punch which after working this speed bag for a month and getting nowhere.

Task 2 Watch the video clip again and answer the questions.

a) From what Maggie has said, try to describe the precious qualities that Maggie has.

____

b) Try to analyze the deep reasons why Frankie insists on finding another manager for Maggie.

____

____

Clip 2 Maggie's first fight and the following winning streak

Words and Expressions:

be subbing for sb.	替补某人	regain your sense	重拾你的力量
knockout mechanism	淘汰机制		

Task 1 Write T(True) or F(False) for the following statement according to the clip.

a) _______ Frankie tells Maggie to keep her left hand up to win the match.

b) _______ The most important rule that Frankie tells Maggie to bear in mind is "Protect yourself at all times".

Task 2 Watch Clip 2 and fill in the missing words.

a) Narrator: The body knows what fighters don't how to **1**__________ itself. A neck can only twist so far. **2**__________ it just a hair more, and the body says: "Hey, I'll take it from here, because you **3**__________ don't know what you're doing."

b) Narrator: Lie down, now, rest and we'll talk about this when you **4**__________ your senses. It's called the **5**__________.

Clip 3 The fight after Frankie moving Maggie up in class

Words and Expressions:

first round	第一回合	take a chance	碰运气
step back	退后		

Task 1 **Watch Clip 3 and fill in the missing words.**

Narrator: Maggie didn't **1**_________ her out till the end of the first **2**_________. After that, no manager wanted to put his fighter in with Maggie. Frankie had to go into his pocket to get her **3**_________ fights sweetening the purse by paying managers on the side. That only worked for so long. Then Frankie did something he **4**_________ doing. He **5**_________.

Task 2 **Watch the video clip again and answer the questions again.**

a) Do you really agree that it is a mistake to move Maggie up in class?

____

____

b) Can you guess the meaning of "Mo cuishle"?

____

Clip 4 Maggie's moving up after a series of strong fights

Words and Expressions:	
propose	建议
in a whole new league	在一个新的队伍

Task 1 **Dub the voice for Frankie and Maggie while the video is played again without a sound.**

Task 2 **Discussion: As we can see, "Mo cuishle" is like magical words that can leave a deep impression on the audience. Have you ever had such magical words in your life? Share it with your classmates and stress the important role it plays in your life.**

____

____

____

Clip 5 The cruel fight against the Blue Bear

Words and Expressions:

disqualify	取消……的资格	neutral corner	中立角
blur	模糊	keep sb. guard up	对某人保持警惕

Task 1 **Write T(True) or F(False) for the following statement according to the clip.**

a) ______ The Blue Bear is the West German champion.

b) ______ Frankie guides Maggie to hit right up the skinny ass of the Blue Bear.

Task 2 **Discussion: Upon seeing the final results, Maggie's lying down, what is on your mind right now or what is your feeling about this?**

Clip 6 The life after Maggie becoming ventilator-dependent quadriplegic

Words and Expressions:

disconnect	失去联系	air machine	飞行器
go through	经过；经历		

Task 1 Answer the questions from this video clip.

a) Looking through the whole movie, what is the role the sentence "Mo cuishle" playing?

____

____

b) The narrator says: "I don't think he had anything left." In your opinion, what is Frankie's last thing remaining left?

____

____

Task 2 Discussion: Do you agree with Frankie's choice? If you were in the same position, would you make the same decision?

____

____

____

____

III Review the movie

1. Cultural Notes

1) Boxing

Boxing is a combat sport in which two people engage in a contest of strength, speed, reflexes, endurance, and will, by throwing punches at each other, usually with gloved hands. Historically, the goals have been to weaken and knock down the opponent.

Since the dawn of history, people have fought in hand-to-hand combat. In BC 688, an Olympic game was held by the ancient Greeks and boxing was accepted as an organized sport. Boxing evolved from prizefights, largely in Great Britain, to the forerunner of modern boxing in the mid-19th century, again initially in Great Britain and later in the United States.

Amateur boxing is both an Olympic and Commonwealth sport and is a common fixture in most international games — it also has its own World Championships. Boxing is supervised by a referee over a series of one-to-three-minute intervals called rounds. The result is decided when an opponent is deemed incapable to continue by a referee, is disqualified for breaking a rule, resigns by throwing in a towel, or is pronounced the winner or loser based on the judges' scorecards at the end of the contest.

2) The Rules of Boxing

The Marquess of Queensberry rules have been the general rules governing modern boxing since their publication in 1867.

A boxing match typically consists of a determined number of three-minute rounds, a total of up to 12 rounds (formerly 15). Between each round there is a minute for the fighters to rest in their assigned corners receiving advice and attention from their coach and staff. A referee is in charge of controlling the fight. The referee needs to work within the ring to judge and control the conduct of the fighters, rule on their ability to fight safely, count knocked-down fighters, and rule on fouls.

To score the bout and assign points to the boxers, up to three judges are typically present at ringside, paying close attention to the punches that connect, defense, knockdowns, and other, more subjective, measures. Because of the open-ended style of boxing judging, many fights have controversial results, in which one or both fighters believe they have been "robbed" or unfairly denied a victory. Each fighter has an assigned corner of the ring, where his or her coach, as well as one or more "seconds" may administer to the fighter at the beginning of the fight and between rounds. Each boxer enters into the ring from their assigned corners at the beginning of each round and must cease fighting and return to their corner at the signal of an end to each round.

The judges are responsible for deciding a bout in which the predetermined number of rounds passes. What they also need to do is to say “go the distance”. The fighter with the higher score at the end of the fight is ruled the winner. With three judges, unanimous and split decisions are possible. A boxer may win the bout before a decision is reached through a knock-out; such bouts are said to have ended “inside the distance”. If a fighter is knocked down during the fight, determined by whether the boxer touches the canvas floor of the ring with any part of their body other than the feet as a result of the opponent’s punch and not a slip, as determined by the referee, the referee begins counting until the fighter returns to his or her feet and can continue.

If the referee counts to ten, then the knocked-down boxer is ruled “knocked out” (whether unconscious or not) and the other boxers are ruled the winner by knockout (KO). A “technical knock-out” (TKO) is possible as well, and is ruled by the referee, fight doctor, or a fighter’s corner if a fighter is unable to safely continue to fight, based upon injuries or being judged unable to effectively defend themselves. Many jurisdictions and sanctioning agencies also have a “three-knockdown rule”, in which three knockdowns in a given round result in a TKO. A TKO is considered a knockout in a fighter’s record. A “standing eight” count rule may also be in effect. This gives the referee the right to step in and administer a count of eight to a fighter that he feels may be in danger, even if no knockdown has taken place. After counting, the referee will observe the fighter, and decide if he is fit to continue. For scoring purposes, a standing eight count is treated as a knockdown.

In general, boxers are prohibited from hitting below the belt, holding, tripping, pushing, biting, or spitting. The boxer’s shorts are raised so the opponent is not allowed to hit to the ground in area with intent to cause pain or injury. Failure to abide by the former may result in a foul. They also are prohibited from kicking, head-butting, or hitting with any part of the arm other than the knuckles of a closed fist (including hitting with the elbow, shoulder or forearm, as well as with open gloves, the wrist, the inside, back or side of the hand). They are prohibited as well from hitting the back, back of the neck or head (called a “rabbit-punch”) or the kidneys. They are prohibited from holding the ropes for support when punching, holding an opponent while punching, or ducking below the belt of their opponent (dropping below the waist of your opponent, no matter the distance between).

If a “clinch” — a defensive move in which a boxer wraps his or her opponents arms and holds on to create a pause — is broken by the referee, each fighter must take a full step back before punching again (Alternatively, the referee may direct the fighters to “punch out” of the clinch). When a boxer is knocked down, the other boxer must immediately cease fighting and move to the furthest neutral corner of the ring until the referee has either ruled a knockout or called for the fight to continue.

Violations of these rules may be ruled "fouls" by the referee, who may issue warnings, deduct points, or disqualify an offending boxer, causing an automatic loss, depending on the seriousness and intentionality of the foul. An intentional foul that causes injury that prevents a fight from continuing usually causes the boxer who committed it to be disqualified. A fighter who suffers an accidental low-blow may be given up to five minutes to recover, after which they may be ruled knocked out if they are unable to continue. Accidental fouls that cause injury to end a bout may lead to a "no contest" result, or else cause the fight to go to a decision if enough rounds (typically four or more, or at least three in a four-round fight) have passed.

Unheard of these days, but common during the early 20th Century in North America, a "newspaper decision" (NWS) might be made after a "no decision" bout had ended. A "no decision" bout occurred when, by law or by pre-arrangement of the fighters, if both boxers were still standing at the fight's conclusion and there was no knockout, no official decision was rendered and neither boxer was declared the winner. But this did not prevent the pool of ringside newspaper reporters from declaring a consensus result among themselves and printing a newspaper decision in their publications. Officially, however, a "no decision" bout resulted in neither boxer winning or losing. Boxing historians sometimes use these unofficial newspaper decisions in compiling fight records for illustrative purposes only. Often, media outlets covering a match will personally score the match, and post their scores as an independent sentence in their report.

3) ***The Lake Isle of Innisfree* by William Butler Yeats**

I will arise and go now, and go to Innisfree,
And a small cabin build there,
of clay and wattles made;
Nine bean-rows will I have there,
a hive for the honey-bee,
And live alone in the bee-loud glade.

And I shall have some peace there,
for peace comes dropping slow,
Dropping from the veils of the morning to where the cricket sings;
There midnight's all a glimmer,
and noon a purple glow,
And evening full of the linnet's wings.

I will arise and go now,
for always night and day,
I hear the lake water lapping with low sounds by the shore;
While I stand on the roadway,
or on the pavements gray,

I hear it in the deep heart's core.

4) **William Butler Yeats**

William Butler Yeats (13 June 1865 — 28 January 1939) was an Irish poet and one of the foremost figures of 20th century literature, a pillar of both the Irish and British literary establishments. In his later years, he served as an Irish Senator for two terms. Yeats was a driving force behind the Irish Literary Revival and, along with Lady Gregory, Edward Martyn, and others, founded the Abbey Theatre, where he served as its chief during its early years. In 1923 he was awarded the Nobel Prize in Literature as the first Irishman so honored for what the Nobel Committee described as "inspired poetry", which in a highly artistic form gives expression to the spirit of a whole nation. Yeats is generally considered one of the few writers who completed their greatest works after being awarded the Nobel Prize; such works include *The Tower* (1928) and *The Winding Stair and Other Poems* (1929). Yeats was a very good friend of American expatriate poet and Bollingen Prize laureate Ezra Pound. Yeats wrote the introduction for Rabindranath Tagore's *Gitanjali*, which was published by the India Society.

He was born in Dublin and was educated there and in London; he spent his childhood holidays in County Sligo. He studied poetry in his youth and from an early age was fascinated by both Irish legends and the occult. Those topics feature in the first phase of his work, which lasted roughly until the turn of the 20th century. His earliest volume of verse was published in 1889, and its slow-paced and lyrical poems display Yeats' debts to Edmund Spenser, Percy Bysshe Shelley, and the poets of the Pre-Raphaelite Brotherhood. From 1900, Yeats's poetry grew more physical and realistic. He largely renounced the transcendental beliefs of his youth, though he remained preoccupied with physical and spiritual masks, as well as with cyclical theories of life.

2. Classical lines from the film

1) Boxing is about respect, getting it for yourself and taking it away from the other guy.
拳击是有关尊严的，赢得你自己的尊严，同时剥夺对手的。

2) Frankie liked to say that boxing is an unnatural act that everything in boxing is backwards. Sometimes the best way to deliver a punch is to step back. But to step back too far, you ain't fighting at all.
弗兰基喜欢说拳击是种不自然的运动，拳击中每样东西都是逆向的。有时打出一记重拳的最好方法就是退后一步，但是退后太多，你就已经退出比赛了。

3) Some people would say that the most important thing a fighter can have is heart. Frankie would say, "Show me a fighter who's nothing but heart and I'll show you a man waiting for a beating."
有些人会说，对于一个拳击手来说，最重要的莫过于热情。弗兰基说，“给我一个只有热情的拳击手，我会告诉他什么叫鼻青脸肿”。

4) If there's magic in boxing, it's the magic of fighting battles beyond endurance, beyond cracked ribs, ruptured kidneys and detached retinas. It's the magic of risking everything for a dream that nobody sees but you.
如果拳击运动中有诀窍的话，那么这种诀窍就是不停地战斗，超越耐力的极限、超越折断的肋骨、破裂的肾脏和脱落的视网膜。这种诀窍是为别人无法了解的梦想而赌上一切。

5) Boxing is an unnatural act. Because everything in it is backwards. You wanna move to the left, you don't step left, you push on the right toe. To move right, you use your left toe. Instead of running from the pain, like a sane person would do you step into it.
拳击是一种不自然的运动，因为一切东西都是相反的。你想向左移动，不是向左迈步，而是右脚趾用力，向右移动就左脚趾用力。你要迎着痛苦而上，而不是像有理智的人那样躲避。

6) To make a fighter, you gotta strip them down to a bare wood. Rest when you're dead. You can't just tell them to forget everything you know. You gotta make them forget it in their bones. Make them so tired that they only listen to you. Only hear your voice. Only do what you say, and nothing else. Show them how to keep their balance and take it away from the other guy. How to generate momentum off your right toe. And how to flex your knees when you fire a jab. How to fight backing up so that the other guy doesn't wanna come after you. Then you gotta show them all over again. Over and over and over till they think they were born that way.
训练一名拳击手，你必须在精神上把他们剥光。死了再休息。你不能只是叫他们忘记以前知道的事情，你要叫他们从骨子里忘记，让他们疲惫到只听你说的话，只能听见你的声音，只做你叫他们做的事情，不做其他事。教他们怎么保持平衡，怎么让对手失去平衡。如何用右脚趾产生动力，出刺拳时如何弯曲膝盖，如何在后腿中攻击好让对手在追击你时有所顾忌，然后你要再全部教他们一遍，一遍又一遍，直到他们感觉一切与生俱来。

7) All fighters are pigheaded some way or other. Some part of them always think that they know better than you about something. The truth is, even if they're wrong, even if that one thing is gonna be the ruin of them, if you can beat that last bit out of them, then they ain't fighters at all.
所有的拳手在这样或那样的方面都是固执的。他们中的一些人会认为他们比你在某方面知道得多。但事实是，尽管他们错了，即便这一件事会毁了他们，如果你能够彻底打败他们，那他们就不是真正意义上的拳手。

8) I can't be like this, Frankie. No matter what I'v done, I'v seen the world. People chanted my name. Well, not my name, some damn name you gave me. But they were chanting for me. I was in magazine. You think I ever dreamed that'd happen? I was born at 2 pounds, 1 and a half ounces. Daddy used to tell me that I fought to get into the world and I'd fight my way out. That's all I wanna do, Frankie. I just don't wanna fight you to do it. I got what I needed. I got it all. Don't let them keep taking it away from me. Don't let me lie here till I can't hear those people chanting no more.
我不能像现在这样，弗兰基。在我已经成就那么多之后，我见识了整个世界。人们高呼我的名字。喔，不是我的本名，是你给我起的该死的名字。可他们为我欢呼。我上过杂志，你以为我以前做过这样的梦吗？我生出来的时候只有2磅1.5盎司，爸爸以前总说我是打拼到这个世界上的，我也会打出一片天地。那是我唯一想做的，弗兰基。我只是不想为那个和你打，我得到了我要的，全部都得到了。别让他们从我身边一点点地拿走。别让我一直躺在这，直到听不见人们的欢呼声为止。

9) Maggie walked through that door with nothing but guts, no chance in the world of being what she needed to be. A year and a half later, she's fighting for the championship of the world. You did that. People die every day, Frankie. Mopping floor, washing dishes. And you know what their last thought is? "I never got my shot." Because of you, Maggie got her shot. If she dies today, you know what her last thought will be? I think I did all right. I know I could rest with that.
麦琪走进那扇门的时候，除了胆量什么都没有，根本没有机会实现她的梦想。一年半以后，她在争夺世界冠军，是你的功劳。每天都有人死去，弗兰基。拖地的时候，刷碗的时候。你知道他们最后一个念头是什么吗？“我从没有过机会。”因为有你，麦琪得到了属于她的机会。如果她今天就死去，你知道她最后一个念头是什么吗？“我觉得我干得不错。我会觉得心安理得的。”

10) Mo cuishle means "my darling, my blood."
莫库什勒意思是“我的挚爱，我的血肉”。

3. Film Review

Sports movies carry rich connotation, such as the persistence of the dream, the realization of people's own value, and the sticking to the national spirit, the defending of racial dignity, even the love for the teammates and respect between the rivals. *Million Dollar Baby* is a typical confrontational sports movie, but has advantages over other sports movies in critical thinking and philosophy, eventually winning the Oscar awards. Taking boxing match as the main line, this movie tells the story of how to deal with the relationship between life and dignity, real dream and true love. In this process, the leading character bursts into laughter or tears and at last the cruelty of reality puts her life to an end.

1) The considerate and warm narrator — the black old boxer Eddie

Will you be attracted to the narrator of a film? Perhaps not, but in this film, it seems so natural to be attracted by the narrator. You will fall into the charm of the vicissitudes of the voice. A black man telling a unique story, a mixed story of sweat, beliefs, dreams and dignity rolls out, in his special perspective. *Million Dollar Baby* considers the black old man as the narrator, and takes the audience's breath away at the first time when they hear the voice of the narrator.

Million Dollar Baby uses the fixed focus technique and tells the story from first-person point of view, selecting the black old boxer Eddie as the narrator of the film. The letter which Eddie wrote to Frankie's daughter is both the start and the end of the whole movie, making the plot of the whole movie complete. It also leaves the spiritual resonance between the audience and the narrator Eddie. Together with Eddie, the audience seems to witness the fighting boxing road of the female boxer Maggie and coach Frankie. In the film, black old boxer Eddie is both a character appearing in the scene and the narrator. Through Eddie, the film forms a fixed "internal perspective". Eddie's got fully display of his subjective feelings, which is also the fundamental key to create the blue narrative atmosphere of the film. Eddie's "internal perspective" gives us a chance to feel the special, deep relationship and emotion between the two close friends. Eddie gets involved in the Frankie's first half life as a coach as well as an agent, and knows all about him because of plenty of entanglement and communication with Frankie. As a spectator, Eddie witnesses the whole process of Maggie learning boxing from Frankie, and he has a comprehensive and profound understanding of the heavy pressure, the hard course and the persistence of Maggie. Therefore, Eddie is the most suitable person to tell the whole story in his comprehensive, objective and convincing words.

2) The familiar but charming narrative themes — dreams and dignity

Million Dollar Baby is a story about women's pursuit of dreams and maintenance of dignity. Its theme is very clear. On the one hand, it shows the thought of the strivers — about how to overcome themselves and how to win the world; on the other hand, it also shows reflection and introspection of ordinary people to their life, about how to recognize the dignity and how to realize their self-value.

In the movie, Maggie's dream of being a fighter never passes away, even during the three years that no one teaches her, holing up in the corner of the boxing hall and enduring ridicule and satire, or in the extreme poorly hunger, or being ruthless refused by her own idol. Maggie never stops her footsteps and still optimistically pursues her dream. When her dream is trampled and she is looked down upon by others, Maggie, the grassroots striver, shows that she is as tough as a rock, facing all man-made or naturally-existed difficulties directly and never gives up. With a set of refining and parallel type lens, such as the pat-time waitress job, the narrow and dark living space, the marginal training venues, the male boxer's jokes, the refusal from the coach, the film wants to show us how the striver, Maggie conquers herself step by step and hears the cheers from all over the world.

In addition, the narrative style of the film has greatly changed, and the dividing line is Maggie's final fight with the Blue Bear. The first half part of the film creates a hard-fought atmosphere. Although there are many kinds of difficulties in front of Maggie, she doesn't give up and spares no effort to climb to the top of the boxing mountain. After Maggie's final fight, the style of narration turns to be warm and sentimental. We feel heart-broken for Maggie and at the same time we are deeply moved by the special emotion between Frankie and Maggie. If we cut the warm caring part off, the film will be incomplete both in the form and style, and will not leave as a deep impression on the audience as before.

Frankie is a lonely winner, who can produce champion but fails to win back her daughter's heart. Though he keeps writing letters to his daughter, these letters are sent back cruelly. He silently collects the returning letters. He goes to church to pray, repent, beg for forgiveness for his fault and he keeps reading Yeats's poetry, hoping that the literature will heal his injured heart. But that will only reinforce the loneliness and empty feelings in his deep heart. His efforts did not pay off. His daughter did not write even one letter back, and at the last minute his fighter Willie leaves him. From the very first moment he meets Maggie, the enthusiastic "old" female fighter, everything seems to start changing. After knowing about Maggie constantly, he finds the resonance, and also sees the enthusiasm for living. So he and Maggie had a strong feeling to fight for life, like a father and a daughter. As their feelings deepen, we can see the sober reflection to the true meaning of life and its value.

3) The unique narrative paradigm — the hero lost its aura.

In the film, the heroine Maggie can finally stand on the glory stage of her career, being the "million dollar baby" if she could beat her final rival. But to our surprise, she does not win as we ever thought. She loses the combat capability in the final battle. The serious injury paralysis makes her despair and eventually dead.

From this shift, it is not hard to see, in recent years, the sports film pays less attention to the game winner of a decisive battle or the gold medal supremacy of heroism. Instead, it turns into a broader view and shoulders social responsibility. Through the objective description, the connotation, rules and regulations of the sports life, we can learn about how to deal with the social and family problems. In this movie, we see the new interpretation about the heroism — the meaning of "hero" is no longer a gold medal, victory or scores, but about a dream, dignity, self-salvation and the value of life. If she has realized the dream, defended the dignity, and known the value of life, she is still a hero, a real hero, though she has finally lost the glory of victory.

4. Extended Reading

Film: *The Blind Side*

The Blind Side is a 2010 American film directed by John Lee Hancock, adapted from *The Blind Side: Evolution of the Game* written by Michael Lewis. It tells us a story about Michael Oher, one of the players of the National Football League, an orphan growing up in an adoptive family. He lives a hard life to realize his dream before he devotes his life to sports life.

Michael Oher is a homeless African-American boy. His father abandoned both his mother and him when he was young. Since his mother was taking drugs, he was forced to be adopted by another family demanded by the United States government. But during that process he has been escaping from the adoptive families. Thanks to the recommendation from his friend's father,

Michael came to a Christian school for studying, but it is not easy for him to adapt to the new environment. At that time, Michael was abandoned by his adoptive families, and the kind Mrs. Tuohy decided to take him. With her help, Michael found his own value gradually and began to fit in the new environment. In the school football team, he was one of the most assiduous players. Due to his unique physical condition, Michael gradually became an excellent left-back in the school team, and so many universities are eager to enroll him. In 2009 at the American football league draft convention, Michael was drafted by a team in Baltimore and became a professional football player.

The film won many prizes, and Sandra Bullock's excellent performance has left a deep impression on the audience.

5. Homework

1) Watch the film *Million Dollar Baby* again and try to write down your feelings after the film.

2) Think about how to deal with the relationship between your dream and the reality.

Unit 11 The Curious Case of Benjamin Button 《本杰明·巴顿的故事》

I Preview the movie

1. Background

Directed by	David Fincher
Based on	The Curious Case of Benjamin Button By F. Scott Fitzgerald
Stars	Brad Pitt Cate Blanche Taraji P. Henson Julia Ormond Jason Flemyng Elias Koteas Tilda Swinton
Distributed by	Paramount Pictures(United States) Warner Bros. Pictures (Worldwide)
Box office	$333.9 million

2. Plot

In 2005, Daisy Fuller lies on her deathbed in a New Orleans hospital. She asks her daughter to read a diary of Benjamin Button. Through the diary, we learn that Benjamin is born on the evening of Nov. 11, 1918 with the appearance and maladies of a grown-up. After giving birth, the boy's mother died, and his father abandons him at a nursing home. Lucky enough, the boy is found by a Queenie and adopted as her own baby.

Different from other children, it is in 1925 that Benjamin learns to walk. It is also regarded as a miracle when he starts to use crutches instead of a wheelchair. On Thanksgiving Day, 1930, Benjamin comes across a pretty girl named Daisy. They start to develop a good relationship. After that, Benjamin works on a tugboat and runs into Thomas Button who doesn't show his real identity to Benjamin. In 1936, Benjamin gains the opportunity of working for a long-term engagement with the tugboat crew and Daisy also gains a job in a dance company in New York. In 1941, Benjamin begins to work for Elisabeth Abbott in Dec. 1941, Japan attacks Pearl harbor, which provokes the U.S. into World War II. Benjamin is rescued by a U.S. navy ship and survives from a campaign.

In May 1945, Benjamin returns to New Orleans and lives with Queenie again. Several weeks later, he meets Daisy again and they enjoy a good meal time. When Daisy finds it hard to seduce Benjamin, she leaves away. Later, Benjamin reunites with Thomas Button who doesn't have much time left in this world. Thomas Button finally reveals his real identity that he is Benjamin' s father.

In 1947, Benjamin visits Daisy without announcing her in advance in New York but leaves soon after he finds that Daisy has fallen in love with other person. In 1945, Daisy suffers a severe car accident in Paris, which makes her impossible to dance again. To Daisy's surprise, Benjamin looks more youthful than before when Benjamin pays a visit to her, but she refuses him to come into her life because of her frustrated result from her injuries.

In 1962, Daisy reunites with Benjamin in New Orleans. Because of their comparable age, they fall in love with each other and then go sailing together. When they come back home, to their regret, Queenie has died already. In 1967, Daisy opens a ballet studio. Later, Daisy gives birth to a girl in 1968. Benjamin worries that he cannot be a good father to his child due to his reverse aging. He sells all his belongings and leaves them to Daisy and his child then departs. He chooses to travel alone during the 1970s. However, when Benjamin returns to Daisy in 1980 again, he finds that Daisy has been married again.

In 1990, Daisy learns from a social worker that Benjamin is a physically pre-teen. When Daisy gets there, they tell her that Benjamin is living in a hospital in poor physical state, and they find her name in Benjamin' s diary. In the end, Daisy moves into the nursing home and takes care of Benjamin for the rest of his life.

In 2003, Benjamin dies in Daisy's arms, physically an infant but chronologically a 84 years old man.

II View the movie

Clip 1 The birth of Benjamin and his adoption by Queenie

Words and Expressions:

nuisance	讨厌的人；麻烦事	be meant to	（因能力、命运等）注定
remembrance	记忆	out of one's mind	发疯的；疯狂的

Task 1 **Watch the video clip and fill in the missing words of the dialogue.**

Dr. Rose: Queenie, some creatures **1**____________.

Queenie: No, this baby, he is a miracle. That's for certain. Just not the kind of **2**_________ one hopes to see. Y'all listen. Y'all listen up here. We're gonna have us a visitor that's gonna be staying with us for a little while. My sister had a child and she couldn't see right by it, so ... He's known as Benjamin. Benjamin. He's not a well child, so we're gonna have to take good care of him.

An old lady: I have 10 children. There's not a baby I can't care for. Let me see him. God in Heaven. He looks just like my **3**_________.

Queenie: Look, he's **4**_________ old. Dr. Rose said he ain't got much more time on this earth.

An old man: Join the club.

Queenie: He's smiling.

Mr. Weathers: Hambert sends his **5**_________ to you. Are you right out of your mind? I know you ain't got all the parts it takes to make one of your own, but this ain't yours to keep. It may not even be humankind.

Queenie: Mr. Weathers, come back here. Please. You never know what's coming for you.

Task 2 **Watch the video clip again and answer the questions.**

a) Why does Queenie pretend to say Benjamin is her sister's child?

____

____

b) "God in heaven, he looks just like my ex-husband". From this humorous saying, can you conclude what kind of atmosphere is in this house?

____

____

Clip 2 Benjamin's leaving from home to serve for the tugboat

Words and Expressions:

familiar 熟悉的　drugstore 药店　postcard 明信片

Task 1 **Mark T(True) or F(False) for the following statements according to the clip.**

a) ______ To some extent, losing someone is a way to test how important they are to us.

b) ______ Benjamin decided to leave home in the 18th year of his life.

Task 2 **Discussion: "Benjamin, we are meant to lose the people we love. How else would we know how important they are to us?" Do you agree with this sentence? How do you understand?**

____

Clip 3 Benjamin's coming back from the sea

Words and Expressions:

worth doing	值得做某事	strike	敲；击；打
mind sb's own business		管好某人自己的事	

Task 1 **Dub the voice for Benjamin and Queenie while the video is played again without a sound.**

Task 2 **Discussion: The sentence "You never know what's coming for you" is just like the classical lines "Life is like a box of chocolate, you never know what you're gonna get" from the film *Forrest Gump*. Can you analyze what is the same thing the two sentences are trying to say?**

Clip 4 Benjamin's unforgettable experience with Daisy

Words and Expressions:

collision	碰撞，冲突	rehearse	排练，预演
drop off	减少	boutique	精品店
pull away	离开；脱身		

Task 1 Answer the questions from this video clip.

a) Where did Daisy rehearse for a performance?

____

b) Why didn't the woman in the boutique wrap the package on time?

____

c) How many kinds of things have been included to lead to Daisy's accident?

____

Task 2 Discussion: Do you think it is a waste of time to describe so many things in detail before Daisy has an accident? If not, list out the reasons.

____

____

____

Clip 5 Benjamin's departure from his family and finally his coming back

Words and Expressions:

chase	追逐，追赶	make the best or worst of	做出最好的或最糟的
startle	惊愕；惊恐	pick up	捡起；偶然学到

Task 1 **Write T(True) or F(False) for the following statement according to the clip.**

a) _______ Caroline was born in 1968.

b) _______ After Benjamin left Daisy and Caroline, he went to India.

Task 2 **Watch the clip again and take down what Benjamin said. (Start with the sentence "to be whoever you want to be".)**

____

____

____

Clip 6 The last moments of Benjamin's life

Words and Expressions:

graveyard	墓地
as if	好像，仿佛

Discussion:

a) The first time Daisy saw young Benjamin, he said "Do I know you?" Can you write down the complex feelings Daisy has through her face?

____

b) Considering Benjamin's whole life, do you think he has a happy life? Do you want to have the same experience as he got?

____

____

III Review the movie

1. Cultural Notes

1) World War I (WWI or WW1)

It is also known that the First World War or the Great War was a global war centering in Europe that began on 28 July, 1914 and lasted until 11 November, 1918. More than 9 million combatants and 7 million civilians died as a result of the war, a casualty rate exacerbated by the belligerents' technological and industrial sophistication, and tactical stalemate. It was one of the deadliest conflicts in history, paving the way for major political changes, including revolutions in many of the nations involved.

The war drew in all the world's economic great powers, which were assembled in two opposing alliances: the Allies (based on the Triple Entente of the United Kingdom, France and the Russian Empire) and the Central Powers of Germany and Austria-Hungary. Although Italy had also been a member of the Triple Alliance alongside Germany and Austria-Hungary, it did not join the Central Powers, as Austria-Hungary had taken the offensive against the terms of the alliance. These alliances were reorganized and expanded as more nations entered the war: Italy, Japan and the United States joined the Allies, and the Ottoman Empire and Bulgaria, the Central Powers. Ultimately, more than 70 million military personnel, including 60 million Europeans, were mobilised in one of the largest wars in history.

2) Franklin Delano Roosevelt

Franklin Delano Roosevelt (30 January, 1882 — 12 April, 1945), commonly known by his initials FDR, was an American statesman and political leader who served as the 32nd President of the United States. A Democrat, he won a record of four elections and served from March 1933 to his death in April 1945. He was a central figure in world events during the mid-20th century, leading the United States during a time of worldwide economic depression and total war. A dominant leader of the Democratic Party, he built a New Deal Coalition that realigned American politics after 1932, as his New Deal domestic policies defined American liberalism for the middle third of the 20th century.

3) Wilhelm Richard Wagner (22 May, 1813 — 13 February, 1883)

Wilhelm Richard Wagner was a German composer, theatre director, polemicist, and conductor who is primarily known for his operas (or, as some of his later works were later known, "music dramas"). Unlike most opera composers, Wagner wrote both the libretto and the music for each of his stage works. Initially establishing his reputation as a composer of works in the romantic vein of Weber and Meyerbeer, Wagner revolutionised opera through his concept of the Gesamtkunstwerk ("total work of art"), by which he sought to synthesise the poetic, visual, musical and dramatic arts, with music subsidiary to drama, and which was announced in a series of essays between 1849 and 1852. Wagner realised these ideas most fully in the first half of the four-opera cycle Der Ring des Nibelungen (The Ring of the Nibelung).

His compositions, particularly those of his later period, are notable for their complex texture, rich harmony and orchestration, and the elaborate use of leitmotifs — musical phrases associated with individual characters, places, ideas or plot elements. His advances in musical language, such as extreme chromaticism and quickly shifting tonal centres, greatly influenced the development of classical music. "His Tristan and Isolde" is sometimes described as marking the start of modern music.

4) Hummingbird

Hummingbirds are New World birds that constitute the family Trochilidae. They are among the smallest of birds, most species measuring in the 7.5-13 cm in range. Indeed, the smallest extant bird species is a hummingbird, the 5-cm bee hummingbird, weighing less than a U.S. penny (2.5g).

They are known as hummingbirds because of the humming sound created by their beating wings which flap at high frequencies audible to humans. They hover in mid-air at rapid wing-flapping rates, typically around 50 times per second, but possibly as high as 200 times per second, allowing them also to fly at speeds exceeding 15 m/s (54 km/h; 34 mph), backwards.

Hummingbirds have the highest metabolism of any homeothermic animal. To conserve energy when food is scarce, they have the ability to go into a hibernation-like state (torpor) where their metabolic rate is slowed to 1/15th of its normal rate.

5) Caviar

Caviar is a delicacy consisting of salt-cured fish-eggs of the Acipenseridae family. The roe can be "fresh" (non-pasteurized) or pasteurized, with pasteurization reducing its culinary and economic value.

Traditionally, the term caviar refers only to roe from wild sturgeon in the Caspian and Black Sea (Beluga, Ossetra and Sevruga caviars). Depending on the country, caviar may also be used to describe the roe of other fish such as salmon, steelhead, trout, lumpfish, whitefish, and other species of sturgeon.

Caviar is considered a delicacy and is eaten as a garnish or a spread.

6) Attack on Pearl Harbor

The attack on Pearl Harbor was a surprise military strike conducted by the Imperial Japanese Navy against the United States naval base at Pearl Harbor, Hawaii, on the morning of December 7, 1941 (December 8 in Japan). The attack led to the United States' entry into World War II.

The attack was intended as a preventive action in order to keep the U.S. Pacific Fleet from interfering with military actions the Empire of Japan was planning in Southeast Asia against overseas territories of the United Kingdom, the Netherlands, and the United States. There were simultaneous Japanese attacks on the U.S.-held Philippines and on the British Empire in Malaya, Singapore.

The attack came as a profound shock to the American people and led directly to the American entry into World War II in both the Pacific and European theaters. The following day, December 8, the United States declared war on Japan. Domestic support for non-interventionism had strongly disappeared. Clandestine support of Britain (e.g., the Neutrality Patrol) was replaced by active alliance. Subsequent operations by the U.S. prompted Germany and Italy to declare war on the U.S. on December 11, which was reciprocated by the U.S. the same day.

There were numerous historical precedents for unannounced military action by Japan. However, the lack of any formal warning, particularly while negotiations were still apparently ongoing, led President Franklin D. Roosevelt to proclaim December 7, 1941, "a date which will live in infamy". Because the attack happened without a declaration of war and without explicit warning, the attack on Pearl Harbor was judged by the Tokyo Trials to be a war crime.

7) David Herbert Richards Lawrence (11 September, 1885 — 2 March, 1930)

D. H. Lawrence was an English novelist, poet, playwright, essayist, literary critic and painter who published as D. H. Lawrence. His collected works, among other things, represent an extended reflection upon the dehumanising effects of modernity and industrialisation. In them, some of the issues Lawrence explored are emotional health, vitality, spontaneity and instinct.

Lawrence's opinions earned him many enemies and he endured official persecution, censorship, and misrepresentation of his creative work throughout the second half of his life, much of which he spent in a voluntary exile which he called his "savage pilgrimage". At the time of his death, his public reputation was that of a pornographer who had wasted his considerable talents. E. M. Forster, in an obituary notice, challenged this widely held view, describing him as "the greatest imaginative novelist of our generation". Later, the influential Cambridge critic F. R. Leavis championed both his artistic integrity and his moral seriousness, placing much of Lawrence's fiction within the canonical "great tradition" of the English novel.

2. Classical lines from the film

1) You never know what's coming for you.
你永不会知道接下来发生什么。(世事难料)

2) There is always something that I should remember for the rest of my life.
总有一些事情是我需要铭记一生的。

3) Everybody feels different about themselves, one way or another. But we're all going the same way. Just taking different roads to get there, that's all. You are on your own roads, Benjamin.
每个人对于自己的感受都不一样，但是我们的终点是一样的。只是走的路不同罢了。你有你自己的道路，本杰明。

4) Benjamin, we're meant to lose the people we love. How else would we know how important they are to us?
本杰明，我们命中注定要失去所爱之人。不然我们怎么知道他们在我们生命中有多重要。

5) I'm blind in the one eye ... I can hardly hear ... I get twitches and shakes out of nowhere ... I lose my line of thought ... but you know what ... God keeps reminding me I'm lucky to be alive ...
当我瞎了一只眼睛，几乎听不见晨间喧嚣，动不动就抽搐，总是丢三落四，上帝却依然扔下闪电来提醒我，能够活着已经是桩幸运的事了。

6) You can be as mad as a mad dog at the way things went. You could swear, curse the fates. But when it comes to the end, you have to let go.
不顺心的时候，你可以像疯狗一样发狂，可以破口大骂、诅咒命运，但最后还是得放手。

7) It's a funny thing about coming home. Looks the same, smells the same, feels the samc. You realize what's changed is you.
回家的感觉很有意思。所有的东西看起来、闻起来、感受起来都一样，你意识到只有你自己是改变了的。

8) Our lives are defined by opportunities. Even the ones we miss.
我们的生活会被机遇所界定，甚至包括那些我们错过的机遇。

9) Plenty of times you be alone. You, different like us, it's gonna be that way. But I tell you a little secret. Fat people, skinny people, tall people, white people ... they just as alone as us ... But they scaredshitless ... Not a thing wrong with being alone ... no sir ...
无论什么肤色，什么体形，人们都是孤独的。但可怕的不是孤独，而是惧怕孤独。其实孤独没什么不好，真的。

10) Sometimes we're on a collision course and we just don't know it. Whether it's by accident or by design, there's not a thing we can do about it.
有时候我们的人生轨道会与别人的交错，只是不自知罢了。无论是出于意外还是有意为之，我们都无力改变。

11) I wish I could have been your father. Nothing I ever did will replace that. For what it's worth, it's never too late or in my case too early to be whoever you want to be. There's no time limit. Start whenever you want. You can change or stay the same. There are no rules to this thing. We can make the best or the worse of it. And I hope you make the best of it. I hope you see things that startle you. I hope you feel things you never felt before. I hope you meet people with a different point of view. I hope you live a life you're proud of. And if you find that you're not, I hope you have the strength to start all over again.
我希望我可以当你爸爸，在没有什么比这更让我魂牵梦绕。只要是有意义的事，再晚去做还是有意义的。不过如果是我说，该说再“早”，再“早”去做都是有意义的。做你想做的人，这件事没有时间的限制，只要愿意，什么时候都可以开始。你能从现在开始改变，也可以一成不变。这件事没有规则可言。你能活出最精彩的自己，也可能搞得一团糟。我希望你能活出最精彩的自己。我希望你能见识到令你惊奇的事物，我希望你能体验未曾体验过的情感，我希望你能遇见一些想法不同的人，我希望你为你自己的人生感到骄傲。如果你发现自己还没有做到，我希望你有勇气重头再来。

3. Film Review

As one of the most anticipated winter films in 2008, *The Curious Case of Benjamin Button* is indeed a masterpiece. The story is attractive and fascinating. In addition, it's got our favorite director, David Fincher. With "Button", Fincher cements his place as of the best directors alive.

As we know, David Fincher is always responsible for the genre of realistic and crime thrillers. So, it's really surprising that he is going to direct such a fantasy film of a lifetime story. Fincher manages to use each resource to craft a most attractive and technically magnificent film of this year with a comparable amount of budget. It's no doubt that it's worth cherishing for ages.

To some extent, the direction of the film is almost perfect. Hopefully, Benjamin Button has garnered David Fincher much more recognition he deserves. On the one hand, he keeps the film grounded in reality; on the other hand, he maintains the undeniable magic within. As a director, you have to win each quality instead of losing either of them, keeping a healthy balance of the two perfectly. He is helped out by a magical score and definitely stunning cinematography which soon regarded as a Fincher film, due to the darkness and lighting of it. He winds this clock so well and with such grace that the movie has this unique flow that is enjoyable from start to end. With nearly 3 hours, not a minute is wasted. Every scene is jaw dropping and some of them will find issue with time, which is used intelligently.

The acting is also a wonderful thing. This is also Brad Pitt's best performance by far. He is so charming yet realistic through the whole process. His nuances are exactly present. And despite the too much use of make-up, CGI plays the leading role of the film with a certain air of likability like he always does. While I think he does a good job with the part he plays, he doesn't have to do much. Benjamin is a rather quiet character in the film. In terms of acting, Cate Blanchett and Taraji P. Henson also have a good performance in the film. Sometimes Blanchett seems much more overrated to some. It's certain that her unrivaled talent at playing a complex and deep character makes her complete it with ease. Taraji P. Henson also will surprise you as Benjamin's mother, because she is not only humorous but also warm and loving. So loving that I feel as if she was my mom.

The Curious Case of Benjamin Button is a film unlike any other films I have ever seen. The true sense leaves me completely speechless. It achieves so much without too much complexity. Everything is top notch from the wonderful directing to the best performances down to the magical score. The film lets us feel not only for the death we will face, but for the incredible life we experience. It prays on the various moral issues we all deal with but also dangles the idea that everyone goes though the same complaints and happiness, just not in the same way. This is a momentous story that deserves nothing less than the title of brilliance.

The movie is rich visually and emotionally, which makes us recall a peculiar man who was born in the early 20th century who ages backwards. His life story is narrated through a diary read by the daughter of his lover, Daisy. Throughout life he experiences the same things we ordinary people face, growing up and then eventually growing old. As a thoughtful observer, he discovers and explores life from different angles. But it is not his life but his love that makes him special and unique. He almost spends a whole life trying to prove how he loves Daisy, but finally only gets a few years really loving her. As their stories tell us, the years of frustration and hardship are all worth it if only for a few moments of happiness.

Despite the wonder of the film, coupled with the realism that Fincher always brings, the true selling point of the film is not only Benjamin' s aging problem, but his romance with beautiful Daisy. The two fall in love, regardless of age, time and place. It's one of the most touching romances of the year.

"Button" has impressed me so much because the film's recurring theme is that age is only a number. And that we should be able to choose what we want to, no matter what our age is. I think it's a best way to illustrate this message through a story where the titular character ages backwards, and have to experience life in such a way: one falls in love when he appears young enough to be his spouse's child or a 5-year-old child plays with the peers when he's confined to a wheelchair due to old age. All these makes people feel upset. Fincher's epic shows our life choices.

"Button" is one of the most technically well-made movie of 2008, and the highlights of it include *Visual Effects and the Makeup*, both of which are Oscar worthy. Pitt plays the character at almost every age, but it's hard for us to tell when the CGI is being used on him. You know it's being used, but you can not tell where and when. It's definitely perfect. No matter a young Pitt or an elder one, it will work well to show you the magic effects.

Despite a long run-time, the film never drags anyway. As to me, I'd like to see more flow of Benjamin as a kid. I mean the last parts of the film when Benjamin gets old, but his body keeps young. This doesn't influence the film in any way, as it's just my own wishes.

In a word, *Benjamin Button* is a film that deals with the human nature and recovers it. Producing every bit of happiness, love, confusion, depression, companionship that life provides us with this film a master piece on most levels.

4. Extended Reading

Film: *Flipped*

Flipped is a 2010 teen, romantic comedy drama film directed by Rob Reiner. It is an adaptation of the novel *Flipped by Wendelin Van Draanen.*

Juli Baker devoutly believes in three things: the sanctity of trees (especially her beloved sycamore), the wholesomeness of the eggs she collects from her backyard flock of chickens, and that someday she will kiss Bryce Loski. Ever since she saw Bryce's baby blues back in second grade, Juli has been smitten. Unfortunately, Bryce has never felt the same. Frankly, he thinks Juli Baker is a little weird after all. What kind of freak raises chickens and sits in trees for fun? Then, in eighth grade, everything changes. Bryce begins to see that Juli's unusual interests and pride in her family are, well, kind of cool. And Juli starts to think that maybe Bryce's brilliant blue eyes are as empty as the rest of Bryce seems to be. After all, what kind of jerk doesn't care about other people's feelings about chickens and trees? With Flipped, mystery author Wendelin Van Draanen has taken a break from her Sammy Keyes series, and the result is flipping fantastic. Bryce and Juli's rants and raves about each other is so true that young readers will quickly identify with at least one of these hilarious feuding egos, if not both. It is a perfect introduction to the adolescent war between the sexes.

5. Homework

1) Watch the film *The Curious Case of Benjamin Button* again and try to write down your feelings after watching.

2) Do you want to be Benjamin? Why or why not?

Unit 12 Mr. Peabody & Sherman 《天才眼镜狗》

I Preview the movie

1. Background

Directed by	Rob Minkoff
Based on	Peabody's Improbable History By Ted Key
Stars	Ty Burrell Max Charles Ariel Winter
Distributed by	20th Century Fox
Box office	$272.9 million

2. Plot

Mr. Peabody is a very smart dog who has been anthropomorphic in the film. After being turned down by every potential owner when he was little, different from other dogs, he spends most time in learning athletics, science and other technologies, which makes him a very skilled and knowledgeable dog. One day, Mr. Peabody finds an orphaned baby. He takes him home and adopts him legally by the name Sherman. Through the process of growing up, Mr. Peabody teaches Sherman a lot of scientific and historical knowledge through a series of adventures using the WABAC.

Sherman attends Susan B. Anthony School in New York City. One day, Sherman falls into conflict with his classmate Penny about certain historical knowledge just because he shows up with his first-hand knowledge innocently. Thus, Penny feels extremely embarrassed and begins to bully and humiliate Sherman by calling him a "dog", which provokes Sherman into biting Penny.

In order to mend fences and solve problems, Mr. Peabody invites the Petersons over for a dinner party. During the meal time, Mr. Peabody has a pleasant time with Penny's parents. At the same time, Sherman shows Penny the WABAC and takes it with her despite Mr. Peabody's warnings. Moments later, Sherman asks Mr. Peabody to help to retrieve Penny who intends to have an engagement with King Tut in Ancient Egypt. Penny wants to leave when she knows that she will be killed and buried with Tut after he died. In order to stop the tragedy's happening, Peabody and Sherman manage to rescue Penny from the wedding and escape in the end despite many adventures.

The battery of the WABAC runs out long before they comes back, so Mr. Peabody gets them to the historical time of Renaissance Florence where they come across Leonardo Da Vinci. Sherman and Penny climb onto Da Vinci's attic and find out his flying machine. Sherman manages to fly it for Penny's encouragement but crash in the end. Da Vinci is so excited that his machine works. But Mr. Peabody insists that Sherman should not risk his safety to do so and also destroy an historical artifact.

After that, they try to return, but a black hole forces them into landing during the Trojan War time. In the war, Mr. Peabody dies during an attempt of rescuing Penny as she is trapped inside a horse when it rolls towards a cliff.

Ms. Grunion always makes an attempt at deprivation of Mr. Peabody's custody. In the process of quarreling, Mr. Peabody's sadness suddenly turns to a rage, which makes him bite Ms. Grunion. Ms. Grunion tries every means to call the police and chase after Mr. Peabody. At the same time, Mr. Peabody, Sherman and Penny in the WABAC are unable to come back in time while several historic figures rain down to the present.

In the end, the time machine crashes and the police gather around it in the street. Animal Control arrests Mr. Peabody and plans to euthanize him for attacking Ms. Grunion. Sherman stands out and says that everything happened is his own fault and insists that he'll rather be the son of a dog instead of a person. Moved by his words, everyone present. Even the police concur. All historical figures support Mr. Peabody's legal custody of Sherman and award him a presidential pardon and eventually Sherman and Penny make it up with each other again.

Mr. Peabody and others try to work out how to close the rip. Sherman advises that they may travel into the future. Mr. Peabody and Sherman drive it and manage to undo the damage. Those historical figures are forced back to their respective times. To everyone's surprise, Ms. Grunion is carried away by Agamemnon to his own time.

II View the movie

Clip 1 Sherman's bite on his classmate Penny Peterson

Words and Expressions:

curriculum	课程	take into account	把……列入考虑
for insurance purpose	为保险起见	point out	指出

Task 1 Watch the video clip and fill in the missing words.

Sherman: I'm sorry I **1**__________ her, Mr. Peabody. I won't do it again.

Mr. Peabody: You're darn tooting, you won't do it again. This kind of wanton **2**__________ is totally **3**__________. And rather **4**__________, given how you feel about Mr. Gandhi. What on earth **5**__________ it?

Sherman: She called me a dog.

Mr. Peabody: All right then. Thank you for telling me. Try and get some sleep.

Sherman: I love you, Mr. Peabody.

Mr. Peabody: I have a deep **6**__________ for you as well, Sherman.

Task 2 Watch the video clip again and answer the questions.

a) Why does Miss Grunion want to take Sherman away?

____

b) Why does Sherman bite Penny?

____

Clip 2 Rescuing Penny in Ancient Egypt

Words and Expressions:

remind of	使回想起，使记起	be allowed to do	被允许做某事
obedient	顺从的；服从的	hit off	将 ... ... 打掉
hold off	推迟		

Task 1 **Write T(True) or F(False) for the following statement according to the clip.**

a) _______ The WABAC can go anytime and anywhere.

b) _______ Mr. Peabody gets along well with Mr. and Mrs. Peterson.

Task 2 **Dub the voice for Mr. Peabody, Sherman and Penny while the video is played again without a sound.**

Clip 3 Successfully helping Penny out and coming into the Renaissance Age

Words and Expressions:

historical artifact	历史手工艺	hooligan	小流氓
smithereens	碎片	brutal	残忍的；野蛮的
Trojan War	特洛伊战争		

Task 1 Watch the video clip and fill in the missing words.

Sherman: I'm sorry I broke the plane, Mr. Peabody.

Mr. Peabody: Well, you should be. You could have been killed.

Penny: What are you talking about? Sherman flew a plane. He was **1**_________!

Mr. Peabody: Sherman destroyed a **2**____________.

Penny: Whatever, you should be happy. It turns out that Sherman is not a **3**_________ and total loser after all.

Sherman: Yeah, Mr. Peabody, it turns out that I'm not a complete and total loser after all.

Mr. Peabody: Miss Peterson, stop turning my son into a hooligan.

Penny: It's not my fault that he is a hooligan.

Sherman: Yeah, it's not her fault I'm a **4**_________.

Mr. Peabody: Well it's certainly not my fault. I've spent the last 7 years teaching Sherman good **5**_________.

Penny: If you are such a great parent, why is Miss Grunion trying to take Sherman away from you?

Sherman: Is that true? Is somebody gonna take me away from you?

Mr. Peabody: No Sherman, I'll never let that happen. You just need to trust me. Oh dear,black hole!

Task 2 Discussion: Do you know anything about the black hole or the Trojan War? Choose one topic and talk about what you know with your partner.

____

____

____

Clip 4 Leaving the Renaissance Age but trapped in the Trojan War

Words and Expressions:

timeline	时间轴；时间表	space-time continuum	空间 — 时间统一体
appetite	食欲；嗜好		

Task 1 **Watch clip 4 and fill in the missing words of the dialogue.**

Mr. Peabody: Miss Grunion! How **1**__________! We were having such a good time. I almost forgot you're coming. Why don't you join the party?

Miss Grunion: I'm not here for a party! I'm here for the **2**__________.

Mr. Peabody: Good! Why don't you start **3**__________ over here? Or here or here or here?

Miss Grunion: Stop waving your hands around!

Miss Grunion, Penny's Parents: Sherman?

Miss Grunion: Wait! Is that?

Penny's Parents: Sherman!

Penny's Father: Dos Shermans? What's going on here, Mr. Peabody?

Mr. Peabody: Nobody move! Sherman, I've got to get you out of here before you touch yourself.

Miss Grunion & Penny's Parents: Oh!

Sherman: Mr. Peabody, you didn't die!

Mr. Peabody: Of course I didn't die! Thank you.

Sherman: How did you get back?

Mr. Peabody: Well, after a few failed experiments, I hit upon a **4**__________ of bone, stone and Yak fat, and **5**__________ a rudimentary WABAC. You know what they say "If at first you don't succeed, Troy, Troy again."

Sherman: This is no time for puns, even good ones. Penny, Sherman quickly!

Task 2 **Watch the video clip again and answer the questions again.**

a) As Penny has admitted that it is her own fault to cause this situation, Miss Grunion does not accept it and still insists on taking Sherman away. Can you conclude the main characteristic of Miss Grunion and analyze which kind of person she stands for?

____

____

b) Why does Mr. Peabody bite Miss Grunion? Is it just because he is a "dog"?

____

____

Clip 5 The appearance of two pairs of Mr. Peabody and Sherman

Words and Expressions:

pay for	偿还	without permission	未经允许
turn one's back on	背弃	pick sb. up	（用车）接某人
mess up	陷入困境，搞糟		

Task 1 **Watch Clip 5 and pay attention to the conversation between Sherman and Miss Grunion. (Take down the conversation from the beginning to the series of "I'm a dog, too.")**

____

____

Task 2 **Discussion: If you were in that scene, would you firmly speak "I'm a dog, too" out? Why?**

Clip 6 The perfect solution of the problem and the happy ending

Words and Expressions:

gravitational field	重力域	reprogram	改编程序
leap	飞跃，跳跃		

Task 1 **Discussion: At last, Sherman has grown up and does something successful. It is closely related to the way Mr. Peabody brings up Sherman. Try to conclude how Mr. Peabody brings up Sherman, and talk about what you have learned from it.**

III Review the movie

1. Cultural Notes

1) French Revolution

The French Revolution was an influential period of social and political upheaval in France that lasted from 1789 until 1799. Inspired by liberal and radical ideas, the Revolution profoundly altered the course of modern history, triggering the global decline of theocracies and absolute monarchies while replacing them with republics and democracies. Through the Revolutionary Wars, it unleashed a wave of global conflicts that extended from the Caribbean to the Middle East. Historians widely regard the Revolution as one of the most important events in human history.

The modern era has unfolded in the shadow of the French Revolution. Almost all future revolutionary movements looked back to the Revolution as their predecessor. Its central phrases and cultural symbols, such as La Marseillaise and Liberté, égalité, fraternité, became the clarion call for other major upheavals in modern history, including the Russian Revolution over a century later. French society itself underwent important transformations as aristocratic and religious privileges disappeared. The values and institutions established by the Revolution dominate French politics to this day. Globally, the Revolution accelerated the rise of republics and democracies. It became the focal point for the development of all modern political ideologies, leading to the spread of liberalism, nationalism, socialism, feminism, and secularism, among many others. The Revolution also witnessed the birth of total war by organizing the resources of France and the lives of its citizens towards the objective of military conquest. Some of its central documents, like the Declaration of the Rights of Man, expanded the arena of human rights to include women and slaves, leading to movements for abolitionism and universal suffrage in the next century.

2) Marie Antoinette

Marie Antoinette (2 November, 1755 – 16 October, 1793), born an Archduchess of Austria, was Dauphine of France from 1770 to 1774 and Queen of France and Navarre from 1774 to 1792. She was the fifteenth and penultimate child of Holy Roman Empress Maria Theresa and Emperor Francis I.

Initially charmed by her personality and beauty, the French people eventually came to dislike her, accusing “L’Autrichienne” [which literally means the Austrian (woman), but also suggests the French word “chienne”, meaning bitch] of being profligate, promiscuous, and of harbouring sympathies for France's enemies, particularly Austria, her country of origin. The Diamond Necklace incident damaged her reputation further. She later became known as Madame Déficit because France's financial crisis was blamed on her lavish spending.

3) Mohandas Karamchand Gandhi

Mohandas Karamchand Gandhi (2 October, 1869 – 30 January, 1948) was the preeminent leader of Indian independence movement in British-ruled India. Employing nonviolent civil disobedience, Gandhi led India to independence and inspired movements for civil rights and freedom across the world. The honorific Mahatma (Sanskrit:"high-souled", "venerable") — applied to him first in 1914 in South Africa — is now used worldwide. He is also called Bapu (Gujarati: endearment for "father", "papa") in India.

4) Wright brothers

The Wright brothers, Orville (19 August, 1871 – 30 January, 1948) and Wilbur (April 16, 1867–May 30, 1912), were two American brothers, inventors, and aviation pioneers who are credited with inventing and building the world's first successful airplane and making the first controlled, powered and sustained heavier-than-air human flight, on December 17, 1903. From 1905 to 1907, the brothers developed their flying machine into the first practical fixed-wing aircraft. Although not the first to build and fly experimental aircraft, the Wright brothers were the first to invent aircraft controls that made fixed-wing powered flight possible.

5) Benjamin Franklin

Benjamin Franklin FRS (17 January, 1706 – 17 April, 1790) was one of the Founding Fathers of the United States and in many ways was "the First American". A renowned polymath, Franklin was a leading author, printer, political theorist, politician, postmaster, scientist, inventor, civic activist, statesman, and diplomat. As a scientist, he was a major figure in the American Enlightenment and the history of physics for his discoveries and theories regarding electricity. As an inventor, he is known for the lightning rod, bifocals, and the Franklin stove, among other inventions. He facilitated many civic organizations, including Philadelphia's fire department and a university.

6) Vincent Willem Van Gogh

Vincent Willem Van Gogh (30 March, 1853 – 29 July, 1890) was a major Post-Impressionist painter. A Dutch artist whose work is notable for its rough beauty, emotional honesty, and bold color — had a far-reaching influence on 20th-century art. After years of painful anxiety and frequent bouts of mental illness, he died aged 37 from a gunshot wound, generally accepted to be self-inflicted (although no gun was ever found).

7) Ludwig van Beethoven

Ludwig van Beethoven (17 December, 1770 – 26 March, 1827) was a German composer and pianist. A crucial figure in the transition between the Classical and Romantic eras in Western art music, he remains one of the most famous and influential of all composers. His best-known compositions include 9 symphonies, 5 concertos for piano, 32 piano sonatas, and 16 string quartets. He also composed other chamber music, choral works and songs.

8) William Shakespeare

William Shakespeare (26 April, 1564 – 23 April, 1616) was an English poet, playwright, and actor, widely regarded as the greatest writer in the English language and the world's pre-eminent dramatist. He is often called England's national poet and the "Bard of Avon". His extant works, including some collaborations, consist of about 38 plays, 154 sonnets, two long narrative poems, and a few other verses, of which the authorship of some is uncertain. His plays have been translated into every major living language and are performed more often than those of any other playwright.

9) Death on the Nile

Death on the Nile is a work of detective fiction by Agatha Christie and first published in the UK by the Collins Crime Club on 1 November, 1937 and in the U.S. by Dodd, Mead and Company the following year. The book features the Belgian detective Hercule Poirot. The action takes place in Egypt, mostly on the Nile River.

10) Tutankhamun

Tutankhamun was an Egyptian pharaoh of the 18th dynasty (ruled ca. 1332 BC – 1323 BC in the conventional chronology, during the period of Egyptian history known as the New Kingdom).

He is popularly referred to as King Tut. His original name, Tutankhaten, means "Living Image of Aten", while Tutankhamun means "Living Image of Amun". In hieroglyphs, the name Tutankhamun was typically written Amen-tut-ankh, because of a scribal custom that placed a divine name at the beginning of a phrase to show appropriate reverence. He is possibly also the Nibhurrereya of the Amarna letters, and likely the 18th dynasty king Rathotis who, according to Manetho, an ancient historian, had reigned for nine years — a figure that conforms with Flavius Josephus's version of Manetho's Epitome.

11) Hatshepsut

Hatshepsut (1508 – 1458 BC) was the fifth pharaoh of the 18th dynasty of Egypt. Hatshepsut came to the throne of Egypt in 1478 BC. Officially, she ruled jointly with Thutmose III who had ascended to the throne as a child one year earlier. Hatshepsut was the chief wife of Thutmose II, Thutmose III's father. She is generally regarded by Egyptologists as one of the most successful pharaohs, reigning longer than any other woman of an indigenous Egyptian dynasty. According to Egyptologist James Henry Breasted, she is also known as "the first great woman in history of whom we are informed".

Hatshepsut was the daughter of Thutmose I and his primary wife Ahmes. Her husband Thutmose II was the son of Thutmose I and a secondary wife named Mutneferet, who carried the title King's daughter and was probably a child of Ahmose I. Hatshepsut and Thutmose II had a daughter named Neferure. Thutmose II fathered Thutmose III with Iset, a secondary wife.

12) The Renaissance

The Renaissance is a period from the 14th to the 17th century, considered as the bridge between the Middle Ages and modern history. It started as a cultural movement in Italy in the Late Medieval period and later spread to the rest of Europe. Some good early examples were the perspective within painting and the recycled knowledge of how to make concrete. Although the invention of metal movable type sped the dissemination of ideas from the 15th century, the changes of the Renaissance were not uniformly experienced across Europe.

As a cultural movement, it encompassed innovative flowering of Latin and vernacular literatures, beginning with the 14th-century resurgence of learning based on classical sources, which contemporaries credited to Petrarch; the development of linear perspective and other techniques of rendering a more natural reality in painting; and, gradual but widespread educational reform.

13) black hole

A black hole is a mathematically defined region of space time exhibiting such a strong gravitational pull that no particle or electromagnetic radiation can escape from it. The theory of general relativity predicts that a sufficiently compact mass can deform space time to form a black hole. The boundary of the region from which no escape is possible is called the event horizon. Although crossing the event horizon has enormous effect on the fate of the object crossing it, it appears to have no locally detectable features. In many ways a black hole acts like an ideal black body, as it reflects no light. Moreover, quantum field theory in curved space time predicts that event horizons emit Hawking radiation, with the same spectrum as a black body of a temperature inversely proportional to its mass. This temperature is on the order of billionths of a kelvin for black holes of stellar mass, making it essentially impossible to observe.

14) Trojan War

In Greek mythology, the Trojan War was waged against the city of Troy by the Achaeans (Greeks) after Paris of Troy took Helen from her husband Menelaus king of Sparta. The war is one of the most important events in Greek mythology and has been narrated through many works of Greek literature, most notably through Homer's *Iliad*.

The war originated from a quarrel between the goddesses Athena, Hera, and Aphrodite, after Eris, the goddess of strife and discord, gave them a golden apple, sometimes known as the Apple of Discord, marked "for the fairest". Zeus sent the goddesses to Paris, who judged that Aphrodite, as the "fairest", should receive the apple. In exchange, Aphrodite made Helen, the most beautiful of all women and wife of Menelaus, fall in love with Paris, who took her to Troy. Agamemnon, king of Mycenae and the brother of Helen's husband Menelaus, led an expedition of Achaean troops to Troy and besieged the city for ten years because of Paris' insult. After the deaths of many heroes, including the Achaeans Achilles and Ajax, and the Trojans Hector and Paris, the city fell to the ruse of the Trojan Horse. The Achaeans slaughtered the Trojans (except for some of the women and children whom they kept or sold as slaves) and desecrated the temples, thus earning the gods' wrath. Few of the Achaeans returned safely to their homes and many founded colonies in distant shores. The Romans later traced their origin to Aeneas, one of the Trojans, who was said to have led the surviving Trojans to modern-day Italy.

15) Spartacus

Spartacus (111–71 BCE) was a Thracian gladiator who, along with the Gauls Crixus, Oenomaus, Castus and Gannicus and was one of the leaders of the men in the Third Servile War, a major slave uprising against the Roman Republic. Little is known about Spartacus beyond the events of the war, and surviving historical accounts are sometimes contradictory and may not always be reliable. All sources agree that he was a former gladiator and an accomplished military leader.

2. Classical lines from the film

1) I dedicated myself to the pursuit of knowledge, culture and athletics.
我把时间和精力投入到追求知识、参加文化和体育活动中。

2) I dedicated myself to the helping mankind. I pioneered new techniques in alternative energy, resolved the geo-political conflicts around the globe, and in my spare time, I invented the first bump planking.
我投入一切精力帮助人类。我在新能源领域开创了新的技术，我解决了全球的地缘政治矛盾，另外我在业余时间发明了“顶拳”。

3) I vowed to be the best father I could be. To prepare him for all the wonders of the world, present and past.
我发誓尽力做最好的父亲。让他看到所有的世界奇观，过去的和现在的。

4) But there is nothing like learning the lessons of history firsthand.
但是，什么都比不上在亲身体验中学习历史。

5) The Queen and aristocratic colonies must pay the price for their gluttony.
女王和贵族亲信们一定要为他们的贪食付出代价。

6) Tomorrow's adventure is one that you are going to take all on your own.
从明天开始，你就要自己去冒险。

7) As with all things Sherman related, I prepared for it.
所有与舍曼相关的事我都有准备。

8) What on earth provoked it?
到底是因为什么?

9) Sigmund Freud says, that if you do not like a person, it's because they remind you of something you don't like about yourself.
弗洛伊德说过，如果你不喜欢一个人，那是因为他们让你想起了你对自己不满意的地方。

10) It means she will be bound to him in eternity through these sacred ceremonies of disembowelment and mummification.
这意味着我们将通过神圣的开膛和木乃伊化仪式，让她能够永生永世和法老在一起。

11) I'm supposed to be having father-son time with Mr. Peabody.
我应该和皮博迪先生享受父子时光。

12) Sherman destroyed a priceless historical artifact.
舍曼毁掉了一件价值连城的历史文物。

13) Sherman, I absolutely forbid you to fight in the Trojan War.
舍曼，我绝对不允许你加入特洛伊战争。

14) If being a dog means you're like Mr. Peabody who never turns his back on you and who's always there to pick you up when you fall and loves you, no matter how many times you mess up, if that is what it means to be a dog, then yeah, I'm a dog, too.
如果作为狗意味着像皮博迪先生一样，永远不会丢下你，当你摔倒的时候他都会扶你起来，无论你把事情搞砸多少次，他都爱你。如果作为狗意味着这样，那么，我也是狗。

15) I have a deep regard for you as well, Mr. Peabody.
我也从心底里尊敬你，皮博迪先生。

3. Film Review

It's certain that *Mr. Peabody & Sherman* is so good that it's hard to surpass again. In addition, *Mr. Peabody & Sherman* also brings another high-quality piece of family entertainment to the silver screen.

Surprisingly, the story of the film is quite strong. Based on the nostalgic cartoon of the same name, *Mr. Peabody & Sherman* focuses on a highly intelligent dog named Mr. Peabody (voiced by Ty Burrell) who adopts an abandoned infant named Sherman (voiced by a child actor Max Charles). Mr. Peabody takes his child on various adventures through a super advanced time machine know as WABAC. After experiencing several incidents, they have to travel to different time periods and eventually fix a potential hole in the space time continuum.

Mr. Peabody is the brainiest dog in the world and also a well-known inventor, athlete and businessman. One day, Peabody comes across an abandoned baby boy in the street and then decides to adopt him. It works out fine until Sherman starts school, forced to mend fences with Penny (voiced by Ariel Winter), a classmate who humiliates him for being a son of a dog. Sherman shows her the time machine invented by Mr. Peabody in order to ensure Sherman to better understand the world and history. Together, Sherman and Penny take it across time and space, experiencing a variety of adventures, and make many jokes.

Bouncing happily from the French Revolution to ancient Greecem, *Mr. Peabody & Sherman* messes mischievously with history — we're showed with a cake-obsessed Marie Antoinette, an explosive Mona Lisa and a stupid Agamemnon. Perhaps these figures will not be familiar to younger audiences, but there's still much more to induce them to laugh. As the film proceeds on, gags and puns are tossed at the audience frequently and it's rather amazing that most of them work very well.

Many recent movies are based on retro cartoons, but not many of them have succeeded in providing a good screenplay to accompany its animated high jinks. *Mr. Peabody & Sherman* is packed with quick witted dialogue and good morals about nontraditional families, fatherhood, and childhood struggles. Mr. Peabody and Sherman are surprisingly etched characters. The fact that Sherman has been raised by a dog does eventually cause a crack between the two. At the beginning of the movie, Sherman is insulted by his classmate Penny for calling a "dog". As he grows up, Sherman wishes to be independent on his own. Peabody, meanwhile, is concerned about Sherman doing things on his own, because he fears that Sherman will no longer need him.

In spite of this, director Rob Minkoff still manages to pull the whole thing off, ending the film in a heartfelt way. He even crafts a father-son moment near the end of the movie that's both shamelessly sweet and a cheeky nod to cinematic history. There is a good reason to illustrate that the cinematic future for *Mr. Peabody & Sherman* is very bright.

I was amused by the movie plot and deeply attracted by the fact that Mr. Peabody, who is a dog, is wiser than the humans he interacts with. I was touched by the father-son relationship between Mr. Peabody and his human child. Though the scene will never happen in reality, the producers of the movie make it possible and believable in the cinema. When seeing the scene that Mr. Peabody gets pretty emotional and sad about his child's growing up, I feel sad in my heart too. The idea of time travel is also very popular and amazing. The voice dubbing is also the highlight of the movie. Ty Burrell is best known for playing the part of Phil Dunphy on the sitcom, *Modern Family* and his performance is equally endearing as Mr. Peabody. Max Charles is naive as the innocent little kid, Sherman. Ariel Winter is also known for playing Alex Dunphy on *Modern Family*, excellent as the curious Penny Peterson. Other famous characters of historical importance are also outstanding. Special mention should be given to Stanley Tucci, Lake Bell & Patrick Warburton for their unforgettable voice overs of Leonardo da Vinci, Mona Lisa and Agamemnon respectively. I would like to end by saying, *Mr. Peabody & Sherman* is a must watch for everyone who enjoys a good animated movie.

4. Extended Reading

Film: *Turbo*

Turbo is a 2013 American 3D computer-animated comedy sports film produced by the Dream Works Animation and distributed by the 20th Century Fox. It is based on an original idea by David Soren, who also directed the film. The film features an ordinary garden snail whose dream to become the fastest snail in the world comes true. The film was released on July 17th, 2013.

Along with Ryan Reynolds, who starts as the eponymous character, the film also features Paul Giamatti, Michael Peña, Snoop Dogg, Maya Rudolph, Michelle Rodriguez and Samuel L.Jackson. It has been followed by a television series, titled *Turbo FAST* (Fast Action Stunt Team), which first aired on Netflix on December 24th, 2013.

5. Homework

1) Watch the film *Mr. Peabody & Sherman* again and try to write down your feelings after watching.

2) Take the way how Mr. Peabody tutors Sherman into account. And if you were a parent, what would you learn from Mr. Peabody?

Script

Unit 1

Clip 1

Mrs. Gump: Okay. Get it, get it ... Wait, is it this way? Hold on. All right. What are y'all staring at? Haven't you ever seen a little boy with braces on his legs before? Don't ever let anybody tell you that they're better than you, Forrest. If God intended everybody to be the same, he'd have given us all braces on our legs.

Forrest: Mama always had a way of explaining things so I could understand them. We lived about a quarter mile off Route 17, about a half mile from the town of Greenbow, Alabama. That's in the county of Greenbow. Our house had been in mama's family since her grandpa's grandpa's grandpa had come across the ocean about a thousand years ago, something like that. Since it was just me and mama and we had all these empty rooms, mama decided to let those rooms out, mostly to people passing through like from, oh, Mobile, Montgomery, places like that. That's how me and mama got money. Mama was a real smart lady.

Mrs. Gump: Remember what I told you, Forrest. You're no different than anybody else is. Did you hear what I said, Forrest? You are the same as everybody else. You are no different.

Clip 2

Forrest: Now, remember how I told you that Jenny never seemed to want to go home? Well, she lived in a house that was as old as Alabama. Her mama had gone up to heaven when she was five and her daddy was some kind of a farmer.

Gump: (knock on the door) Jenny?

Forrest: He was a very loving man. He was always kissing and touching her and her sisters. And then this one time, Jenny wasn't on the bus to go to school.

Gump: Jenny, why didn't you come to school today?

Little Jenny: Shh! Daddy's taking a nap.

Father: Jenny!

Little Jenny: Come on!

Father: Jenny! Where'd you run to? You'd better get back here, girl. Where are you at? Jenny! Jenny! Where are you at? Jenny!

Little Jenny: Pray with me, Forrest. Pray with me.

Father: Jenny!

Little Jenny: Dear God, make me a bird, so I can fly far, far far away from here. Dear God, make me a bird ... So I can fly far. far far away from here.

Forrest: Mama always said that God is mysterious. He didn't turn Jenny into a bird that day. Instead, he had the police say Jenny didn't have to stay in that house no more. She went to live with her grandma, just over on Greekmore Avenue, which made me happy 'cause she was so close.

Clip 3

Gump: Okay.

(In training)

Drill Seargeant: Gump! What's your sole purpose in this army?

Forrest: To do whatever you tell me, Drill Sergeant!

Drill Sergeant: God damn it! Gump. You're a goddamn genius. That is the most outstanding answer I've ever heard. You must have a goddamn I.Q. of 160. You are goddamn gifted, Private Gump. Listen up, people ...

Forrest: Now for some reason, I fit in the army like one of them, round pegs. It's not really hard. You just make your bed real neat and remember to stand up straight, and always, answer every question with "Yes, Drill Sergeant".

Drill Sergeant: Is that clear?

All Soldiers: Yes, Drill Sergeant!

Bubba: What you do is, you just drag your nets along the bottom. On a good day, you can catch over a hundred pounds of shrimp. Everything goes all right, two men shrimping ten hours ... less what you spend on gas, you can ...

Forrest: Done! Drill Sergeant.

Drill Sergeant: Gump! Why did you put that weapon together so quickly, Gump?

Forrest: You told me to, Drill Sergeant.

Drill Sergeant: Jesus says Christ! This is a new company record. If it wouldn't be a waste of such a damn fine enlisted man, I would recommend you for OCS, Private Gump. You are going to be a general, someday, Gump. Now, disassemble your weapon and continue.

Bubba: Anyway, like I was saying, shrimp is the fruit of the sea. You can barbecue it, boil it, broil it, bake it, saute it. There's, uh, shrimp kabobs, shrimp Creole, shrimp gumbo, pan fried, deep fried, stir-fried. There's pineapple shrimp, lemon shrimp, coconut shrimp, pepper shrimp, shrimp soup, shrimp stew, shrimp salad, shrimp in potatoes, shrimp burger, shrimp sandwich. That — that's about it.

Clip 4

Gump: Where's Mama?

Louise: She's upstairs.

Mrs. Gump: Hi, Forrest.

Doctor: I'll see you tomorrow.

Mrs. Gump: All right.

Doctor: We sure got you straightened out, didn't we, boy?

Gump: What's the matter, Mama?

Mrs. Gump: Calm down, Forrest. Come on in, sit down over here.

Gump: Why are you dying, Mama?

Mrs. Gump: It's my time. It's just my time. Oh, now ... don't you be afraid, sweet heart. Death is just a part of life, something we are all destined to do. I didn't know it, but I was destined to be your Mama. I did the best I could.

Gump: You did good, Mama.

Mrs. Gump: Well, I happen to believe you make your own destiny. You have to do the best with what God gave you.

Gump: What's my destiny, Mama?

Mrs. Gump: You're gonna have to figure that out for yourself. Life is a box of chocolates, Forrest. You never know what you're going to get.

Forrest: Mama always had a way of explaining things so I could understand them.

Mrs. Gump: I will miss you, Forrest.

Forrest: She had got the cancer and died on a Tuesday. I bought her a new hat with little flowers on it. And that's all I have to say about that. Didn't you say you were waiting for the number seven bus?

Woman: There'll be another one along shortly.

Clip 5

Jenny: Forrest! How are you doing? Come in, come in.

Forrest: I got your letter.

Jenny: Oh! I was wondering about that.

Forrest: Is this your house?

Jenny: Yeah, it's messy right now. I just got off work.

Forrest: It's nice. You've got air-conditioning.

Jenny: Thank you.

Forrest: I ate some.

Jenny: Hey, I kept ... I kept a scrapbook of your clippings and everything. There you are. And this, I got you running.

Forrest: I ran a long way. For a long time.

Jenny: And there ... Listen, Forrest, I don't know how to say this ... I just ... I want to apologize for anything that I ever did to you 'cause I was messed up for a long time and ...

Baby-sitter: Yoohoo!

Jenny: Hey.

Boby-sitter: Hi!

Jenny: Hey you! This is an old friend from Alabama.

Baby-sitter: Ah, how do you do?

Jenny: Listen, next week my schedule changes, so I'll be able to ...

Baby-sitter: No problem. Gotta go, Jen. I'm double parked.

Jenny: Okay.

Baby-sitter:	Bye!
Jenny:	Thanks.
Jenny:	This is my very good friend, Mr. Gump. Can you say hi to him?
Little Forrest:	Hello, Mr. Gump.
Forrest:	Hello.
Little Forrest:	Can I go watch TV now?
Jenny:	Yes. you can, just keep it low.
Forrest:	You're a Mama, Jenny.
Jenny:	I'm a Mama. His name is Forrest.
Forrest:	Like me!
Jenny:	I named him after his daddy.
Forrest:	He got a daddy named Forrest, too?
Jenny:	You're his daddy, Forrest. Hey, Forrest, look at me. Look at me, Forrest. There's nothing you need to do. OK? You didn't do anything wrong. OK? Isn't he beautiful?
Forrest:	He's the most beautiful thing I have ever seen. But, is he smart or is he ...
Jenny:	He's very smart. He's one of the smartest in his class. Yeah, it's OK. Go talk to him ...
Forrest:	What are you watching?
Little Forrest:	Bert and Ernie.
Jenny:	Forrest, I'm sick.
Forrest:	What, do you have a cough due to a cold?
Jenny:	I have some kind of virus, and the doctors don't, they don't know what it is and there isn't anything they can do about it.
Forrest:	You could come home with me, Jenny. You and Little Forrest could come stay at my house in Greenbow. I'll take care of you if you're sick.
Jenny:	Would you marry me, Forrest?
Forrest:	OK.

Clip 6

Forrest: You died on a Saturday morning and I had you placed here under our tree. And I had that house of your father bulldozed to the ground. Mama always said dying was a part of life. I sure wish it wasn't. Little Forrest is doing just fine. He's about to start school again soon. I make his breakfast, lunch and dinner every day. I make sure he combs his hair and brushes his teeth every day. I teach him how to play ping-pong. He's really good. We fish a lot, and every night we read a book. And he's so smart, Jenny. You'd be so proud of him. I am. He wrote you a letter. He says I can't read it. I'm not supposed to. So I'll just leave it here for you. Jenny, I don't know if mama was right or if it's Lieutenant Dan. I don't know if we each have a destiny or if we're all just floating around accidental-like on a breeze. But I ... I think that maybe it's both. Maybe both are happening at the same time. I miss you, Jenny. If there's anything you need, I won't be far away.

Unit 2

Clip 1

Man 1: Dog Fancy, please.

News vendor: Dog Fancy, yep?

Man 1: Thank you very much.

Truman: Get me a paper, will you, Errol? And one of these for my wife. Loves her fashion mags.

News vender: That'll be all for you, Truman?

Truman: That's the whole kit and caboodle.

News vendor: Catch you later.

Passer-by: Good morning.

Truman: OK. Yeah. Hank!

Man 2: Good morning, Truman.

Man 3: Good morning, Truman.

Truman: Hey, how are you guys?

Man 4: Beautiful day, isn't it?

Truman: Oh, Always.

Man 3: And how's your lovely wife?

Truman: Good. Good. How are yours?

Man 3: Oh, Couldn't be better.

Man 4: Good. Good.

Man 3: Nice talking to you, Truman.

Truman: You too. You too.

Man 4: We must go now.

Truman: Hey. Think about that policy. Huh? OK. That's two for one. That's a good deal. Doppelganger special.

Man 4: Right.

Truman: Hey, fellas. You going in? Go ahead. Hey. No. You first, please. I'm not that anxious to get there.

Truman: Yes, hello. Could I have directory assistance for Fiji, please? Fiji islands.

Co-worker: Truman, did you see this?

Truman: I'm sorry, ma'am, if he's in a coma, he's probably uninsurable. Hello. Yes, Fiji, please. Do you have a listing for Lauren Garland? Nothing listed. OK. Do you have a Sylvia Garland? "S"for Sylvia. Nothing. Okay, thank you.

Truman: Lawrence.

Lawrence: Hey, Burbank. I've got a prospect in Wells Park I need you to close.

Truman: Wells Park? On a Harbour lsland?

Lawrence: You know another one?

Truman: Well, I can't do it. l have an appointment. Dentist, uh ... yeah.

Lawrence: You're going to lose a lot more than your teeth if you don't meet your quota. Look, Truman, they're making cutbacks at the end of this month.

Truman: Cutbacks?

Lawrence: Yeah. And you need this. Besides, a half hour across the bay, a little sea air, will do you good.

Truman: Hey, thanks.

Clip 2

Truman's mother: It doesn't sound insane at all, Truman. I see him ten times a week in 100 different faces. I almost hugged a perfect stranger in the salon last Thursday.

Truman: It was Dad, I swear, dressed like a homeless man. And you know what else was strange? A businessman and a woman with a little dog came out of nowhere and forced him onto a bus.

Truman's mother: Well, it's about time they cleaned up the trash downtown before we become just like the rest of the country.

Truman: They never found Dad's body. Maybe somehow ...

Truman's mother: Oh, God!

Truman: I'm telling you if it wasn't him, it was his twin! Did Dad have a brother?

Truman's mother: Truman, you know perfectly well that your father was an only child, just like you. Now Sweetie, you're just feeling bad because of what happened. You sailing off into that storm. But I've never blamed you, Truman. And I don't blame you now.

Clip 3

Meryl: Truman, you've studied enough.

Truman: No, I've got to commit this to memory.

Marlon: Come on, Truman, one ice-cold brewsky.

Meryl: Come on.

Truman: You're gonna have to copy off me, so be careful.

Marlon: I know it.

Meryl: You know, you're a better person than I am. See you later.

Truman: OK.

Meryl: Bye.

Truman: Bye.

Marlon: See you later, loser.

Truman: Hi. Konnichi-wa.

Lauren:	What?
Truman:	Oh, you take Japanese.
Lauren:	Oh, yes, yeah.
Truman:	Lauren, right? It's on the ...
Lauren:	Lauren, right, right.
Truman:	I'm Truman Burbank.
Lauren:	Yeah, I know. You know, Truman, I'm not allowed to talk to you.
Truman:	Really? Yeah well. I can understand that I'm a pretty dangerous character.
Lauren:	I'm sorry it's not up to me.
Truman:	Girls have got to be careful. You have a boyfriend, right?
Lauren:	No, it's not that.
Truman:	Caution. Was it Meryl, the girl that was with me? We're not ... we don't ... We're not ... We are just ... We're friends.
Lauren:	It's nothing like that.
Truman:	It's how I look? Not your type?
Lauren:	No.
Truman:	I like your pin. I was wondering that myself ... Would you wanna, maybe, possibly sometime go out for some pizza or something? Like, Friday? Saturday?
Lauren:	I can't.
Truman:	Sunday, Monday, Tuesday? We have finals tomorrow.
Lauren:	Yeah, I know. If we don't go now, it won't happen. Do you understand? So what do you want to do?
Truman:	Please keep your hands inside the car! This is my favorite pizza place. Tony, one large, extra plankton!
Lauren:	We have so little time. They can be here any minute.
Truman:	Who are they?
Lauren:	They don't want me talking to you.
Truman:	Then don't talk.

Lauren:	They're here. Truman.
Truman:	What do they want?
Lauren:	Listen to me. Everybody knows that, everybody knows everything you do. They're pretending, Truman. Do you understand? Everybody is pretending.
Truman:	Lauren. I don't know.
Lauren:	No, no, no, my name's not Lauren, it's Sylvia. My name is Sylvia.
Truman:	Sylvia.
Lauren:	Yeah.
Man:	Lauren, sweetheart, not again.
Truman:	Hey, wait a minute, who are you?
Man:	I'm her father.
Truman:	What?
Lauren:	I've never seen him before.
Truman:	We don't do anything.
Man:	Honey, honey, please.
Lauren:	He is lying. Truman, please don't listen to him. Everything I've told you is the truth. This, it's fake. It's all for you.
Truman:	I don't understand.
Lauren:	The sky and the sea. Everything, It's a set! It's a show. Everybody's watching you. Please, don't listen to him. He's gonna lie to you. They're watching us now.
Truman:	What's going on? I really like to know what's going on.
Man:	Schizophrenia. She has episodes. We've tried everything. Hypnotism, shock therapy.
Lauren:	Don't listen to him, Truman, Truman!
Man:	Don't worry, you're not the first. You're not the first. She brings all her boyfriends down here.
Lauren:	What's he saying! Truman, he's lying! Get out of here. Come and find me.
Man:	Don't worry, we're going to Fiji.

Truman: I'll see you in school.

Man: Fiji. We're moving to Fiji.

Clip 4

Truman: Let's go now. I'm ready to go now. Why wait?

Meryl: What?

Truman: Early bird gathers no moss. Rolling stone catches the worm. Right?

Meryl: Truman, what are you doing? Truman.

Truman: Where shall we go? Where shall we go?

Meryl: Truman, where are we going?

Truman: I don't really know. I guess I'm being spontaneous. Somebody help me! I'm being spontaneous! Forget Fiji. We can't drive to Fiji, can we?

Meryl: No.

Truman: What about Atlantic City?

Meryl: Oh, No, you hate to gamble.

Truman: That's right, I do, don't I?

Meryl: So why do you want to go there?

Truman: Because I never have. That's why people go places, isn't it?

Meryl: Truman, Truman, I think I'm going to throw up.

Truman: Me too. Blocked at every turn. Beautifully synchronized, don't you agree?

Meryl: You're blaming me for the traffic?

Truman: Should I?

Meryl: Truman, let's go home.

Truman: You're right. We could be stuck here for hours. It'll be like this all the way to Atlantic City. Let's go back. I'm sorry. I don't know what got into me.

Meryl: Can you please slow down?

Truman: Yes, I can.

Meryl: Truman, Truman, that's our turn-off.

Truman:	I changed my mind. What's New Orleans like this time of year? Mardis Gras! Look, Meryl. Same road, no cars. It's magic.
Meryl:	You let me out, Truman. You're not right in the head. If you want to destroy yourself, you do it on your own.
Truman:	I think I'd like a little company.
Meryl:	Oh, Truman. You knew this would happen. You know you can't drive over water. Let's go home, where you'll feel safe.
Truman:	Give me your hand.
Meryl:	Sweetie.
Truman:	You drive!
Meryl:	Truman! We shouldn't be doing this, Truman, We're breaking the law! Oh, my!
Truman:	You can do it!
Meryl:	Please don't! Please!
Truman:	You can make it!
Meryl:	Oh, Truman! We're over! We're over the bridge! We're over the bridge! We're over the bridge! We're over the bridge!
Truman:	We're over!
Meryl:	Truman, Truman, what about that sign?
Truman:	I'm sure they are exaggerating. We'll be fine.
Meryl:	They are exaggerating? Do you believe that? Oh my! On my! Truman, we're on fire!
Truman:	It's OK.
Meryl:	We're on fire!
Truman:	It's OK. It's just smoke. You okay?
Meryl:	Yes!
Truman:	Wanna do it again?
Meryl:	No! Truman, stop! Oh, God. So what we're going to do for money when we get to New Orleans?
Truman:	I have my Seahaven bank card.

Meryl: So we're just gonna eat into our savings, is that it? You know I'll have to call your mother when we get there. She's going to be worried sick. I don't know how she is going to take this.

Truman: What now?

Meryl: Truman, looks like a leak at the plant.

Policeman: Back up. Back up. Leak at the plant. Get to shut down.

Truman: Is there any way around?

Policeman: The whole area is being evacuated.

Meryl: Is there anything I can do?

Policeman: No, ma'am. Thank you for your help. You're welcome, Truman.

Truman: Truman!

Clip 5

Talk show caller: 1.7 billion were there for his birth. 220 countries tuned in for his first step. The world stood still for that stolen kiss. And as he grew, so did the technology. An entire human life recorded on an intricate network of hidden cameras and broadcast live and unedited, 24 hours a day, 7 days a week, to an audience around the globe. Coming to you now from Seahaven island, enclosed in the largest studio ever constructed, and along with the Great Wall of China, one of only two man-made structures visible from space, now in its 30th great year, it's The Truman Show!

Mike Michaelson: What a week it's been! I don't know about you. I was on pins and needles the entire time. Hello and good evening, I'm your host, Mike Michaelson and Welcome to TruTalk, our forum for issues growing out of the show. But tonight, something very special indeed: a rare and exclusive interview with the show's conceiver and creator. So come with us now as we go live to the lunar room on the 221st floor of the Omni-Cam Ecosphere. That's where we'll find the world's greatest televisionary. The designer and architect of the world within a world that is Seahaven Island: Christof. Before we begin, I'd like to thank you on behalf of our audience for granting this exclusive interview. We know how demanding your schedule is and we all know how jealously you guard your privacy. This, sir, is indeed an honor.

Christof: Don't mention it.

Mike Michaelson: Well, the catalyst for the recent dramatic events on the show has been, of course, Truman's father, Kirk, and his attempts to infiltrate the show. But before we get into that, I think it's worth noting this is not the first time that someone from the outside has attempted to reach Truman, is it?

Christof: We have had our close calls in the past.

Man: Truman, it's television! Yes! I did it! I'm on The Truman Show!

Mike Michaelson: But there's never been anything to compare with this most recent breach in security. The first intruder to be a former cast member.

Christof: A dead one at that.

Mike Michaelson: Gotta say, writing Kirk back in, masterstroke.

Christof: Since Kirk started this whole crisis in Truman's life, I came to the conclusion that he was the only one who could end it.

Kirk: Truman! Truman, no! That's off limits!

Truman: Why? What's over there?

Kirk: Nothing. It's dangerous, that's all. You've got to know your limitations. Truman.

Mike Michaelson: But let's remind viewers of exactly why Dad was written out in the first place.

Christof: As Truman grew up, we were forced to manufacture ways to keep him on the island.

Truman: I'd like to be an explorer like the great Magellan.

Teacher: Oh, you're too late. There's really nothing left to explore.

Christof: Finally I came up with the concept of Kirk's drowning.

Mike Michaelson: Most effective, Truman's been terrified of the water ever since.

Christof: When Kirk read the synopsis for the Death At Sea episode, he was disappointed, to say the least. And I'm sure that's what caused him to break back onto the set.

Mike Michaelson: But how do you intend to explain his 22-year absence?

Christof: Amnesia.

Mike Michaelson: Brilliant. Let's take some those viewer phone calls. Charlotte, North Carolina, you're on with Christof.

Charlotte: Yeah. Hi, Christof. I was just wondering how many cameras you got there in that town?

Christof: Somewhere in the vicinity of 5,000.

Charlotte: Oh! That's a lot of cameras.

Christof: Remember, we started with just one. He was curious from birth. Premature by two weeks, it was almost as if he couldn't wait to get started.

Mike Michaelson: And of course his eagerness to leave his mother's womb was the very reason he was, the one was selected.

Christof: In competition with five other unwanted pregnancies — the casting of a show determined by an air date, Truman was the one who arrived on cue.

Mike Michaelson: Incidentally I believe Truman is the first child who has been legally adopted by a corporation.

Christof: That's correct.

Mike Michaelson: The show has generated enormous revenues now, equivalent to the Gross National Product of a small country.

Christof: People forget it takes the population of an entire country to keep the show running.

Mike Michaelson: Since the show is on 24 hours a day without commercial interruption, all those staggering revenues are generated by product placement.

Christof: That's true. Everything on the show is for sale, from the actors' wardrobe, food products, to the very homes they live in.

Mike Michaelson: And of course all of it available in the Truman catalog.

Clip 6

NET EXEC: How do we stop him?

SIMEON: Okay. Uh ... we're going to be accessing the weather program now. So, hold on to your hats.

CHRISTOF: You got that?

SIMEON: No, I think we're going to want to localize the storm over the boat. You can get the coordinates for that.

CHLOE: There's no rescue boat. He won't know what to do.

CHRISTOF: He'll turn back. He'll be afraid.

SIMEON: There she blows.

TRUMAN: Come on! Ahh! Ugh! Ahh!

CHRISTOF: Give me some lightning ... Again! Hit him again!

MOSES: For God's sake, Chris! The whole world is watching! We can't let him die in front of a live audience!

CHRISTOF: He was born in front of a live audience!

TRUMAN: Ahh!

Man in Bathtub: You can do it! Hold on!

TRUMAN: Ugh! (after braving the first wave) Is that the best you can do!? You're gonna have to kill me.

(sings)

What should we do with a drunken sailor? What should we do with a drunken sailor?

NET EXEC: Oh behalf of the studio, I demand that you were transmission.

CHRISTOF: Keep running.

TRUMAN: What should we do with a drunken sailor, early in the morning? ...

CHRISTOF: Increase the wind. Increase the wind!

NET EXEC: I'm telling you for the last time.

CHRISTOF: How close is he?

SIMEON: Very close.

CHRISTOF: Capsize him. Tip him over.

NET EXEC: Damn you, Christof!!!

CHLOE: No! You can't! He's tied himself to the boat!

CHRISTOF: Shut up!

SIMEON: He's gonna drown and he doesn't even care.

CHRISTOF: Do it.

SIMEON: No.

CHRISTOF: Do it!

Clip 7

CHRISTOF: I want to talk to him. (to Truman) Truman.

TRUMAN: (gasps in shock)

CHRISTOF: You can speak. I can hear you.

TRUMAN: Who are you?

CHRISTOF: I am the creator of a television show that gives hope and joy and inspiration to millions.

TRUMAN: And who am I?

CHRISTOF: You're the star.

TRUMAN: Was nothing real?

CHRISTOF: You were real. That's what made you so good to watch. Listen to me, Truman. There's no more truth out there than there is in the world I created for you. The same lies. The same deceit. But in my world, you have nothing to fear. I know you are better than you know yourself.

TRUMAN: You never had a camera in my head!

CHRISTOF: You're afraid. That's why you can't leave. It's okay, Truman. I understand. I have been watching you your whole life. I was watching when you were born. I was watching when you took your first step. I watched you on your first day of school. heh heh. The episode when you lost your first tooth. heh heh heh. You can't leave, Truman.

SYLVIA: Please, God.

CHRISTOF: You belong here ...

SYLVIA: You can do it.

CHRISTOF: With me. Talk to me. Say something. Well, say something, goddamn it! You're on television! You're live to the whole world!

TRUMAN: In case I don't see ya, good afternoon, good evening and good night. Hahaha! Yeah!

Unit 3

Clip 1

Chris: Man, I got two questions for you: What do you do? And how do you do it?

Man: I'm a stockbroker.

Chris: Stockbroker. Oh, goodness. Had to go to college to be a stockbroker, huh?

Man: You don't have to. Have to be good with numbers and good with people. That's it.

Chris: Hey, you take care. I'll let you hang on to my car for the weekend. But I need it back for Monday.

Man: Feed the meter.

Chris: I still remember that moment. They all looked so damn happy to me. Why couldn't I look like that?

Chris: I'm gonna try to get home by 6. I'm gonna stop by a brokerage firm after work.

Linda: For what?

Chris: I wanna see about a job there.

Linda: Yeah? What job?

Chris: You know, when I ... when I was a kid, I could go through a math book in a week. So I'm gonna go see about what job they got down there.

Linda: What job?

Chris: Stockbroker.

Linda: Stockbroker?

Chris: Yeah.

Linda: Not an astronaut?

Chris: Don't talk to me like that, Linda. I'm gonna go down and see about this, and I'm gonna do it during the day.

Linda: You should probably do your sales calls.

Chris: I don't need you to tell me about my sales calls, Linda. I got three of them before the damn office is even open.

Linda: Do you remember that rent is due next week? Probably not. We're already two months behind. Next, next week we'll owe three months. I've been pulling double shifts for four months now, Chris. Just, just sell what's in your contract. Get us out of that business.

Chris: Linda, that is what I am trying to do. This is what I'm trying to do for my family, for you and for Christopher.

Linda:	What's the matter with you?

Clip 2

Twistle:	Taxi!
Chris:	Mr. Twistle.
Twistle:	Yeah, hi.
Chris:	Hi. Chris Gardner.
Twistle:	Yeah, hi. Listen. What can I do for you?
Chris:	I submitted an application for the intern program about a month ago ... and I would just love the opportunity to sit with you briefly ...
Twistle:	Listen, I'm going to Noe Valley, Chris. Take care of yourself.
Chris:	Mr. Twistle. Actually, I'm on my way to Noe Valley also. How about we share a ride?
Twistle:	All right, get in.
Chris:	So when I was in the Navy, I worked for a doctor ... who loved to play golf, hour ... hours every day ... and I would actually perform medical procedures ... when he'd leave me in the office. So I'm ... I'm used to being in a position where ... where I have to make decisions and ... Mr. Twistle, listen. This is ... , this is a very important ...
Twistle:	I'm sorry. I'm sorry. This thing's impossible.
Chris:	I can do it.
Twistle:	No, you can't. No one can. That's bullshit.
Chris:	No, I'm pretty sure I can do it.
Twistle:	No, you can't.
Chris:	Let me see it. Give it here. Oh, yeah. Oh, wow, you really messed it up.
Twistle:	Sorry.
Chris:	It looks like it works around a swivel, so the center pieces never move. So if it's yellow in the center, that's the yellow side. If it's red in the center, that's the red side.
Twistle:	Okay.
Chris:	So ... You can slow down.
Twistle:	Listen, we can drive around all day. I don't believe you can do this.

Chris:	Yeah, I can.
Twistle:	No, you can't.
Chris:	Yes, I can.
Twistle:	No, you can't. I'm telling you, no one can. See? That's all I ever do. You almost have this side. Holy cow. You almost had that one.
Chris:	I'm gonna get it.
Twistle:	Look at that. You're almost there.
Taxi Driver:	17.10.
Twistle:	This is me. Good job. Goodbye.
Chris:	Yeah. I'll see you ... see you soon.
Taxi Driver:	Where are you going, sir? Excuse me, sir. Where are you going, please?
Chris:	Two ... A couple of blocks. Just flip around.
Taxi Driver:	Okay. Hey! Stop it! Hey! Where are you going? Come here!
Chris:	No! No, no, no!
Taxi Driver:	You asshole, give me my money! Give me my money.
Chris:	Please stop. Please, please, please!
Taxi Driver:	Son of a bitch.
Chris:	Please! He should've paid you! He should've paid you!
Taxi Driver:	Come here!
Chris:	I'm sorry. I'm so sorry.
Taxi Driver:	I'll kick your ass!
Chris:	I'm sorry!
Taxi Driver:	Idiot.

Clip 3

Charlie:	Hey, listen. I need the rent. I can't wait anymore.
Chris:	Yeah, I'm good for that, Charlie. I'm gonna get it.

Charlie:	Why don't you go two blocks over at the Mission Inn Motel? It's half what you pay here. Listen, Chris. I need you out of here in the morning.
Chris:	The hell am I supposed to be out of here tomorrow?
Charlie:	I got painters coming in.
Chris:	All right, look. I need more time.
Charlie:	No.
Chris:	All right, I'll paint it myself. All right, but I just ... I gotta have some more time ... I got my son up in here.
Charlie:	All right. One week. And you paint it.
Policeman:	Chris Gardner?
Chris:	Yeah. What happened?
Policeman:	Payable to the City of San Francisco.
Chris:	Does it have to be the full amount?
Policeman:	Well, you gotta pay each parking ticket, otherwise, you're staying.
Chris:	This is all I got.
Policeman:	You verify at 9:30 tomorrow morning.
Chris:	What?
Policeman:	You gotta stay until this thing clears.
Chris:	No. No, I, I can't, I can't spend the night here. I have to pick up my son.
Policeman:	You verify at 9:30 tomorrow morning.
Chris:	Sir, I have a job interview at Dean Witter at 10:15 tomorrow morning. I cannot stay ...
Policeman:	9:30 tomorrow morning.
Chris:	What am I supposed to do with my son? What am I supposed to do with my son?
Woman:	Is there anyone else who can take ... ?
Chris:	I take care of him.
Policeman:	Maybe we can go and have Social Services pick him up.
Chris:	All right. Can I have my phone call, please?

Linda: Hello.

Chris: Hey.

Linda: What do you want?

Chris: Ahh, You gotta get Christopher from daycare. I can't. Just keep him for the night and I'm ... And ... Just one night.

Linda: What happened?

Chris: I'll pick him up from daycare tomorrow. I'm gonna go right ... You can just ... You can drop him off and I'll pick him up.

Linda: No.

Chris: Come on, Linda. Why, why you doing that?

Linda: No, I wanna take him to the park. To Golden Gate after daycare tomorrow. How is he?

Chris: He is fine. All right, just ... All right, take him to the park. And bring him back, all right? Just bring ... bring me my son back. Okay? Linda?

Linda: I'll bring him back around 6.

Chris: All right, all right. Thank you. Bye.

Clip 4

Chris: I'm Okay? Excuse me. Excuse me.

Secretary: Mr. Gardner. This way. It'll be right this way.

Man: What is the word on that one?

Secretary: Chris Gardner.

Chris: Chris Gardner. How are you? Good morning. Chris Gardner. Chris Gardner. Good to see you again. Chris Gardner. Pleasure.

Chris: I've been sitting there for the last half-hour ... trying to come up with a story ... that would explain my being here dressed like this. And I wanted to come up with a story that would demonstrate qualities ... that I'm sure you all admire here, like earnestness or diligence. Team-playing, something. And I couldn't think of anything. So the truth is ... I was arrested for failure to pay parking tickets.

Jay: Parking tickets?

Chris: And I ran all the way here from the Polk Station, the police station.

Interviewer: What were you doing before you were arrested?

Chris: I was painting my apartment.

Interviewer: Is it dry now?

Chris: I hope so.

Interviewer: Jay says you're pretty determined.

Jay: He's been waiting outside the front of the building ... with some 40-pound gizmo for over a month.

Interviewer: He said you're smart.

Chris: Well, I like to think so.

Interviewer: And you want to learn this business?

Chris: Yes, sir, I wanna learn this business.

Interviewer: Have you already started learning on your own?

Chris: Absolutely.

Interviewer: Jay?

Jay: Yes, sir.

Interviewer: How many times have you seen Chris?

Jay: I don't know. One too many, apparently.

Interviewer: Was he ever dressed like this?

Jay: No. No. Jacket and tie.

Interviewer: First in your class in school? High school?

Chris: Yes, sir.

Interviewer: How many in the class?

Chris: Twelve. It was a small town.

Interviewer: I'll say.

Chris: But I was also first in my radar class ... in the Navy, and that was a class of 20. Can I say something? I'm the type of person ... if you ask me a question, and I don't know the answer ... I'm gonna tell you that I don't know. But I bet you what. I know how to find the answer, and I will find the answer. Is that fair enough?

Interviewer: Chris. What would you say if a guy walked in for an interview without a shirt on ... and I hired him? What would you say?

Chris: He must've had on some really nice pants.

Clip 5

Chris: This part of my life is called "Internship".

Frakesh: The 1200 building is Medley Industrial and Sanko Oil. The building across the street is Lee-Ray Shipping. In a couple weeks, you'll get call sheets with the phone numbers of employees from every Fortune 500 company in the financial district. You will be pooling from 60 Fortune companies. You will mainly be cold-calling potential clients. But if you have to have lunch with them, have breakfast with them, if you even have to baby-sit for them, you will do whatever it takes to familiarize them with our packages. We need you to match their needs and goals to one of our many financial plans. In essence, you reel them in. We'll cook the fish. Some of you guys are here because you know somebody. Some of you guys are here because you think you're somebody. There's one guy in here who's gonna be somebody. That person's gonna be the guy who can turn this into this. 800,000 in commission dollars. You, you, help me hand these out. This is going to be your Bible. You'll eat with it. You'll drink with it.

Chris: It was simple. X number of calls equals X number of prospects. X number of prospects equals X number of customers. X number of customers equals X number of dollars in the company's pocket.

Frakesh: Your board exam. Last year, we had an intern score a 96.4 percent on the written exam. He wasn't chosen. It's not a simple pass-fail. It's an evaluation tool we use to separate applicants. Be safe, score a hundred. Okay, let's take a break. Be back in 10.

Chris: Hey. Mr. Frohm. Chris.

Frohm: Hi. Chris, how are you?

Chris: I'm good. How are you doing?

Frohm: Fine, thank you for asking.

Chris: Yeah, First day in there. It was exciting.

Frohm: You're not quitting on us yet, are you?

Chris: No, sir. Ten-minute break. Pop out, get a quick bite and then back in there for board prep.

Frohm: Oh, man, I remember mine. And ours were only an hour, not three like yours. We didn't do world markets. We didn't bother with taxes, and it was still a pain in the ass.

Clip 6

Chris: Thank you very much. Bye bye.

Frakesh: Chris. Come.

Mr Frohm: Hi, Chris.

Chris: Mr. Frohm, good to see you.

Mr Frohm: Nice shirt.

Chris: Thank you, sir.

Jay: Chris.

Chris: Hey, Jay.

Man: Chris.

Mr Frohm: Chris, sit down, please.

Chris: I thought I'd wear a shirt today. You know, being the last day and all.

Mr Frohm: Well, thank you. Thank you. We appreciate that. But ... wear one tomorrow though, okay? Because tomorrow's going to be your first day ... if you'd like to work here as a broker. Would you like that, Chris?

Chris: Yes, sir.

Mr Frohm: Good. We couldn't be happier. So welcome. Was it as easy as it looked?

Chris: No, sir. No, sir, it wasn't.

Mr Frohm: Good luck, Chris.

Chris: Thank you. Thank you.

Mr Frohm: Oh, Chris. I almost forgot.

Chris: Thank you.

(This part of my life ... this little part ... is called "Happiness".)

Chris: Christopher. Christopher. Come here.

Unit 4

Clip 1

Red: And that's how it came to pass, that on the second-to-last day of the job, the convict crew that tarred the plate factory roof in the spring of 49 wound up sitting in a row at 10:00 in the morning, drinking icy-cold Bohemian style of beer, courtesy of the hardest screw that ever walked a turn at Shawshank State Prison.

Hadley: Drink up while it's cold, ladies.

Red: The colossal prick even managed to sound magnanimous.

Red: We sat and drank with the sun on our shoulders and felt like free men. We could have been tarring the roof of one of our own houses. We were the lords of all creation.

Red: As for Andy, he spent that break hunkered in the shade, a strange little smile on his face, watching us drink his beer.

Heywood: Hey, want a cold one, Andy.

Andy: No, thanks. I gave up drinking.

Red: You could argue he'd done it to curry favor with the guards. Or maybe make a few friends among us cons. Me? I think he did it just to feel normal again ... if only for a short while.

Clip 2

Brook: Dear fellas, I can't believe how fast things move on the outside.

Man: Watch it, old-timer! Want to get killed?

Brook: I saw an automobile once when I was a kid ... but now they're everywhere. The world went and got itself in a big damn hurry. The parole board got me into this halfway house ... called "The Brewer" ... and a job ... bagging groceries at the Food-Way. It's hard work and I try to keep up ... but my hands hurt most of the time.

Woman: Make sure your man double-bags. Last time, you didn't double bag and the bottom near came out.

Man: Make sure you double-bag like the lady says. Understand?

Brook: Yes, sir. Surely will.

Brook: I don't think the store manager likes me very much. Sometimes after work, I go to the park and feed the birds. I keep thinking ... Jake might just show up and say hello. But he never does. I hope, wherever he is, he's doing okay and making new friends. I have trouble sleeping at night. I have bad dreams like I'm falling. I wake up scared. Sometimes it takes me a while to remember where I am. Maybe I should get me a gun and rob the Food-Way so they'd send me home. I could shoot the manager while I was at it. Sort of like a bonus. I guess I'm too old for that sort of nonsense anymore. I don't like it here. I'm tired of being afraid all the time. I've decided ... not to stay. I doubt they'll kick up any fuss ... not for an old crook like me.

Clip 3

Red: He's got his fingers in a lot of pies, from what I hear.

Andy: What you hear isn't half of it. He's got scams you haven't even dreamed of. I kickbacks on his kickbacks. There's a river of dirty money flowing through this place.

Red: Can be a problem having all that money. Cause sooner or later you're gotta have to explain where it came from.

Andy: That's where I come in. I channel it. Filter it. Funnel it. Stocks, securities, tax-free municipals. I send that money out into the real world and when it comes back.

Red: Clean as a virgin's honeypot, huh?

Andy: Cleaner. By the time Norton retires, I will have made him a millionaire.

Red: If they ever catch on him, he's gonna wind up here wearing a number himself.

Andy: Oh Red, I thought you had a little more faith in me than that.

Red: I know you're good, but all that paper leaves a trail. Now anybody gets curious, FBI, IRS, whatever. It's going to lead to somebody.

Andy: Sure it is. But not to me, and certainly not to the warden.

Red: All right, who?

Andy: Randall Stevens.

Red: Who?

Andy: The "silent" silent partner. He's the guilty one, your honor. The man with the bank accounts. It's where the filtering process starts. They trace anything, so it's gonna lead to him.

Red: But who is he?

Andy: He's a phantom, an apparition. Second cousin to Harvey the Rabbit. (off Red's look) I conjured him out of thin air. He doesn't exist, except on paper.

Clip 4

Andy: My wife used to say I'm a hard man to know. Like a closed book. Complained about it all the time. She was beautiful. God, I loved her. But I just didn't know how to show it. That's all. I killed her, Red. I didn't pull the trigger. But I drove her away. That's why she died because of me, the way I am.

Red: That don't make you a murderer. Bad husband, maybe. Feel bad about it if you want, but you didn't pull the trigger.

Andy: No. I didn't. Somebody else did. And I wound up in here. Bad luck, I guess.

Red: Yeah.

Andy: It floats around. It's got to land on somebody. It was my turn. That's all. I was in the path of the tornado. I just didn't expect the storm would last as long as it has. Think you'll ever get out of here?

Red: Me? Yeah. One day when I got a long, white beard and two or three marbles rolling around upstairs. They'll let me out.

Andy: Tell you where I'd go. Zihuatanejo.

Red: Zihua ... ?

Andy: Zihuatanejo. It's in Mexico. A little place on the Pacific Ocean. You know what the Mexicans say about the Pacific? They say it has no memory. That's where I want to live the rest of my life. A warm place with no memory. Open up a little hotel right on the beach. Buy some worthless old boat and fix it up new. Take my guests out charterfishing.

Red: Zihuatanejo?

Andy: In a place like that, I could use a man that knows how to get things.

Red: I don't think I could make it on the outside, Andy. I've been in here most of my life. I'm an institutional man now. Just like Brooks was.

Andy: Well, you underestimate yourself.

Red: I don't think so. In here I'm the guy who can get things for you, sure, but outside all you need is the Yellow Pages. Hell, I wouldn't even know where to begin. Pacific Ocean? Shit! Scare me to death, somethin' that big.

Andy: Not me. I didn't shoot my wife and I didn't shoot her lover. Whatever mistakes I made I've paid for them and then some. That hotel, that boat ... I don't think that's too much to ask.

Red: I don't think you ought to be doing this to yourself, Andy! This is shitty pipe dreams! I mean Mexico's way down there, and you're in here, and that's the way it is!

Andy: Yeah, right. That's the way it is. It's down there, and I'm in here. I guess it comes down to a simple choice, really. Get busy living ... or get busy dying.

Clip 5

In 1966, Andy Dufresne escaped from Shawshank Prison. All they found of him was a muddy set of prison clothes, a bar of soap and an old rock hammer, damn near worn down to the nub. I remembered thinking it'd take a man 600 years to tunnel through the wall with it. Old Andy did it in less than 20. Oh, Andy loved geology. I imagine it appealed to his meticulous nature. An ice age here million years of mountain building there. Geology is the study of pressure and time. That's all it takes, really. Pressure and time. That and a big goddamn poster. Like I said in prison, a man will do anything to keep his mind occupied. Turns out Andy's favorite hobby was toting his wall out into the exercise yard, a handful at a time. I guess after Tommy was killed. Andy decided he'd been here long enough.

Clip 6

There's not a day goes by I don't feel regret. Not because I'm in here, or because you think I should. I look back on the way I was then. Then a young, stupid kid who committed that terrible crime. I want to talk to him. I want to try and talk some sense to him. Tell him the way things are. But I can't. That kid's long gone and this old man is all that's left. I got to live with that. Rehabilitated? It's just a bullshit word. So you go on and stamp your form, sonny, and stop wasting my time. Because to tell you the truth, I don't give a shit.

Clip 7

I find I'm so excited. I can barely sit still or hold a thought in my head. I think it's the excitement only a free man can feel. A free man at the start of a long journey whose conclusion is uncertain. I hope I can make it across the border. I hope to see my friend, and shake his hand. I hope the Pacific is as blue as it has been in my dreams. I hope.

Unit 5

Clip 1

William Wallace: I am William Wallace! And I see a whole army of my countrymen here in defiance of tyranny. You have come to fight as free men, and free men you are! What will you do with that freedom? Will you fight?

Soldiers: No! No!

Veteran Soldier: Against that? No, we will run, and we will live.

William Wallace: Aye. Fight and you may die. Run, and you'll live. At least a while. And dying in your beds many years from now, would you be willing to trade all the days from this day to that for one chance, just one chance to come back here and tell our enemies that they may take our lives, but they'll never take our freedom!

Clip 2

William: You ask your King to his face. Ask him. And you see if his eyes can convince you of the truth.

Isabella: Hamilton ... Leave us.

Hamilton: My lady ...

Isabella: Leave us. Now. Let us talk plainly. You invade England. But you cannot complete the conquest. So far from your shelter and supply. The king desires peace.

William: Longshanks desires peace?

Isabella: He declares it to me. I swear it. He proposes that you withdraw your attack. In return, he grants you title, estates, and this chest of gold which I am to pay to you personally.

William: A lordship and titles ... gold ... that I should become Judas.

Isabella: Peace is made in such ways.

William: Slaves are made in such ways. The last time Longshanks spoke of peace, I was a boy. And many Scottish nobles who would not be slaves, were lured by him under a flag of truce, to a barn ... where he had them hanged. I was very young, but I remember Longshanks' notion of peace.

Isabella: I understand you have suffered. I know ... about your woman.

William: She was my wife. We got married in secret. Because I would not share her with an English lord. They killed her ... to get to me. I have never spoken of it. I don't know why I tell you now, except ... I see her strength in you. One day, you'll be a queen ... And you must open your eyes. You tell your King that William Wallace will not be ruled and nor will any Scot while I live.

Clip 3

Leper: We must have alliance with England to prevail here. You achieved that. You saved your family and increased your land. In time, you will have all the power in Scotland.

Robert: Lands. Titles. Men. Power. Nothing.

Leper: Nothing?

Robert: I have nothing. Men fight for me because if they do not I throw them off my land and I starve their wives and their children. Those men who bled the ground red at Falkirk ... They fought for William Wallace, and he fights for something that I've never had, and I took it from him when I betrayed him, and I saw it in his face on the battlefield. And it's tearing me apart.

Leper: Well, all men betray. All lose heart.

Robert: I don't want to lose heart. I want to believe ... as he does. I will never be on the wrong side again.

Clip 4

Longshanks: If what Lord Hamilton tells me is correct, he warmed to our future queen. He would trust her. So we'll dispatch her with the notion that she comes in peace.

Hamilton: My lord, the princess might be taken hostage or her life be put in jeopardy.

Longshanks: Oh. My son would be most distressed by that. Uh, but in truth, if she were to be killed, we would soon find the King of France a useful ally against the Scots. You see, as king, you must find the goods in any situation.

Assassin: It's William Wallace, sure. He's giving up his sword. Be ready.

William: My lady. I received your message. This is ... the second time you've warned me of danger. Why?

Isabella: There will be a new shipment of supplies coming north next month ... foods and weapons. They will ...

William: No, stop. Why do you help me? Why do you help me?

Isabella: Because of the way you are looking at me now.

Clip 5

Robert: Father! You rotting bastard! Why? Why?

Leper: Longshanks acquired Wallace. So did our nobles. That was the price of your crown.

Robert: Die! I want you to die!

Leper: Soon enough I'll be dead. And you'll be king.

Robert: I don't want anything from you. You're not a man! And you're not my father.

Leper: You're my son, and you've always known my mind.

Robert: You deceived me.

Leper: You let yourself be deceived. In your heart, you always knew what had to happen here. At last, you know what it means to hate. Now you're ready to be a king.

Robert: My hate ... will die with you.

Clip 6

Executioner: William Wallace, you stand in taint of high treason.

William: Against whom?

Executioner: Against your King. Have you anything to say?

William: Never in my whole life ... did I swear allegiance to him.

Executioner: It matters not. He is your King. Confess, and you may receive a quick death. Deny, and you must be purified by pain. Do you confess? Do you confess? Then on the morrow, you shall receive your purification.

Clip 7

William: Not every man really lives.

Isabella: Drink this. It will dull your pain.

William: No. It will numb my wits. I must have them all. For if I'm senseless, or if I wail, then Longshanks will have broken me.

Isabella: I can't bear the thought of your torture. Take it.

William: All right.

Clip 8

Isabella: I have come to beg for the life of William Wallace.

Prince: You're quite taken with him, aren't you?

Isabella: I respect him. At worst, he was a worthy enemy. Show mercy, O thou great King, and win the respect of your own people. Even now ... you are incapable of mercy. And you ... To you, that word is as unfamiliar as love.

Prince: Before he lost his powers of speech, he told me his one comfort was that he would live to know Wallace was dead.

Isabella: You see ... Death comes to us all. But before it comes to you, know this: Your blood dies with you. A child who is not of your line grows in my belly. Your son will not sit long on the throne, I swear it.

Unit 6

Clip 1

Katherine Waston: From the beginning, man has always had the impulse to create art. Can anyone tell me what this is?

Joan: Wounded Bison, Altamira, Spain ... about 15,000 B.C. Joan Brandwyn.

Katherine Waston: Very good, Joan.

Katherine Waston: Despite the age of these paintings, they are technically very sophisticated because ...

Joan: Because of the shading and the thickness of the lines moves over the hump of the bison. Is that right?

Katherine Waston: Yes, that's exactly right. Next slide. This one you are probably less familiar with. It was discovered by archeologists ...

Betty: In 1879, Lascaux, France. Dates back to 10,000 B.C. Singled out because of flowing lines depicting the movement of the animal.

Katherine Waston: Impressive. Name?

Betty: Herd of Horses.

Katherine Waston: I meant yours.

Giselle: We call her Flicka.

Betty: Elizabeth Warren. They call me Betty.

Katherine Waston: Very good. Betty is also correct. Just because something is ancient doesn't mean that it is primitive.

Katherine Waston: For example. Next slide, please.

Susan Delacorte: My cerinus and His Queen. 2470B. C. It's a funerary statue of the pharaoh and queen ... originally intended to preserve the pharaoh's Ka.Soul.

Katherine Waston: Have any of you taken Art History before?

Girls: No.

Katherine Waston: Let's go on. Slide.

Girls: Seated Scribe. Egypet. 2400B.C. Peasant Couple Plowing. Sixteenth century B.C. Egypt. Snake Goddess. Minoan. 1600B.C. Fresco, Minoan. 1600B.C. Funeral Mask. My cenaean. 1200.

Katherine Waston: Could someone please get ... ? Thank you. By a show of hands only ... how many of you have read the entire text?

Susan Delacorte: And the suggested supplements.

Giselle: Long way from Oakland state?

Katherine Waston: Well, you girls do prepare.

Betty: If you've nothing else for us, we could go to independent study.

Clip 2

Betty: What is that?

Katherine Waston: You tell me. Carcass by Soutine,1925.

Susan Delacorte: It's not on the syllabus.

Katherine Waston: No, it's not. Is it any good? Come on, ladies. There's no wrong answer. There's also no textbook telling you what to think. It's not that easy, is it?

Betty: All right. No. It's not good. In fact, I wouldn't even call it art. It's grotesque.

Connie: Is there a rule against not being grotesque?

Giselle: I think there's something aggressive about it ... and erotic.

Betty: To you, everything is erotic ...

Giselle: Everything is erotic.

Katherine Waston: Girls.

Susan Delacorte: Aren't there standards?

Betty: Of course there are. Otherwise a tacky velvet painting could be equated to a Rembrandt.

Connie: My uncle Ferdie has two tacky velvet paintings. He loves those clowns.

Betty: There are standards, technique, composition, color, even subject. So if you're suggesting that rotted side of meat is art ... much less good art, then what are we going to learn?

Katherine Waston: Just that. You have outlined our new syllabus, Betty. Thank you. What is art? What makes it good or bad? And who decides? Next slide, please. Twenty-five years ago someone thought this was brilliant.

Connie: I can see that. Who?

Katherine Waston: My mother. I painted it for her birthday. Next slide. This is my mom.

Betty: Is it art?

Susan Delacorte: It's a snapshot.

Katherine Waston: If I told you Ansel Adams had taken it, would that make a difference?

Betty: Art isn't art until someone says it is.

Katherine Waston: It's art!

Betty: The right people.

Katherine Waston: Who are they?

Giselle: Betty Warren! So we're lucky we have one right here.

Betty: Screw you.

Katherine Waston: Could you go back to the Soutine, please? Just look at it again. Look beyond the paint. Let us try to open our minds to a new idea. All right, back to chapter three. Has anyone read it? Okay.

Clip 3

President Jocelyn Carr: I've been getting some calls about your teaching methods, Katherine. They're a little unorthodox ... for Wellesley. We are traditionalists, Katherine.

Katherine Waston: Yes, I noticed.

President Jocelyn Carr: So if you'd like to stay here ...

Katherine Waston: Is that a question?

President Jocelyn Carr: More of a discussion.

Katherine Waston: About my staying here?

President Jocelyn Carr: You'll have your formal review in May. Until then ... a little less modern art.

Clip 4

Joan: Beautiful! You've got everything you've ever dreamed of.

Betty: You will too.

Joan: I've got a secret to tell you. You swear you won't gab to anyone? I got accepted early to Yale Law School.

Betty: To what?! Why?! You don't want to be a lawyer.

Joan: Maybe I do.

Betty: You won't switch brands of cold creams without asking me, but you applied to school?

Joan: On a lark. We never thought I'd get in.

Betty: Who's "we"?

Joan: Miss Watson. She practically filled out my application for me.

Betty: You've got to be kidding me! What right does she have? You're getting married!

Joan: First of all, there's no ring on this finger. Second, I can do both. I can.

Betty: How does Tommy feel about this?

Joan: He doesn't know. No one does.

Betty: Not even her?

Joan: No.

Clip 5

Connie: You're a sight for sore eyes.

Betty: I would've been here sooner, silly me, I thought class was held in the classroom.

Katherine Waston: Glad you could join us, Mrs. Jones. We thought we'd lost you.

Connie: There's a sort of unwritten rule for married girls.

Katherine Waston: Don't bother. Since your wedding, you've missed six classes, a paper and your midterm.

Betty: Well, thank God, I didn't miss the paint-by-numbers lecture. I was on my honeymoon and then I had to set up house.What does she expect?

Katherine Waston: Attendance.

Connie Baker: Most of the faculty turn their heads when the married students miss a class or two.

Katherine Waston: Then why not get married as freshmen? That way you could graduate without actually ever stepping foot on campus.

Betty Warren: Don't disregard our traditions just because you're subversive.

Katherine Waston: Don't disrespect this class just because you're married.

Betty Warren: Don't disrespect me just because you're not.

Katherine Waston: Come to class, do the work, or I'll fail you.

Betty Warren: If you fail me, there will be consequences.

Katherine Waston: Are you threatening me?

Betty Warren: I'm educating you.

Katherine Waston: That's my job.

Clip 6

Katherine Waston: Come in. Seven law schools within 45 minutes of Philadelphia. You can study and get dinner on the table by 5:00.

Joan: It's too late.

Katherine Waston: No. Some of them accept late admissions. I was upset at first. I can tell you that now. When Tommy came to me that he got accepted to Penn, I thought: Oh, god. "Her fate is sealed. She works so hard. How can she throw it all away?" I realized you won't have to. You could bake your cake and eat it, too. It's just wonderful.

Joan: We're married. We eloped over the weekend. It turned out he was petrified of a big ceremony ... so we did a sort of spur-of-the-moment thing. Very romantic. Look.

Katherine Waston: It's beautiful.

Joan: It was my choice. Not to go. He would have supported it.

Katherine Waston: But you don't have to choose.

Joan: No, I have to. I want a home; I want a family. That's not something I'll sacrifice.

Katherine Waston: No one's asking you to sacrifice that, Joan. I just want you to understand that you can do both.

Joan: Do you think I'll wake up one morning and regret not being a lawyer?

Katherine Waston: Yes, I'm afraid that you will.

Joan: Not as much as I'd regret not having a family. Not being there to raise them. I know exactly what I'm doing, and it doesn't make me any less smart. This must seem terrible to you.

Katherine Waston: I didn't say that. I ...

Joan: Sure you did. You always do. You stand in class and tell us to look beyond the image, but you don't. To you, a housewife is someone who sold her soul for a center hall colonial. She has no depth, no intellect, no interests. You're the one who said I could do anything I wanted. This is what I want.

Katherine Waston: Congratulations. Be happy.

Clip 7

Bill: Katherine! You are okay?

Katherine Waston: I met Stan. Hell of a nice guy.

Bill: Yeah. What a talker. Yeah. We go back a long way.

Katherine Waston: All the way to Long lsland. Secret's out. What an incredible lie.

Bill: Look, I spoke the language; I had the uniform; People just assumed things. I didn't correct them. I guess I should've done.

Katherine Waston: I guess you should've done.

Bill: Oh, Katherine. Look ... I'm sorry. Okay? I made a mistake. Just give me a chance ...

to straighten things out, okay?

Katherine Waston: Why couldn't you just be honest?

Bill: You don't make it easy. You're so perfect, you. It's impossible to be honest with you. I ...

Katherine Waston: For you, it is.

Bill: Well, it's not just me, Katherine. Joan failed you, too, right?

Katherine Waston: That's an awful thing to say.

Bill: I know, but it's the truth. If you want honesty, I can be real honest. You didn't come to Wellesley to help people find their way. I think you came to wellesley to help people find your way.

Clip 8

Betty's mother: Elizabeth, I don't see Spencer.

Betty: Excuse me, Mother. Miss Watson, can you help me get in touch with that friend of yours ... in Greenwich Village?

Betty's mother: What do you need in Greenwich Village?

Betty: An apartment. I filed for a divorce this morning. And since we know I'm not welcome at your house ... You remember Giselle Levy? What did you call her? "A New York kike." That's it. Well, we're going to be roommates.

Giselle: Hi. You ready?

Betty: Yeah.

Giselle: You okay?

Katherine Waston: Greenwich Village?

Betty: Yeah. For a while. Then, who knows? Maybe law school. Yale, even.

Katherine Waston: Well ... I wouldn't want to come up against you in any court anywhere.

Betty: Maybe I can drop by next year? Keep you on your toes. You will be here? Miss Watson?

Katherine Waston: (a letter to Betty) Dear Betty: I came to Wellesley because I wanted to make a difference. But to change for others ... is to lie to yourself, my teacher.

Unit 7

Clip 1

Clarisse: Amelia, have you ever heard of Edward Christoff Phillipe Gerard Renaldi?

MIA: No.

Clarisse: He was the crown prince of Genovia.

MIA: Um, what about him?

Clarisse: Edward Christoff Phillipe Gerard Renaldi was your father.

MIA: Yeah, sure. My father was the prince of Genovia. Uh-huh. You're joking.

Clarisse: Why would I joke about something like that?

MIA: No no! Cuz if he's really a prince, then I ...

Clarisse: Exactly. You're not just Amelia Thermopolis. You are Amelia Mignonette Thermopolis Renaldi Princess of Genovia.

MIA: Me? A ... a ... princess? Shut up!

Clarisse: I beg your pardon? Shut up?

SERVENT: Your Majesty, in America it doesn't always mean "Be quiet." Here it could mean "Wow," "GEE whiz," "Golly".

Clarisse: Oh, I ... I understand. Thank you. Nevertheless, you are the princess. And I am Queen Clarisse Renaldi.

MIA: Why on earth would you pick me to be your princess?

Clarisse: Since your father died, you are the natural heir to the throne of Genovia. That's our law. I'm royal by marriage. You are royal by blood. You can rule.

MIA: Rule? Oh, no. Oh no. No, no, no. Now you have really got the wrong girl. I never lead anybody not at not at Brownies, not at Camp Fire Girls ... Queen Clarisse, my expectation in life is to be invisible, and I'm good at it.

Clarisse: Amelia, I had other expectations also. In my wildest dreams I never expected this to happen. But you are the legal heir, the only heir to the Genovian throne and we will accept the challenge of helping you become the princess that you are. Oh, I can give you books. You will study languages, history, art, political science. I can teach you to walk, talk, sit, stand, eat, dress like a princess. Given time, I think you'll find the palace in Genovia a very pleasant place to live.

MIA: Live in Genovia?

Clarisse: It's a wonderful country. Amelia, really.

MIA: Whoa, whoa, just — rewind and freeze. I'm no princess. I'm still waiting for normal body parts to arrive. I refuse to move to and rule a country and — Do you want another reason? I don't want to be a princess!

Clarisse: Oh, oh. Amelia! Amelia! Amelia! Come back!

Clip 2

MIA: What's going on?

Lilly: Maybe it's a protest.

MIA: Maybe. Excuse me. Hi. Who are you all waiting for?

Lana: There she is right there! That's Mia Thermopolis!

Reporter 1: Waiting for you.

Reporter 2: Right here, princess. Talk to me.

MIA: Lilly, Lilly, did you tell?

Lilly: I didn't say anything!

Reporter 3: Princess Mia! Princess Mia. Who's your favorite actor?

Michael: Why are they calling her "princess"?

Lilly: Mia!

Reporter: Princess Mia! What do you do about pimples?

Lilly: Come on. Let's just go, please!

Reporter: Can we quote you, your Majesty?

Miss Gupta: Come on, Mia. Let's get inside.

Lana: Oh, Mia! Oh! Wait! Wait! Wait! Excuse me, sir? Hi!

Miss Gupta: The phone's ringing off the hook.

MIA: What? Oh!

O'CONNELL: Mia, your mother's on her way.

Miss Gupta: Gupta. Mm-hmm. Mm-hmm. Mm-hmm. The queen is coming to Grove High School.

Woman: A limo with flags.

Reporter 4: A Genovian limousine has arrived. The queen is getting out.

Reporter 5: Your Majesty, why all the secrets? All we keep hearing is "No comment." "No comment." Do you have a comment?

Reporter 6: Your Majesty. Will you be visiting the White House?

Reporter 7: Are you taking the princess home?

MIA: Mom, I don't know who told on me.

Clarisse: We'll get to the bottom of this.

Miss Gupta: Here's your tea, Your Majesty. I'm sorry we don't have finer china.

Clarisse: But that's perfectly all right.

Miss Gupta: Here.

Clarisse: Joseph?

Joe: Speak.

MIA: Paolo?

Paolo: Majesty, it was I who told the press about you, Principessa. I outed you. So to speak. I don't mean to imply ...

Paolo: Grazie.

Joe: Prego.

Paolo: But not for money. Principessa. Paolo hates money. He spits on money. There was no money. Well, there was some money. After all, a man likes me. Each ring is ... the point is, it was pride and ego who drove me to know that royalty would see one day the beauty was mine! The hair was mine. That I, Paolo Puttanesca, was responsible for ...

Paolo: Grazie.

Joe: Prego.

Paolo: By the way, your hair — magnificent. The next time, we go a little lighter?

Reporter: Your majesty, would you like to say anything?

GUPTA: Isn't that just awful? Doesn't anyone respect royalty anymore? What is it like in Genovia, your majesty? Do people just fawn over you?

Clarisse: I wonder, would you give us a moment alone?

GUPTA: I am the vice-principle ...

Clarisse: Joseph, would you take this fine educator and show her your security plans for Amelia's safety?

Joe: What? Uh. Yes, of course, of course. yes.

Gupta: Your Majesty, thank you. Mercy.

Joe: Your security system is a bit lax.

Gupta: Oh, is it?

HELEN: A week ago, Mia was a normal little kid.

Clarisse: She has never been normal. She was born royal. And we cope with the press every single day and we will do it again.

HELEN: You don't have to do this. You can get out of this whole thing right now.

Clarisse: Your mother is right, Amelia. We had a bargain.

MIA: All right. I will think about it and let you know soon.

Clarisse: Good. A diplomatic answer. Polite, but vague.

Clip 3

Clarisse: I do believe I'm beginning to feel that corn dog.

Mia: Uh, uh, uh.

Clarisse: Maybe you can just sneak gently through?

Mia: OK. OK. I'll try.

Clarisse: Good! Right, now, blaze on up.

Mia: I, I got it!

Clarisse: Yes. You've got it!

MIA: I got it!

Clarisse: You've got it! Uhh!

Mia: Oh! I haven't got it!

Clarisse: Uh-oh! Mia! Mia! Brake! Brake! Look out! Down here.

Mia: Uh!

Nun 1: 9-1-1, I need to report an accident.

People on the trolley: You didn't hear the bell!?

Nun 1: They put me on hold.

Nun 2: Oh, for the love of god!

Bruce: Put down destruction of public property.

Arthur: I will, I will. And last but not least, driving without a license, accompanied by an adult whose license expired 45 years ago.

Clarisse: I've been trying to tell you, officer. Licenses don't expire in Genovia. Not for the queen. Don't I have diplomatic immunity?

Arthur: You do. But her, we have to take downtown.

MIA: What?

Arthur: I'm sorry, miss.

Clarisse: It's all right, officer. I understand I ... I understand perfectly.

MIA: You do?

Clarisse: Mia, no town, no city, no country can function peacefully if its officers and its transportation engineers don't follow the letter of the law. Why, I would be proud to have two such fine, honorable gentlemen serving in Genovia.

Arthur: Aw, shucks, ma'ma.

Bruce: Ma'am, we're not all that.

Clarisse: Oh, but you most certainly are. As a matter of fact, I would like to bestow upon you the honor of the Genovian Order of the Genovian Order of the Rose.

Mia: Oh-oh! Ooh!

Clarisse: Would you please kneel? Does anybody have a saber?

Old woman: Oh, I've got an umbrella.

MIA:	I have an emergency brake.
Clarisse:	This will do fine, thank you. With the power vested in me by the royal crown of Genovia I dub thee.
Arthur:	Arthur Washington San Francisco, ma'am.
Clarisse:	Arthur Washington. And I dub thee ...
Bruce:	Bruce Macintosh of San Leandro.
Clarisse:	Bruce Macintosh, masters of the Order of the Rose. And all of you bear witness to this auspicious moment in history. Please rise.
Arthur:	Wait till I go home and tell Bernice.
Clarisse:	Now, Mia, I know you don't want to go all the way downtown, but ...
Arthur:	That really won't be necessary. No one got hurt, did they?
Bruce:	We're insured.
Arthur:	Chivalry ain't dead you know, so ...
Clarisse:	Noble Arthur. How very kind.
Arthur:	Do you need a lift home?
Clarisse:	Oh, that would be very helpful, thank you. Come along, Mia. Good-bye, trolley people!
MIA:	Please take the car to Doctor Motors?
People:	Goodbye! So long! Goodbye! Goodbye!
Charisse:	Goodbye!
MIA:	You were awesome! You are the coolest queen ever!
Clarisse:	All in a day's work.
People:	Wave goodbye, that's a queen.
MIA:	Would you like to slide in first?
Clarisse:	I never slide. Goodbye! Thank you!
People:	Goodbye!
Man:	Hey, Bruce! How about gettin' on you royal carriage and gettin' us out of here.

Clip 4

Girl:	Awesome!
PHOTOGRAPHER:	Hey, Princess! Give us a smile!
MIA:	How did they find me here?
Josh:	What?
MIA:	How did they find me here?!
Brian:	Hey, wave, everybody! You're on TV!
PHOTOGRAPHER:	Wait, Princess, don't be shy! Come back!
BRIAN:	Hey, chopper boy, look over here! Royal deejays!
MIA:	Josh! No, oh! I am so sorry about all this.
Josh:	No, it's fine. It's fine. They can't get us in here.
MIA:	We were having such a good time ... and then they came and ruined it.
Josh:	I know, I know. Look, they can't see us ... we can't see them. We're all alone in this little shack. Actually, you know what? It's kind of cozy in here ... and there's no one I'd rather be here with than you, Mia.
MIA:	Really?
Josh:	Yeah.
MIA:	Josh? This isn't romantic.
Josh:	You're right.
MIA:	Um ... it just ... No. It's my foot. It's caught in a volleyball net.
Josh:	Yeah. Here.
MIA:	Oh!
GIRL A:	Hey! My dad thinks I'm a princess!
GIRL B:	I'm a friend of Mia's!
Josh:	I tell you what. While we're waiting, how about a foot massage?
MIA:	That would be so wonderful. Thank you.
Josh:	No. Actually, I mean you give me one.

MIA: Oh, yeah.

(The next scene)

Lily: And indeed, it is the queen of hearts! Thank you, Jeremiah ... for your potpourri of prestidigitations for the past hour. Obviously, Princess Mia has a problem appearing here tonight and I'm sure she has a good excuse. I'm Lilly Moscovitz for "Shut Up and Listen." Thank you and good night.

(Back to the beach)

Josh: Mia ... the coast is clear.

MIA: Really?

Josh: They're gone. Yeah.

MIA: Oh, good.

Josh: So, what do you say we go find a more romantic spot?

MIA: OK.

PHOTOGRAPHER: Quiet! Quiet!

(Cameras clicking)

(Shouting)

JOSH: No! Stay!(Overlapping questions)

REPORTER 1: Give her a smooch!

REPORTER 2: Come on! Give her a big, sloppy wet one!

(Josh kisses Mia)

PHOTOGRAPHER: Hold it!

FEMALE PHOTOGRAPHER: Hit him again! Hit him again!

MIA: Go away! No, no, no! Go away, all of you! Leave me alone!

REPORTER: The princess has left the building.

REPORTER B: Who have we got? What's your name?

NELSON: Where do you go to school?

Josh: Josh Bryant.

Reporter: Josh! Right picture! Right here!

Lana: What are we, friends with Mia now?

Josh: I go to Grove High School.

Clip 5

MIA: Thank you, Dad, but I can't be a princess. OK? I don't make speeches. And I'm not Clarisse Renadi and ... and I just ... I can't do it, OK? I'm scared.

Charlotte: Joseph.

Joe: Charlotte, Miss Kawa.

Charlotte: Hello!

Miss Kawa: Nice to meet you.

Miss Kawa: Pardon me. I have to get the band ready.

Joe: Of course.

Charlotte: Should you be going to get Princess Mia?

Joe: Well, Mia told Clarisse her mother would be bringing her.

Charlotte: Helen just arrived and said Mia was waiting for you.

Joe: She's going to run.

Mia: Come on, Fat Louie. Time to pack. Let's get your things. Louie, what have you got there? Come on, Louie. We're going on a trip. We're going to Colorado where we can climb some real rocks. We are so out of here, Louie.

Phillipe: My dearest daughter, today is your sixteenth birthday. Congratulations. I present you with this diary to fill the pages with your special thoughts, special thoughts of your wonderful life. It is a custom in my family to pass on a piece of wisdom when one reaches this age. I pass it on to you as my father passed it on to me. Amelia, courage is not the absence of fear but rather the judgement that something else is more important than fear. The brave may not live forever, but the cautious do not live at all. From now on, you'll be traveling the road between who you think you are, and who you can be. The key is to allow yourself to make the journey. I also want you to know. I loved your mother very much and still think of her often. Happy birthday, my Mia. All my love, your father.

Clip 6

Joe: Get in!

(Her Majesty, the Queen)

Clarisse: My fellow Genovians and honored guests, good evening. I apologize for the delay and ... oh, hello ... And may I say ... welcome to our grand Genovian Independence Day ball.

Charlotte: Hurry! Hurry! No, no, no! No time to change. You look fine.

Joe: Pretty and fine. Just fine.

MIA: Oh!

Joe: No, no, no. No running.

Charlotte: Here we go.

Joe: Please, no running. Good.

Charlotte: It's nice.

Clarisse: Thank you so much for your patience. I have an announcement to make. My granddaughter ... (Ahen)

Lilly: She' here.

Jeremiah: I see.

Lily: She's here.

Clarisse: I would like to announce that my granddaughter has arrived with a fascinating explanation as to her wardrobe I'm sure.

REPORTER: She's styling a wet, sort of grunge-look hairdo ... and is wearing a sweatshirt, jeans and Docs.

Clarisse: Mia, would you care to say a few words?

MIA: Um, yes.

Lilly: Why don't we dress like her?We look like idiots.

MIA: Thank you, your Majesty.

Woman: Do you think they're trying to save money on the gown?

MIA: Hi, er ... Hello, I'm Mia. It stopped raining.

DUKE: Get your tiara ready.

MIA: I'm really no good at speechmaking. Normally I get so nervous that I faint or run away or sometimes I even get sick. But you really didn't need to know that. But I'm not so afraid anymore. My father helped me. Earlier this evening, I had every intention of giving up my claim to the throne and my mother helped me by telling me that it was OK and by supporting me like she has for my entire life. But then I wondered how I'd feel after abdicating my role as Princess of Genovia. Would I feel relieved or would I feel sad? And then I realized how many stupid times a day I use the word "I", and that probably all I ever do is think about myself. And how lame is that when there are 7 billion other people out there on the planet ... ooh, sorry. sorry. I'm going too fast. But then I thought if I cared about the other 7 billion out there instead of just me, that's probably a much better use of my time. See, if I were Princess of Genovia then my thoughts and the thoughts of people smarter than me would be much better heard and just maybe those thoughts could be turned into actions. So this morning when I woke up I was Mia Thermopolis. But now I choose to be forevermore Amelia Mignonette Thermopolis Renaldi, Princess of Genovia.

Woman: I hope you didn't order your stationary yet.

Clarisse: This was my very first tiara. I was rather fond of it. I'm hoping you will be, too.

MIA: Oh, grandma, but you had it already. How did you know I'd even be here?

Clarisse: Because I recognize the same spirit in you as someone else I know.

MIA: Who?

Clarisse: Me.

Unit 8

Clip 1

Emily: She wants to see you.

Andrea: Oh! Oh!

Emily: Move. This is foul. Don't let her see it.

Andrea: That's my ...

Emily: Go.

Miranda: Who are you?

Andrea: Uh, my name is Andy Sachs. I recently graduated from Northwestern University.

Miranda: And what are you doing here?

Andrea: Well, I think I could do a good job as your assistant. And, um ... Yeah, I came to New York to be a journalist, and sent letters out everywhere, and then finally got a call from Elias Clarke, and met with Sherry up at Human Resources and basically, it's this or Auto Universe.

Miranda: So you don't read *Runway*?

Andrea: Uh, no.

Miranda: And, before today, you had never heard of me?

Andrea: No.

Miranda: And you have no style or sense of fashion.

Andrea: Well, um, I think that depends on what you're ...

Miranda: No, no. That wasn't a question.

Andrea: Um, I was editor in chief of *The Daily Northwestern*. I also, um, won a national competition for college journalists with my series on the janitors' union, which exposed the exploitation of ...

Miranda: That's all.

Andrea: Yeah, you know, okay. You're right. I don't fit in here. I am not skinny or glamorous and I don't know that much about fashion. But I'm smart. I learn fast and I will work very hard.

(Nigel walks in.)

Nigel: I've got the exclusive on the Cavalli for Gwyneth. But, the problem is, with that huge feathered headdress that she's wearing, she looks like she's working the main stage at the Golden Nugget.

Andrea: Thank you for your time.

Nigel: Who is that sad little person? Are we doing a before-and-after piece I don't know about?

(Andrea is ready to step out of the building)

Emily: Andrea.

Andrea: Hmm?

Clip 2

Emily: Excuse me, where do you think you're going?

Andrea: She hates me, Nigel.

Nigel: And that's my problem because ... Oh, wait, no. It's not my problem.

Andrea: I don't ... I ... I don't know what else I can do, because if I do something right, it's unacknowledged. She doesn't even say thank you. But if I do something wrong, she is vicious.

Nigel: So quit.

Andrea: What?

Nigel: Quit.

Andrea: Qui —

Nigel: I can get another girl to take your job in five minutes ... one who really wants it.

Andrea: But I now ... I don't wanna quit. That's not fair. But I — You know, I'm just saying that I would just like a little credit for the fact that I'm killing myself trying.

Nigel: Andy, be serious. You are not trying. You are whining. What is it that you want me to say to you, huh? Try me say "Poor you. Miranda's picking on you. Poor you, poor Andy"? Wake up, six. She's just doing her job. Don't you know you are working at the place that published some of the greatest artists of the century? Halston, Lagerfeld, de la Renta. And what they did, what they created, was greater than art because you live your life in it. Well, not you, obviously, but some people. You think this is just a magazine, hmm? This is not just a magazine. This is a shining beacon of hope for ... Oh, I don't know. Let's say, a young boy growing up in Rhode Island with six brothers pretending to go to soccer practice, when he was really going to sewing class and reading Runway under the covers at night with a flashlight. You have no idea how many legends have walked these halls. What's worse, you don't care. Because this place, where so many people would die to work, you only deign to work. And you want to know why she doesn't kiss you on the forehead and give you a gold star on your homework at the end of the day. Wake up, sweetheart.

Andrea: Okay, so I'm screwing it up.

Nigel: Mmm.

Andrea: But I don't want to. I just wish that I knew what I could do to ... Nigel? Nigel, Nigel.

Nigel: No.

Clip 3

Miranda: Andrea, don't forget to tell Emily. Do it now.

Andrea: Don't pick up. Don't pick up. Don't pick up. Don't pick.

Emily: Hi.

Andrea: Emily.

Emily: Hi, hi. Sorry I'm late. It's just Miranda wanted some scarves from Hermes. She did tell me yesterday, but I forgot like an idiot. So I freaked out, of course.

Andrea: Emily — Emily, I need to talk to you.

Emily: But then I called Martine at home, and she opened the shop early. Whoa! I'm sorry. She opened the shop early for me, so I got them, which is great.

Andrea: Yeah, okay, um, Emily, when you come in ... there's something we, I have to talk to you about.

Emily: Well, I hope it's not another Miranda problem.

Andrea: Not exactly.

Emily: Well, good, because I've got so much to deal with before I go. I swear to God, I mean —

(The crowed: Oh, my God!)

Andrea: Emily?

(In the hospital)

Emily: I don't care if she was gonna fire you or beat you with a red-hot poker. You should have said no.

Andrea: Emily, I didn't have a choice. You know how she is.

Emily: Please. That is a pathetic excuse.

(The doctor walks in.)

Emily: Thanks. Do you know what really just gets me about this whole thing? Is that, you know, you're the one who said that you don't really care about this stuff. And you don't really care about fashion. You just wanna be a journalist. Oh, what a pile of bollocks!

Andrea: Emily, I know you're mad. I don't blame you.

Emily: Face it, Andy, you sold your soul the day you put on that first pair of Jimmy Choo's. I saw it. And do you know what really just kills me about this whole thing? Is the clothes that you're gonna get. I mean, you don't deserve them. You eat carbs, for Christ's sake! God! It's so unfair.

Andrea: Emily ...

Emily: Just go.

Andrea: Emily, I ...

Emily: I said, go.

Dong: You are going to Paris for the couture shows?

Andrea: Mn-hmm.

Dong: That's the coolest fashion.

Clip 4

Andrea: And now you're gonna give me a hard time too?

Nate: Hey, Andy. Andy! Andy, what the hell is wrong with you?

Andrea: I — I didn't have a choice, okay? I ... Miranda asked me, and I couldn't say no.

Nate: I know. That's your answer for everything, lately, "I didn't have a choice." Like this job was forced on you. Like you don't make decisions yourself.

Andrea: Nate, I get it, OK? You're mad because I work late all the time and I missed your birthday party. And I'm sorry.

Nate: Oh, come on. What am I for?

Andrea: You — You hate *Runway* and Miranda. And you think fashion is stupid. You've made that clear.

Nate: Andy, I make portwine reductions all day. I'm not exactly in the Peace Corps. You know, I wouldn't care if you were out there pole-dancing all night as long as you did it with a little integrity. You used to say this was just a job. You used to make fun of the Runway girls. What happened? Now you've become one of them.

Andrea: That's absurd.

Nate: Hey, that's okay. That's fine. Just own up to it. And then we can stop pretending like we have anything in common anymore.

Andrea: You don't mean that, do you?

Nate: No, I do.

Andrea: Well, maybe this trip is coming at a good time. Maybe we should take a break. Nate?

(Andrea's phone rings.)

Andrea: I'm sorry. Just one second.

Nate: You know, in case you were wondering the person whose calls you always take, that's the relationship you're in. I hope you two are very happy together.

Clip 5

Miranda: You thought I didn't know. I've known what was happening for quite some time. It just took me a little while to find a suitable alternative for Jacqueline. And that James Holt job was just so absurdly overpaid that, of course, she jumped at it. So I just had to tell Irv that Jacqueline was unavailable. The truth is, there is no one that can do what I do, including her. Any of the other choices would have found that job impossible and the magazine would have suffered, especially because of the list. The list of designers, photographers, editors, writers, models, all of whom were found by me, nurtured by me and have promised me they will follow me whenever and if ever I choose to leave *Runway*. So he reconsidered. But I was very, very impressed by how intently you tried to warn me. I never thought I would say this, Andrea, but I really ... .I see a great deal of myself in you. You can see beyond what people want, and what they need and you can choose for yourself.

Andrea: I don't think I'm like that. I ... I couldn't do what you did to Nigel Miranda. I couldn't do something like that.

Miranda: You already did. To Emily.

Andrea: That's not what I ... No, that was different. I didn't have a choice.

Miranda: Oh, no, you chose. You chose to get ahead. You want this life. Those choices are necessary.

Andrea: But what if this isn't what I want? I mean, what if I don't wanna live the way you live?

Miranda: Oh. Don't be ridiculous, Andrea. Everybody wants this. Everybody wants to be us.

Clip 6

Greg: Andy. Greg Hill.

Andrea: Hello.

Greg: Come on. These clips are excellent. This thing on the janitors' union. That's exactly what we do here. My only question is: Runway? You were there for less than a year. What the hell kind of a blip is that?

Andrea: Learned a lot. In the end, though, I kind of screwed it up.

Greg: I called over there for a reference, left word with some snooty girl. Next thing you know, I got a fax from Miranda Priestly herself, saying that of all the assistants she's ever had you were by far her biggest disappointment. And, if I don't hire you, I am an idiot. You must have done something right.

Unit 9

Clip 1

Mark: Done!

Wardo: Hey, what's going on?

Mark: Perfect timing. Eduardo's here and he's going to have the key ingredient.

Wardo: Hey, Mark.

Mark: Wardo.

Wardo: You and Erica split up?

Mark: How did you know that?

Wardo: It's on your blog.

Mark: Yeah.

Wardo: Are you all right?

Mark: I need you.

Wardo: I'm here for you.

Mark: No, I need the algorithm you use to rank chess players.

Wardo: Are you OK?

Mark: We're ranking girls.

Wardo: You mean other students.

Mark: Yeah.

Wardo: You think this is such a good idea?

Mark: I need the algorithm.

Wardo: Mark ...

Mark: I need the algorithm.

Wardo: Give each girl a base rating of 1400. At any given time "Girl A" has a rating R-a and "Girl B" has a rating R-b.

Mark: When any two girls are matched up, there's an expectation of which will win based on their current rating, right?

Wardo: Yeah. And all those expectations are expressed this way.

Mark: Let's write it.

(The next scene.)

Boys: One on the left. The right. Yeah, still the right.

Dustin: Wardo. Who should we send it to first?

Wardo: Dwyer.

Chris: Neal.

Wardo: Who will you send it to?

Mark: Just a couple of people. Question is, who are they gonna send it to?

Boy 1: Hey, guys, check this out.

Boys: Someone go to the left. Dude, do left.

Boy 1: Look at these girls. Right or left? Left is hot.

Boys 2: Left is hot.

Boy 3: Left?

Boys: Yeah, yeah, yeah.

Boy 1: Right or left?

Girl 1: It's my roommate.

Boys: Oh, my God. The girl on the left.

Girl 2: This is pathetic.

Boys: Right.

Boys: Left. Left. Left?

Erica's roommate: Oh, shit. Albright. He blogged about you. You don't wanna read it.

Boys: Left. How about the right one? Left.

Wardo: That's awful, a lot of traffic. Do you really agree we shouldn't shut it down before getting into trouble?

Clip 2

Mark: Yeah.

Tyler: Mark, this is Divya Narendra, our partner.

Mark: Hi.

Divya: We were really impressed with Facemash. And then we checked you out, and you also built Course Match.

Tyler: I know CourseMatch.

Divya: You go online and see what courses your friends are taking.

Cameron: Really smart, man.

Divya: Mark.

Mark: Yeah.

Divya: We were talking about CourseMatch.

Mark: It was kind of a no-brainer.

Divya: But you invented something in high school, too, right?

Mark: Oh. An app for an MP3 player that recognizes your taste in music.

Divya: Anybody try to buy it?

Mark:	Microsoft.
Divya:	Wow. How much?
Mark:	Didn't sell it. Uploaded it for free.
Divya:	For free?
Mark:	Yeah.
Divya:	Why?
Cameron:	Okay, well, uh, we have something that we've been working on for a while and we think it's great. It's called Harvard Connection. You create your own page. Interests, bio, friends, pics.
Tyler:	And then people can go online, see your bio, request to be your ...
Mark:	Yeah, how is that different from MySpace or Friendster?
Tyler:	Harvard. edu.
Cameron:	Harvard.edu is the most prestigious e-mail address in the country.
Tyler:	The whole site's kind of based on the idea that girls ...
Cameron:	Not to put anything indelicately.
Divya:	Girls wanna go with guys who go to Harvard.
Cameron:	Divya and my brother don't have trouble putting things indelicately.
Tyler:	The main difference between what we're talking about and MySpace or Friendster, or any of those social networking sites is ...
Mark:	Is exclusivity. Right?
Divya:	Right.
Tyler:	Yeah. We'd love you to work with us, Mark.
Cameron:	And we need a gifted programmer who's creative.
Tyler:	And we know that you can take it in the shins.
Divya:	Women's groups are ready to declare a fatwa. But, you know, this could help rehabilitate your image.
Mark:	Wow. You would do that for me?
Divya:	We'd like to work with you.

Cameron: Our ... Our first programmer had graduated and went to work for Google. Our second programmer has just got overwhelmed with schoolwork. We will need you to build the site and write the code, and we'll provide all the ...

Mark: I'm in.

Cameron: What?

Mark: I'm in.

Cameron: Awesome.

Lawyer: That's what you said?

Mark: It was three or four.

Clip 3

Wardo: Mark! Be right back.

Mark: I think I've come up with something.

Wardo: Hang on. I gotta tell you something that you're not gonna believe.

Mark: What?

Wardo: I got punched by the Phoenix.

Mark: Are you kidding?

Wardo: No.

Wardo: I mean, it's just the first of a four-step process, but they slid the invitation under my door tonight. I got to my first punch party tomorrow.

Mark: So ... You got punched by the Phoenix.

Wardo: Yeah, but, you know, it was probable just a diversity thing. It was just a diversity thing. Just ride that horse until ... What did you wanna talk to me about? Mark?

Mark: Year.

Wardo: You said you'd come up with something.

Mark: Yeah, I think I've come up with something. Come outside and let's talk.

Wardo: It's 20 degrees outside.

Mark: I can't stare at that loop of Niagara Falls, which has absolutely nothing to do with the Caribbean.

(Outside)

Mark: People came to Facemash in a stampede, right?

Wardo: Yeah.

Mark: But it wasn't because they saw pictures of hot girls. You can go anywhere on the Internet and see pictures of hot girls.

Wardo: Yeah.

Mark: It was because they saw pictures of girls that they knew. People want to go on the Internet and check out their friends, so why not build a website that offers that? Friends, pictures, profiles, whatever you can visit. Browse around. Maybe it's someone you just met at a party. But I'm not talking about a dating site. I'm talking about taking the entire social experience of college and putting it online.

Wardo: I can't feel my legs.

Mark: I know. I'm totally psyched about this, too. But, Wardo?

Wardo: Yeah?

(In the office)

Wardo: "It would be exclusive."

(Outside)

Mark: You would have to know the people on the site to get past your own page, like getting punched.

Wardo: Now, that's good.

Mark: Wardo, it's like a final club, except we're the president.

(Back in the office)

Wardo: I told him that I thought it sounded great. It was a great idea. There was nothing to hack. People were gonna provide their own pictures, their own information. And people had the ability to invite, or not to invite, their friends to join. See, in a world where social structure was everything, that was the thing. It was a big project, and he was going to have to write tens of thousands of lines of code, so I wondered why he was coming to me and not his roommates, Dustin Moskovitz and Chris Hughes. They were programmers.

(Outside)

Mark: We're gonna need a little start-up cash to rent the servers and get it online.

(Back in the office)

Wardo: So that was why.

Gretchen: Did he offer terms?

Wardo: Yes.

(Outside)

Mark: We'll split it 70/30. 70 for me, 30 for you for putting up the $1,000 and for handling everthing on the business end. You're CFO.

(Back in the office)

Gretchen: And you said?

Wardo: I said, "Let's do it."

Gretchen: Okay. Did he add anything else?

Wardo: Yes.

(Outside)

Mark: It probably was a diversity thing. But so what?

Gretchen: Why do you think he said that?

Sy: Gretchen, excuse me for interrupting, but whose discovery is this?

Gretchen: Sy, if you'll let me continue with my line of questioning.

Sy: What are you suggesting?

Mark: Suggesting that I was jealous of Eduardo for getting punched by the Phoenix and began a plan to screw him out of a company — I hadn't even invented yet.

Gretchen: Were you?

Sy: Gretchen.

Mark: Jealous of Eduardo?

Sy: Oh, stop typing. We're off the record.

Mark: Ma'am, I know you've done your homework, and so you know that money isn't a big part of my life. But at the moment, I could buy Mount Auburn Street, take the Phoenix Club and turn it into my ping-pong room.

(Outside)

Wardo: I'll let you know how the party is.

Clip 4

Wardo: He took us through his episode with Napster.

Sean: I didn't wanna spend my twentieth as a professional defendant. Who knew? The music industry doesn't have a sense of humor. We tried to sell the company to pay the 35 million they said we owed in royalties, but I guess to them that was a little like selling a stolen car to pay for the stolen gas. So we said: Screw it, we declared bankruptcy.

Christy: But you made a name for yourself.

Sean: And you are dry. Tori!

Christy: No, no, I'm good.

Wardo: And then he went on to his second business venture, which was an online Rolodex that he got thrown out of by Case Equity.

Sean: And I wanted to do it nice this time. I put on a tie and I shined my shoes, but nobody wants to take orders from a kid. So let me tell you what happens to a 20-year-old at the top of a hot dot-com.

Wardo: I'm not a psychiatrist, but ...

Sy: I'm glad we've got that on record.

Gretchen: You're not a psychiatrist, but what?

Wardo: A psychiatrist would say that he was paranoid.

Sean: They'll hire private detectives who'll follow you day and night. You're a target for high-priced escorts. I can't prove it, but I know they tap my phones. Whatever it is that's gonna trip you up. You've done already. Private behavior is a relic of a time gone by. They don't want you, they want your idea. And they want you to say "thank you" while you ... Excuse me ... wipe your chin and walk away.

Mark: That's what happened to you?

Wardo: And delusional.

Sean: Yes. But there'll be payback at Case. I brought down the record companies with Napster and Case'll suffer for their sins, too.

Wardo: Sorry, you didn't bring down the record companies. They won.

Sean: In court.

Wardo: Yeah.

Sean: You wanna buy a Tower Records, Eduardo?

Wardo: And he told story after story about life in Silicon Valley, and parties at Stanford and down in LA, and friends who'd become millionaires. But mostly how Mark had to ... he had to come to California. And then he cut around to The Facebook.

Sean: So, tell me about your progress.

Wardo: Well, we're in 29 schools now. We got over 75,000 members.

Sean: Tell me about the strategy you're using.

Mark: Okay. For instance, we wanted Baylor in Texas, but Baylor already had a social network on campus. So instead of going right after them, we made a list of every school within 100 miles.

Sean: You put The Facebook on those campuses first.

Mark: Pretty soon all the Baylor kids were seeing their friends on our site and we were in.

Sean: It's called a little bait for a big one. That's smart, Mark.

Wardo: Thanks, that was mine.

Christy: Easy.

Wardo: Hey, you know what? Settle an argument for us. I say it's time to start making money from The Facebook, but Mark doesn't want advertising. Who's right?

Sean: Well ... Neither of you yet. The Facebook is cool. That's what it's got going for it.

Mark: Yeah.

Sean: You don't wanna ruin it with ads because ads aren't cool.

Mark: Exactly.

Sean: It's like you're throwing the greatest party on campus and someone's saying it's gotta be over by 11:00.

Mark: That's exactly right.

Sean: You don't even know what the thing is yet.

Mark: Exactly.

Sean: How big it can get and how far it can go. This is no time to take your chips down. A million dollars isn't cool. You know what's cool?

Wardo: You?

Wardo: A billion dollars. And that shut everybody up.

Sean: And that's where you're headed. A billion-dollar valuation. Unless you take bad advice, in which case you may as well have come up with a chain of very successful yogurt shops. When you go fishing, you can catch a lot of fish or you can catch a big fish. You ever walk into a guy's den and see a picture of him standing next to 14 trout?

Christy: No, he's holding a 3,000-pound marlin.

Sean: Yep.

Mark: That's a good analogy.

Wardo: Okay. But we all know marlins don't really weigh 3,000 pounds, right?

Christy: Have you seen the big ones up close?

Wardo: No, I haven't, but I don't think the guy's holding a marlin the size of a Range Rover. That would be a really big fish and a very strong guy.

Christy: You think we might be getting away from the point?

Sean: I don't have a dog in this fight. I'm just a fan who came to say hi.

Wardo: He owned Mark after that dinner. He picked up the check. He told Mark they'd talk again soon, and he was gone. But not before he made his biggest contribution to the company.

Sean: Drop the "The." Just "Facebook." It's cleaner.

Mark: Shit.

Clip 5

Cameron: Just brutal, brutally close. Brutally excruciating. Jesus.

Divya: The guy is the prince of a country the size of Nantucket. Relax, it's fine.

Mr. Winklevoss: Boys. Divya.

Winklevosses: Dad.

Divya: Mr. Winklevoss.

Mr. Winklevoss: That was a tough beat.

Cameron: I'm sorry that you and Mom had to fly out here to see that.

Mr. Winklevoss: No, don't ever apologize to me for losing a race like that. Don't ever apologize to anyone for losing a race like that.

Mr Kenwright: Boys.

Tyler: Mr. Kenwright. Dad, this is Mr. Kenwright, head of the host family for this week.

Mr Kenwright: Pleasure to meet you.

Mr. Winklevoss: Good to meet you.

Mr Kenwright: I've just had a phone chat with my daughter. She told me that she and her friends are already talking about the race, which they've just seen via their computers. A new website called Facebook. Do you have this in America?

Mr. Winklevoss: I'm gonna find your mother.

Mr Kenwright: Have I said something wrong?

Divya: Your daughter doesn't go to school in the States?

Mr Kenwright: No, no. Cambridge. Majoring in French literature, though I wasn't aware there was such a thing.

Tyler: And they have Facebook at Cambridge?

Mr Kenwright: And apparently Oxford and the London School of Economics. That's where her friends are.

Divya: That's awesome.

Mr Kenwright: Good race, boys. Take the bitter with the better, eh?

Cameron: I'm gonna go watch the race film. If this is online, I wanna see it.

Tyler: Stop it. Stop it, Cam. Knock it off. I don't mind that we lost to the Dutch today by less than a second. That was a good race, and that was a fair race. And they'll see us again. What I mind, and what you should mind, is showing up on Monday for a race that was run on Sunday. We tried talking to him ourselves. We tried writing a letter. We tried the Ad Board. And we tried talking to the president of the university. Now, I am asking you for the last time. Let's take the considerable resources at our disposal and sue him in a federal court.

Divya: Come on.

Cameron:	I need a real drink. Screw it. Let's gut that freaking nerd.
Tyler:	That's what I'm talking about.
	(Girls are laughing.)
Sean:	Check it out. I saw him today, Manningham, Mitchall Manningham.

Clip 6

Wardo:	In late November, I got the e-mail from Mark telling me to come out for the millionth-member party.
Gretchen:	What else did the e-mail say?
Wardo:	It said that we had to have a business meeting, that Mark and Sean had played some kind of revenge stunt on Case Equity, and that Manningham was so impressed that he was now making an investment offer that was hard to turn down. So I went to California, and I went straight to the new offices. I didn't know whether to dress for the party or for the business meeting, so I kind of dressed for both. But it didn't matter.
Gretchen:	Why not?
Wardo:	Because I wasn't called out there for either one.
Gretchen:	What were you called out there for?
Wardo:	An ambush.
Facebook lawyer:	Mr. Saverin. Hey. Right over here.
Wardo:	Hey, man. How are you?
Facebook lawyer:	Good. How are you?
Wardo:	Good, good, good, good, good. Good to see you.

(Back to the deposition.)

Wardo:	At first I thought he was joking, giving me more contracts to sign. But then I started reading. Wait, what is this?
Facebook lawyer:	Well, as you know, we had some new investors that have come in.
Wardo:	What is this?
Facebook lawyer:	Mr. Saverin.

Wardo:	Mark! Mark?
Sean:	He's wired in.
Wardo:	Sorry?
Sean:	He's wired in.
Wardo:	Is he?
Sean:	Yes.
Wardo:	How about now? Are you still wired in?
Sean:	Call security.
Wardo:	You issued 24 million new shares of stock!
Mark:	You were told that if new investors came along ...
Wardo:	How much were your shares diluted? How much were his?
Gretchen:	What was Mr. Zuckerberg's ownership share diluted down to?
Wardo:	It wasn't.
Gretchen:	What was Mr. Moskovitz's ownership share diluted down to?
Wardo:	It wasn't.
Gretchen:	What was Sean Parker's ownership share diluted down to?
Wardo:	It wasn't.
Gretchen:	What was Peter Thiel's ownership share diluted down to?
Wardo:	It wasn't.
Gretchen:	And what was your ownership share diluted down to?
Wardo:	0.03%.
Mark:	You signed the papers.
Wardo:	You set me up.
Mark:	You're gonna blame me because you were the business head of the company, and you made a bad business deal with your own company?
Wardo:	It's gonna be like I'm not a part of Facebook.

Sean:	It won't be like you're not a part of Facebook. You're not a part of Facebook.
Wardo:	My name's on the masthead.
Sean:	You might wanna check again.
Wardo:	Just because I froze the account?
Sean:	You think we were gonna let you parade around in your ridiculous suits, pretending you were running this company?
Wardo:	Sorry, my Prada's at the cleaner's! Along with my hoodie and my fuck-you flip-flops, you pretentious douche bag!
Sean:	Security's here. You'll be leaving now.
Wardo:	I'm not signing those papers.
Sean:	We will get the signature.
Wardo:	Tell me this isn't about me getting into the Phoenix. You ... You did it. I knew you did it. You planted that story about the chicken!
Mark:	I didn't plant that story about the chicken.
Sean:	What's he talking about?
Wardo:	You had me accused of animal cruelty.
Sean:	Seriously. What the hell's the chicken?
Wardo:	And I'll bet what you hated the most is that they identified me as a co-founder of Facebook, which I am. You'd better lawyer up, asshole. Because I'm not coming back for 30%. I'm coming back for everything.
Sean:	Get him out of here.
Wardo:	It's okay. I'm going.
Sean:	Hang on. Almost forgot. Here's your $19,000. I wouldn't cash it, though. I drew it on the account you froze.
Wardo:	I like standing next to you, Sean. It makes me look so tough.

Unit 10

Clip 1

Frankie: You are not breathing right. That's why you are panting. So it's your birthday, ha? How old does that make you?

Maggie: I'm 32, Mr. Dunn. And I'm here celebrating the fact that I spent another year scraping dishes and waitressing which is what I've been doing since 13. And according to you, I'll be 37 before I can even throw a decent punch which after working this speed bag for a month and getting nowhere ... I now realize may be God's simple truth. Other truth is ... My brother's in prison. My sister cheats on welfare by pretending one of her babies is still alive. My daddy's dead, and my mama weighs 312 pounds. If I was thinking straight, I'd go back home, find a use trailer, buy a deep fryer and some Oreos. The problem is ... This is the only thing I ever felt good doing. If I'm too old for this, then I got nothing. That's enough truth to suit you?

Frankie: This is your speed bag?

Maggie: Put yours behind the counter. Wish I could say I wore it out.

Frankie: OK, just hold it. Hold it. I'll show you a few things and then we'll get you a trainer.

Maggie: No, sorry.

Frankie: You are in a position to negotiate?

Maggie: Yes, sir. Because I know if you train me right, I'm gonna be a champ. I have seen you looking at me.

Frankie: Yeah, out of pity.

Maggie: Don't you say that. Don't you say that if it ain't true. I want a trainer. I don't want charity and I don't want favors. If you're not interested, then I got more celebrating to do.

Frankie: Stop, stop, stop. Goddamn it, stop. What the hell are you doing? Okay. If I'm gonna take you on ...

Maggie: You will never regret it.

Frankie: Look, just listen to me. If I take you on ...

Maggie: I promise I'll work so hard.

Frankie: God, this is a mistake already.

Maggie: Hum ... hum. I'm listening, boss.

Frankie: If I take you on, you don't say anything, you don't question me, you don't ask why, you don't say anything except maybe, " Yes, Frankie." And I'm gonna try to forget the fact that you're a girl.

Maggie: It's all I ask.

Frankie: And don't come crying to me if you get hurt. All righty.

Maggie: We got a deal.

Frankie: No, not quite. I'm gonna teach you how to fight, then we'll get you a manager, and I'm off down the road.

Maggie: Well, I hate to argue with you, but ...

Frankie: Don't argue with me. That's the only way we're doing it. I teach you all you need know and then you go off and make a million dollars. I don't care. Get your teeth knocked out, I don't care. I don't wanna hear about it either way. That's just the way it's gonna be. It's the only way I'll do it.

Clip 2

Eddie: Sally's a good manager. I must think she can take her.

Frankie: Jesus age. Your left, keep your left up.

Eddie: You think she can hear you from back here?

Eddie: Of course, if Maggie loses, it wouldn't mean anything to Sally. Might even help him. Lonnie's girl gets another win. Lonnie might let Sally's lightweight fight Joey Adagio for the title.

Frankie: Sally's trying to set a fight with Adagio?

Eddie: Hey, what do I know? I just come because I enjoy the fights.

Frankie: Mother of God.

Judge: Okay, break.

Frankie: Hey. Come here, come here.

Sally: Hey. Get over here.

Frankie: You're dropping your left hand. Quit dropping your left hand.

Sally: Hey, Frankie, you mind if I talk to my fighter?

Frankie: You're doing a hell of a job of it, Sally. Is this the way you advise your lightweight?

Judge: One.

Judge: What the hell are you doing?

Frankie: I'm talking. What are you doing?

Judge: Is this your fighter?

Sally: It's my fighter.

Maggie: It ain't fitting real well, Sally.

Sally: Fine, you take her. She can't fight worth a shit anyway.

Judge: Somebody tell me what's going on.

Frankie: Look, I was late. Sally was just subbing for me.

Judge: You're telling me this is your fighter?

Frankie: Yeah, this is my fighter.

Judge: Then you got 10 seconds.

Maggie: I keep holding my left up, then I throw a punch and it keeps dropping.

Frankie: Yeah, let it drop.

Maggie: That'd be a lot easier.

Frankie: She thinks she knows you. Every time you drop it, she comes right over the top. So you just wait for her, see? That's all she's thinking about. And when she cocks that big right hand. You hear me?

Maggie: I hear, boss.

Frankie: When she does, step to the side and come with a good-night hook. Got one?

Maggie: Got it right here.

Frankie: Okay.

Judge: Fight, or I'm calling it.

Frankie: Go give it to her.

Voiceover: The body knows what fighters don't how to protect itself. A neck can only twist so far.

Twist it just a hair more, and the body says: "Hey, I'll take it from here, because you obviously don't know what you're doing."

Judge: Neutral corner.

Eddie: See the way she did that?

Frankie: Yeah.

Eddie: Sugar Ray would do that. Girl's got sugar.

Voiceover: Lie down, now, rest and we'll talk about this when you regain your senses. It's called the knockout mechanism.

Frankie: Don't get all carried away, now.

Eddie: You did good.

Maggie: Thanks, boss.

Frankie: You, you forgot the rule. Now what is the rule?

Maggie: Keep my left up?

Frankie: It's to protect yourself at all times. Now, what is the rule?

Maggie: Protect myself at all times.

Frankie: Good, good.

Maggie: You gave me away. How was that protecting me?

Frankie: It wasn't.

Maggie: It's okay. I'll work my left, boss.

Frankie: Drink your water.

Maggie: Other than that, how'd I do?

Frankie: Fine, you did fine.

Maggie: You gonna leave me again?

Clip 3

Judge: Five, six, seven, eight, nine, ten. It's over.

Voiceover: Maggie didn't knock her out till the end of the first round. After that, no manager wanted to put his fighter in with Maggie. Frankie had to go into his pocket to get her decent fights sweetening the purse by paying managers on the side. That only worked for so long. Then Frankie did something he hated doing. He took a chance.

Judge: Box.

Voiceover: He moved her up in class. That could have been a mistake.

Audience: Watch the right. Watch it, watch it.

Judge: Break, break. Step back. Break. Time.

Frankie: Damn, damn, damn. Hey, guys, two seconds, will you? Just two seconds.

Judge: Okay.

Frankie: Your nose is broken.

Maggie: Oh, damn. Fix it.

Frankie: I can't, I can't.

Maggie: You can fix it.

Frankie: I can't, I've gotta call it.

Maggie: I assume what you can do. Fix it.

Frankie: Look, I can snap it back into place, but I can't stop the bleeding. The ring doctor's gonna call it.

Maggie: Please, Frankie, if you can stop the blood, I can beat her.

Frankie: Bite down on this. Inhale.

Maggie: What?

Frankie: Breathe in.

Frankie: Okay, huh?

Judge: Yeah, it's okay.

Frankie: All right, you got 20 seconds before this turns into a geyser and it's gonna spray all over the front row. Twenty seconds, that's all you've got. Now get going.

Judge: Go to your corner. Three, four, five, come on, breathe. Breathe, six, seven, eight, nine, ten.

Clip 4

Sever: Ten minutes, love.

Maggie: Thank you. Man says he loves me.

Frankie: He's probably not the first one to say that.

Maggie: First since my daddy. I win, you think he'll propose?

Frankie: You win, I'll propose. Look, I got you a gift here.

Maggie: I think they gave you somebody else's.

Frankie: No, no, this is it.

Maggie: What's it mean?

Frankie: I don't know. Just something in Gaelic.

Maggie: It's beautiful.

Frankie: Yeah, I thought so.

Frankie: Yeah. Real silk thread.

Compere: From the United States of America, the challenger Maggie Fitzgerald.

Woman: Mo cuishle. Did you see what was on her robe?

Woman&Man: Mo cuishle. Mo cuishle. Mo cuishle.

Voiceover: She wasn't the main attraction. She was on the undercard of a middleweight title fight. But ask someone who was there, they couldn't tell you who else fought that night.

Judge: Box.

Woman&Man: Come on, Mo cuishle!

Audierce: Mo cuishle! Mo cuishle! Mo cuishle! Mo cuishle! Mo cuishle! Mo cuishle! Mo cuishle! Mo cuishle!

Maggie: She's tough. I can't get inside. I can't get close enough to hit her.

rankie: You know why that is?

Maggie: Why?

rankie: She's a better fighter than you are. That's why She's younger. She's stronger. And she's more experienced. Now what are you gonna do about it? Get in there.

Judge: Box.

Judge: Three, four, five, six, seven, eight, nine, ten.

Audierce: Mo cuishle! Mo cuishle! Mo cuishle! Mo cuishle ...

Maggie: I could ask someone, you know.

Frankie: Good. You find out, you let me know.

Voiceover: Whatever it meant, the name stuck. Maggie fought in Edinburgh and Paris, Brussels and Amsterdam. It was always Mo cuishle. Seems there are Irish people everywhere or people who wanna be. By the time they came back to the states, Maggie was in a whole new league.

Clip 5

Blue bear's trainer: Looking good.

Judge: You pull that crap one more time, you're disqualified.

Frankie: It's gonna be all right.

Maggie: Got no doubt, boss.

Frankie: Okay, just watch yourself. Stay away from this damn.

Judge: Go to the neutral corner. Neutral corner.

Judge: Four, five, six ...

Frankie: Stay down, you bitch.

Judge: Seven, eight, nine.

Audierce: Yeah, yeah.

Judge: Right there, right there.

TV voice: Fitzgerald continues to pummel the Blue Bear, the East German champion.

Audierce: Yeah, come on.

Frankie: I got it, I got it.

Maggie: Eyes are blurring, boss.

Frankie: How many eyes you need to finish this?

Maggie: One's enough.

Frankie: Good.

Maggie: Now ... what do I do about the Bear?

Frankie: Do you know that step into the outside and hook into the liver?

Maggie: I've been doing it. She's made of steel.

Frankie: I don't want you to go to the liver this time. I want you to heel, right upon her skinny ass, understand? Right in the sciatic nerve. Just keep digging it in there digging it in. And just keep sticking her. You hear that?

Maggie: What about the ref?

Frankie: Keep yourself between the ref and the Bear and everything will just be fine.

Blue bear's trainer: This is yours. You keep your guard up. You keep it up.

Audience: Oh. Yeah!

Judge: Break, break!

Audience: Mo cuishle! Mo cuishle! Mo cuishle! Mo cuishle!

TV voice: Doctor.

Doctor: Come on. Breathe. That's it. Breathe. Good. Look at me. Concentrate on me. Breathe. Good. That's it. Breathe.

Clip 6

Frankie: All right. I'm gonna disconnect your air machine and you're gonna go to sleep. And I'll give you a shot, and you'll stay asleep. Mo cuishle means "my darling, my blood".

Voiceover: He gave her a single shot. It was enough adrenaline to do the job a few times over. He didn't want her going through this again. Then he walked out.

Unit 11

Clip 1

Dr. Rose: Never seen anything like it. Nearly blind from cataracts. I'm not sure if he can hear. His bones indicate severe arthritis. His skin has lost all elasticity, and his hands and feet are ossified. He shows all the deterioration, the infirmities, not of a newborn but a

	man well in his 80s on his way to the grave.
Queenie:	He's dying?
Dr. Rose:	His body is failing him before his life's begun.
Dr. Rose:	Where did he come from?
Queenie:	My sister's child from Lafayette. She had an unfortunate adventure. The poor child, he got the worst of it. Come out white.
Dr. Rose:	There are places for unwanted babies like these, Queenie. No room for another mouth to feed here. The Nolan Foundation, despite their good intentions, thinks this place is a large nuisance as it is, a baby.
Queenie:	You said he don't have long.
Dr. Rose:	Queenie, some creatures aren't meant to survive.
Queenie:	No, this baby, he is a miracle. It has decided just not the kind of miracle one hopes to see. Y'all listen. Y'all listen up here. We're gonna have us a visitor that's gonna be staying with us for a little while. My sister had a child and she couldn't see right by it, so ... He's known as Benjamin. Benjamin. He's not a well child, so we're gonna have to take good care of him.
Old Lady:	I have 10 children. There's not a baby I can't care for. Let me see him. God in heaven. He looks just like my ex-husband.
Queenie:	Look, he's prematurely old. Dr. Rose said he ain't got much more time on this earth.
Old Man:	Join the club.
All:	He's smiling.
Mr. Webber:	Hambert sends his remembrances to you. Are you right out of your mind? I know you ain't got all the parts it takes to make one of your own, but this ain't yours to keep. It may not even be humankind.
Queenie:	Mr. Weathers, come back here. Please. You never know what's coming for you.

Clip 2

Old Lady:	Benjamin, we are meant to lose the people we love. How else would we know how important they are to us?
Benjamin:	And one fall day, a familiar visitor came knocking on our door.
Benjamin:	You want to go with me to the drugstore?

Benjamin: She taught me how to play the piano.

All: Amen amen.

Benjamin: And she taught me what it meant to miss somebody.

Benjamin: Let's go.

Benjamin: I had gone to a brothel and had my first drink, said goodbye to one friend and buried another. In 1936, when I was coming to the end of the 17th year of my life, I packed my bag, said goodbye.

Man: Bye, Benjamin.

Benjamin: Goodbye.

Benjamin: I knew, life being what it was, I'd probably never see them again.

Lady: Bye, Mr. Benjamin.

Mr. Webber: Good luck to you, son.

Benjamin: Thank you.

Benjamin: I love you, Mama.

Queenie: I love you, too, baby. I want you to say your prayers every night, hear? Be safe, hear?

Daisy: Benjamin! Where you going?

Benjamin: To sea. I'll send you a postcard.

Daisy: From everywhere. Write me a postcard from everywhere.

Daisy: Can you imagine? He sent me a postcard from everywhere he went, every place he worked. Newfourdland, Baffin Bay, Glasgow, Liverpool, Narvik. He had gone with that Captain Mike.

Benjamin: Captain Mike had contracted for three years with Moran Brothers Tug ard Salvage. The old ship had been refitted with a diesel engine and a new sea winch. We went around Florida and up the Atlantic Seaboard. We were a crew of seven now. Captain Mike and me, Cookie, Prentiss Maryes from Wilmirgton, Delaware, Brody twins, Rich and Vic, who got along fine at sea but, for some reason, one they were or dry lard could't stard the sight of each other.

Clip 3

Benjamin: When I was 26 years old, I came home.

Other Waitress: I'm ready! I'm ready!

Queenie: I'm coming!

Other Waitress: I'm ready!

Queenie: All right, I'm coming, Miss Alfalina.

Benjamin: Queenie?

Queenie: Yes? Sweet Jesus! Oh, you're home! Oh, Lord, you came back! Let me look at you.

Benjamin's Sister: Who's that, Mama?

Queenie: Child, it's your brother, Benjamin.

Benjamin's Sister: I didn't know he was my brother.

Queenie: There's a shitload of things you don't know, child. Get on out there and finish sweeping. Come here, wash your hands, help me with the table. Go on, now. Turn around. You look like you've been born again. Younger than the springtime. I think that preacher laid hands on you gave you a second life. I knew it that moment I saw you. You were special. I tell you what, my knees are sore 'cause I've been on them every night asking the Lord, I said "God, just bring him home safely." Remember what I told you?

Benjamin: You never know what's coming for you.

Queenie: That's right. Sit down. Well, you learned anything worth repeating?

Benjamin: I'm sure I saw some things.

Queenie: Oh, you're seeing some pain. Some joy, too?

Benjamin: Sure, sure, I did.

Queenie: Yeah, that's what I want to hear. Look at you.

Benjamin: Where's Tizzy?

Queenie: Oh, baby. Mr. Weathers died in his sleep one night last April.

Benjamin: Mama, I'm so sorry.

Queenie: Don't you worry about that, baby. Yeah, well, it's only one or two of them left now. They are all just about new. Guess they're waiting their turn like everybody else, huh? I'm so glad you're back home with me! Now we're gonna have to find you a wife and a new job! That's right. Come on in here, help me with this table. Benjamin, you're wasting your time, baby. She's stone deaf. Oh, and you'll be staying in what was Mrs. DeSeroux's old room. You're too big to be rooming with anybody else.

Benjamin: It's a funny thing about coming home. Looks the same, smells the same, feels the same.

Man: Did I ever tell you I've been struck by lightning seven times? Once when I was sitting in my truck just minding my own business.

Benjamin: You'll realize what's changed is you.

Benjamin: And late one morning, not long after I have been back.

Clip 4

Benjamin: Sometimes we're on a collision course and we just don't know it. Whether it's by accident or by design, there's not a thing we can do about it. A woman in Paris was on her way to go shopping. But she had forgotten her coat, went back to get it. When she had gotten her coat, the phone had rung. So she had stopped to answer it and talked for a couple of minutes. While the woman was on the phone, Daisy was rehearsing for a performance at the Paris Opera House. And while she was rehearsing, the woman, off the phone now had gone outside to get a taxi. Now a taxi driver had dropped off a fare earlier and stopped to get a cup of coffee. And all the while, Daisy was rehearsing. And this cab driver, who dropped off the earlier fare and stopped to get the cup of coffee, he picked up the lady who was going shopping and missed getting the earlier cab. The taxi had to stop for a man crossing the street who left for the work five minutes later than he normally did, because he forgot to set his alarm. While that man late for work, was crossing the street. Daisy had finished rehearsing and was taking a shower. And while Daisy was showering, the taxi was waiting outside a boutique for the woman to pick up a package, which hadn't been wrapped yet, because the girl who was supposed to wrap it had broken up with her boyfriend the night before and forgot. When the package was wrapped, the woman, who was back in the cab was blocked by a delivery truck. All the while, Daisy was getting dressed. The delivery truck pulled away, and the taxi was able to move, while Daisy, the last to be dressed, waited for one of her friends who had broken a shoelace. While the taxi was stopped, waiting for a traffic light, Daisy and her friend came out the back of the theater. And if only one thing had happened differently, if that shoelace hadn't broken or that delivery truck had moved moments earlier or that package had been wrapped and ready because the girl hadn't broken up with her boyfriend or that man had set his alarm and got up five minutes earlier or that taxi driver hadn't stopped for a cup of coffee or that woman had remembered her coat and got into an earlier cab. Daisy and her friend would have crossed the street and the taxi would have driven by. But life being what it is, a series of interesting lives and incidents out of anyone's control, that taxi did not go by, and that driver was momentarily distracted, and that taxi hit Daisy, and her leg was crushed.

Clip 5

Carolire: I left with just the clothes on my back. I don't wanna read this now. Can you just tell me where he went?

Daisy: I don't really know.

Carolire: It's for me. 1970. I was two. "Happy Birthday". I wish I could have kissed you good night. They're all for me. Five. I wish I could have taken you to your first day of school. Six. I wish I could have been there to teach you to play the piano. 1981,13th. I wish I could have told you not to chase some boy. I wish I could have held you when you had a broken heart. I wish I could have been your father. Nothing I ever did will replace that. I guess he went to India. For what it's worth, it's never too late or in my case too early.

Benjamin: Or in my case too early, to be whoever you want to be. There's no time limit. Start whenever you want. You can change or stay the same. There are no rules to this thing. We can make the best or the worst of it. And I hope you make the best of it. I hope you see things that startle you. I hope you feel things you never felt before. I hope you meet people with a different point of view. I hope you live a life you're proud of. And if you find that you're not, I hope you have the strength to start all over again.

Daisy: He had been gone a long time.

Daisy: I'll see you next Thursday.

Kids: Good night, Miss Daisy.

Daisy: Oh good night, sweetheart. I'm sorry, we're closing. Can I help you? Are you here to pick somebody up? Why did you come back?

Daisy's daughter: Mom?

Clip 6

Daisy: Do you mind if I sit with you? I would love to hear you play.

Benjamin: Do I know you?

Daisy: And everyday I would stop by to make sure that he was comfortable.

Benjamin: No, I wasn't.

Care Staff: You just finished eating.

Benjamin: Don't think I don't know what you're doing! You're all fucking liars!

Care Staff: He doesn't believe he just had his breakfast.

Daisy: Now, why don't we see if we can't find something else for you to do?

Care Staff: I have a feeling that there's a lot of things I can't remember.

Daisy: Well, like what, sugar?

Benjamin: It's like there's this whole life I had and I can't remember what it was.

Daisy: It's okay. It's okay to forget things.

Daisy: Many times, he would simply forget who or where he was.

Care Staff: There he is. He's up there on the roof.

Daisy: It wasn't easy.

Daisy: Benjamin!

Benjamin: I can see everything! I can see the big river!

Daisy: That's right! You can see everything, sweetheart.

Benjamin: I can see the graveyard Mama's buried and all those other people.

Daisy: I want you to come down!

Benjamin: What if I could fly?

Daisy: I knew a man who could fly. You come down and I'll tell you all about him. Somebody go up there.

Daisy: He was five when I moved in. Nearly the same age I was when I had met him.

Daisy: This is the picture of Old Man Kangaroo at 5:00 in the afternoon when he had got his beautiful hind legs. The days passed and I watched as he forgot how to walk and how to talk.

Daisy: What's my name? I'm Daisy. Can you say "Daisy"?

Daisy: In 2002, they put up a new clock in that train station. And in the spring of 2003, he looked at me and I knew that he knew who I was. And then he closed his eyes as if to go to sleep.

Unit 12

Clip 1

Principal Purdy: Mr. Peabody. Thank you for coming in on such a short notice to discuss the problem with Sherman.

Mr. Peabody: Oh, it's not a problem at all, Principal Purdy. I fully expected this.

Principal Purdy: You did?

Mr. Peabody: Yes, and as with all things Sherman related, I prepared for it.

Mr. Peabody: Here is a curriculum, that takes Sherman advanced preparation into account but won't require you to have him skip one or more grades.

Principal Purdy: Mr. Peabody ...

Mr. Peabody: Here are some pre-algebra worksheets and an advanced reading list and a link to a website I created so we can start studying mandarin Chinese. It is, after all, the language of the future.

Principal Purdy: Mr. Peabody!

Mr. Peabody: I'm not saying he shouldn't study French too, Principal Purdy. I'm saying have him do both.

Principal Purdy: Mr. Peabody!

Mr. Peabody: What? Not enough? Swahili?

Principal Purdy: Sherman got into a fight today.

Mr. Peabody: Oh, dear ...

Principal Purdy: Pictures were taken, for insurance purposes.

Principal Purdy: He bit her.

Miss Grunion: I must say, it doesn't look good for you, Mr. Peabody. After all ... you are a dog.

Mr. Peabody: Who may I ask are you?

Miss Grunion: I am Miss Grunion from the Bureau of Child Safety and Protection.

Principal Purdy: We are required by law to contact them whenever there is an incident.

Mr. Peabody: Sherman has never done anything like this before. I'm sure he must have had a reason.

Principal Purdy: Well, the girl was being a bit of a bully.

Miss Grunion: Quiet, Purdy! It's normal for children to tease. It's not normal for them to bite. Clearly it's because of how he's being raised. In my opinion, a dog can never be a suitable parent to a little boy.

Mr. Peabody: I must point out, Miss Grunion, that I won the right to adopt Sherman in a court of law.

Miss Grunion: And the court can take it away from you! I'll be coming to your home tomorrow evening, to conduct an investigation. If I discover that you are in anyway an unfit parent I will see to it, Sherman is removed from your custody, permanently. I hope I made myself clear.

Mr. Peabody: Crystal.

Sherman: I'm sorry I bit her, Mr. Peabody. I won't do it again.

Mr. Peabody: You're darn too-ting. You won't do it again. This kind of wanton violence is totally unacceptable. And rather uncharacteristic, given how you feel about Mr. Gandhi? What on earth provoked it?

Sherman: She called me a dog.

Mr. Peabody: Well. All right then. Thank you for telling me. Try and get some sleep.

Sherman: I love you, Mr. Peabody.

Mr. Peabody: I have a deep regard for you as well, Sherman.

Clip 2

Sherman: You know, Penny Sigmund Freud says, that if you do not like a person it's because they remind you of something you don't like about yourself.

Penny: What do you know about Sigmund Freud?

Sherman: More than you think.

Penny: Sure. Just like you know all that stuff about George Washington not really cutting down the cherry tree. What a crock!

Sherman: But it's true!

Penny: How do you know?

Sherman: I just know!

Penny: Did you read it in a book?

Sherman: No.

Penny: See it in a movie?

Sherman: No.

Penny: Did your brainiac dad tell you?

Sherman: No!

Penny: So how do you know, Sherman? — How — Do — You — Know?

Sherman: He told me.

Penny: Who told you?

Sherman: George Washington.

Penny: George Washington.

Sherman: Yeah.

Penny: Liar.

Mr. Peabody: Don't tell her about the WABAC.

Sherman: He calls it the "WABAC".

Penny: So where have you gone it in?

Sherman: Not where, Penny. When.

Penny: Okay, smart guy. when.

Sherman: Oh, 1965, 1776, 1620, 1492, 1215, 4 ...

Penny: Can it go back to an hour ago?

Sherman: Why?

Penny: Because I can take it home. Pretend to be sick and not come to this lame dinner party.

Sherman: Hum, hum, Mr. Peabody says you should never use the WABAC to travel to a time when you existed.

Penny: How come?

Sherman:	There'll be two of you.
Penny:	Oh, Yeah. I guess the world's not ready for that.
Sherman:	Oh, well. Now that we've seen it, maybe we should go back.
Penny:	Are you kidding? Where should we go first?
Sherman:	Mr. Peabody says I'm not allowed to drive it until I'm older.
Penny:	You do everything Mr. Peabody says?
Sherman:	Yeah ...
Penny:	You know what that makes you, Sherman?
Sherman:	An obedient son.
Penny:	No. A dog.
Penny's Father:	Nice control!
Penny's Father:	Look at him, go!
Mr. Peabody:	Take it, Patty.
Mr. Peabody:	Hands up, Paul!
Penny's Mother:	Here you go.
Penny's Father:	Oh,Yeah!
Penny's Father:	Look at this.
Penny's Mother:	It's fun.
Mr. Peabody:	This is a little home-spun concoction I'd like to call: "Einstein on the beach".
Penny's Mother:	Yummy.
Mr. Peabody:	To the kids.
Penny Parents:	To the kids!
Sherman:	Mr. Peabody!
Mr. Peabody:	Sherman?
Sherman:	Can I talk to you for a second?
Mr. Peabody:	Of course. Excuse me.

Mr. Peabody: I've really hit off with Penny's parents.

Mr. Peabody: I think we can file this night under "Unqualified Success".

Sherman: I'd hold off filing it just yet.

Mr. Peabody: What do you mean?

Mr. Peabody: Where is Penny?

Sherman: Ancient Egypt ...

(GASPS)

Penny's Father: You used the WABAC? (GROWLS)

Penny's Father: What's happening, big guy? We're running low. (CONTINUES GROWLING)

Mr. Peabody: I'll be right there, Paul. How would you?

Clip 3

Sherman: I'm sorry I broke the plane, Mr. Peabody.

Mr. Peabody: Well, you should be. You could have been killed.

Penny: What are you talking about? Sherman flew a plane. He was amazing!

Mr. Peabody: Sherman destroyed a priceless historical artifact.

Penny: Whatever, you should be happy. It turns out that Sherman is not a complete and total loser after all.

Sherman: Yeah, Mr. Peabody, it turns out that I'm not a complete and total loser after all.

Mr. Peabody: Miss Peterson, stop turning my son into a hooligan.

Penny: It's not my fault he is a hooligan.

Sherman: Yeah, it's not her fault I'm a hooligan.

Mr. Peabody: Well it's certainly not my fault. I've spent the last 7 years teaching Sherman good judgment.

Penny: If you are such a great parent, why is Miss Grunion trying to take Sherman away from you?

Sherman: Is that true? Is somebody gonna take me away from you?

Mr. Peabody: No, Sherman, I'll never let that happen. You just need to trust me. Oh, dear, a black hole!

Penny: What's happening?

Mr. Peabody: If I cannot pull us out of here, we are going to be smashed to smithereens on the event horizon. There's not enough power to resist the gravitational pull. I've got to divert everything to the reverse thrusters.

Sherman: Why didn't you tell me?

Mr. Peabody: Tell you what?

Sherman: Why didn't you tell me that Miss Grunion was trying to take me away from you?

Mr. Peabody: It's not your job to worry about these things.

Sherman: You just didn't think I could handle it.

Mr. Peabody: We'll discuss it later. Now sit down.

Sherman: I don't want to discuss it later!

Mr. Peabody: Sherman, sit.

Sherman: You can't talk to me like that. I'm not a dog.

Mr. Peabody: What did you say?

Sherman: I said I'm not a dog!

Mr. Peabody: You are right, Sherman, you're not. You're just a very bad boy!

—T minus 10, 9, 8, 7, 6, 5, 4, 3, 2, 1.

Mr. Peabody: Sherman? Penny? Sherman, are you okay? Sherman?

Penny: He's gone. Where are we, anyway?

Mr. Peabody: Oh no. We are on the brink of one of history's most ferocious conflicts.

Clip 4

Sherman: So I came back and got you.

Penny: Then we ran out of gas.

Sherman: In Florence.

Penny: Went into a black hole.

Sherman: And then you died in ancient Troy.

Mr. Peabody: Died? I have a hard time believing that.

Penny and Sherman: It's true.

Sherman: But now you are here, and everything's gonna be OK!

Mr. Peabody: I told you never to come back to a time when you existed because there would be two of you.

Sherman: Yeah, but the other one of me is in ancient Egypt.

Sherman: Ah ... Who are you?

Mr. Peabody: He's you, but from another timeline.

Sherman: But I thought you said never to come back to a time when you existed!

Mr. Peabody: Exactly!

Sherman: I know, I know. But what was I supposed to do?

Sherman: Mr. Peabody died in ancient Troy.

Mr. Peabody: Died? I have a hard time believing that.

Mr. Peabody: Thank you!

Penny: What are we going to do?

Mr. Peabody: Well, for starters, both Shermans can't stay here.

Sherman: Why? We could get bunk beds.

Sherman: I was thinking the same thing!

Sherman: That's so weird. It's like we are twins.

Sherman: I was thinking that, too!

Mr. Peabody: See?

Mr. Peabody: We can't have two Shermans in the same timeline. It puts too much strain on the space-time continuum.

Mr. Peabody: What to do? What to do?

Mr. Peabody: The Petersons can't know any of this.

Penny's Father: Hey, Peabody!

Mr. Peabody: Hey!

Penny's Mother: How's it going?

Penny's Father: Patty and I are working up an appetite.

Penny's Mother: Mmm. The smells coming from your kitchen are yummy! Especially that baked Alaska!

Penny's Mother: Yeah, so what's going on here?

Penny's Father: Yeah, what's with the getups?

Penny: Toga party!

Penny's Mother: Toga party?

Mr. Peabody: Yes. It is a toga party!

Penny's Father: But what about dinner? I'm starving.

Penny's Father: Why don't we head into the dining room and tuck into those quails you've been yakking about?

Mr. Peabody: No!

Penny's Mother: Why not?

Mr. Peabody: Because it's so fun right here!

Mr. Peabody: Miss Grunion! How delightful! We were having such a good time. I almost forgot you're coming. Why don't you join the party?

Miss Grunion: I'm not here for a party! I'm here for the investigation.

Mr. Peabody: Good! Why don't you start investigating over here? Or here or here or here?

Miss Grunion: Stop waving your hands around!

Penny's Father&Penny's Mother: Sherman?

Miss Grunion: Wait! Is that?

Penny's Father&Miss Grunion: Sherman?

Penny's Father: Dos Shermans? What ... What's going on here, Peabody? (注：Dos Shermans. 为西班牙语)

Mr. Peabody: Nobody move! Sherman, I've got to get you out of here before you touch yourself.

Miss Grunion & Penny's Father & Penny's Mother: Oh!

Sherman: Mr. Peabody! You didn't die!

Mr. Peabody:	Of course I didn't die! Thank you.
Sherman:	How did you get back?
Mr. Peabody:	Well, after a few failed experiments, I hit upon a combination of bones, stone and yak fat, and constructed a rudimentary WABAC.
Mr. Peabody:	You know what they say "If at first you don't succeed, Troy, Troy again."
Mr. Peabody:	This is no time for puns! Even good ones.
Mr. Peabody:	Penny, Sherman, quickly!
Miss Grunion:	You're not going anywhere. I've seen quite enough to remove the boy, both boys, from this home.
Penny:	No, don't! Miss Grunion please! This is all my fault! I started it. I'm so sorry Sherman.
Miss Grunion:	You have nothing to apologize for, Penny. A dog should never been allowed to adopt a boy in the first place. Now come on.
Mr. Peabody:	Miss Grunion, be careful!
Penny:	What's happening?
Sherman:	Mr. Peabody! Help!
Mr. Peabody:	Sherman?
Penny's Father:	Hey! Where did the other two go?
Mr. Peabody:	Our cosmic doubles combined in order to reconcile a paradox in the space-time continuum.
Penny's Father:	OK, that makes sense.
Miss Grunion:	I don't know what just happened here, but I know it was wrong! This boy is coming with me!
Sherman:	Mr. Peabody!
Mr. Peabody:	No, Miss Grunion!
Sherman:	Oh, let me go.
Mr. Peabody:	Get back here!
Sherman:	Oh, you are hurting me!

Mr. Peabody: Oh. He bit me! He bit me!

Clip 5

Mr. Peabody: Please, before it's too late.

Sherman: Wait! Give him another chance.

Miss Grunion: He's through with chances. Now he has to pay for his mistakes.

Sherman: But I'm the one who made all the mistakes. I'm the one who used the WABAC without permission. The only mistake Mr. Peabody ever made was me.

Mr. Peabody: Sherman!

Miss Grunion: You're absolutely right, Sherman. What kind of a father could this dog ever be to a boy?

Sherman: Maybe you're right, Miss Grunion, but there is one thing you haven't considered.

Miss Grunion: What's that?

Sherman: I'm a dog, too. If being a dog means you're like Mr. Peabody who never turns his back on you and who's always there to pick you up when you fall and loves you, no matter how many times you mess up. If that's what it means to be a dog, then yeah, I'm a dog, too!

Other man: I'm a dog, too!

Other man: I'm a dog, too!

Other man: I'm a dog, too!

Other man: I'm a dog, too!

Other man: I'm a dog as well! A poodle dog!

Penny's Mother: I am a dog, too!

Penny's Father: Ditto on that dog thing!

Other man: I'm a dog, too!. .. I'm a dog, too!

Penny: I'm a dog, too!

Spartacus: I'm Spartacus.

Miss Grunion: All right, fine. You are all dogs. But you can't change the law.

Penny: I know someone who can.

All: George Washington!

Washington: We hold these truths to be self-evident, that all men and some dogs are created equal. I hereby award Mr. Peabody a presidential pardon.

Abraham Lincoln: Me, too.

Bill Clinton: I've done worse.

All: Yeah.

Clip 6

Sherman: I have an idea.

Sherman: Hey, everybody! I have an idea!

Mr. Peabody: Yes, what is it, Sherman?

Sherman: Why not go to the future?

Mr. Peabody: The future?

Sherman: I've never been there before. So it's probably not as messed up.

Mr. Peabody: Sherman, that's it! Are you thinking what I'm thinking?

Sherman: Not usually!

Mr. Peabody: It's exactly what you all just said except the total opposite! If we set the WABAC for the future and go very very fast, you'll create our own gravitational field, that's equal and opposite to the rip in the space-time continuum!

Spartacus: Ah, ha, ha, ha. Oh, my ... I don't get it.

Sherman: We're gonna fly up there, and punch that big hole in the face.

Spartacus: Yes!

Mr. Peabody: Sherman, you're a genius!

Other man: But, Peabody, how far into the future must you go?

Mr. Peabody: Just a few seconds ought to do it.

Mr. Peabody: And then we'll slingshot right back!

Penny: Are you sure this is going to work?

Sherman: Don't worry, Penny. Just remember, I'm a genius!

Mr. Peabody: Sherman, I need to reprogram the WABAC.

Sherman: All right, Mr. Peabody.

Mr. Peabody: That means you have to drive. In order to make the leap into the future, the WABAC have to go very fast, faster than it's ever gone before. Are you ready, Sherman?

Sherman: I'm ready.

Penny: Come on, Sherman, you can do it.

Sherman: Now, Mr. Peabody?

Mr. Peabody: Sherman, we need more speed.

Sherman: Now?

Mr. Peabody: Just a little more. Not yet, Sherman. Not yet. Now!

Keys

Unit 1

Clip 1

Task 1: 1. staring at 2. braces 3. they're better than you 4. intended 5. You're no different than anybody else is

Task 2: a) They let the rooms out.

b) (Omitted)

Clip 2

Task 1: a) T b) T

Task 2: a) She would like to be away from home.

b) Nothing happened.

Clip 3

Task 1: a) T b) F c)F

Task 2: a) He thinks that Forrest is a talent in military.

b) In Vietnam. The Vietnam War.

Clip 4

Task 1: 1. What's the matter 2. Calm down 3. It's my time 4. It's just my time 5. Death is just a part of life 6. we are all destined to do 7. I did the best I could 8. you make your own destiny 9. You have to do the best with what God gave you. 10. figure that out 11. Life is a box of chocolates 12. little flowers

Task 2: (Omitted)

Task 3: (Omitted)

Clip 5

Task 1: a) There is a boy in the room.

b) He has eaten some of the chocolate.

c) All about Forrest's experience in these years.

d) The kid gets his name after Forrest.

e) He is worried that his son is not smart.

Clip 6

Task 1: You died on a Saturday morning and I had you placed here under our tree. And I had that house of your father bulldozed to the ground. Mama always said dying was a part of life. I sure wish it wasn't. Little Forrest is doing just fine. He's about to start school again soon. I make his breakfast, lunch and dinner every day. I make sure he combs his hair and brushes his teeth every day. I teach him how to play ping-pong. He's really good. We fish a lot, and every night we read a book. And he's so smart, Jenny. You'd be so proud of him. I am. He wrote you a letter. He says I can't read it. I'm not supposed to. So I'll just leave it here for you. Jenny, I don't know if mama was right or if it's Lieutenant Dan. I don't know if we each have a destiny or if we're all just floating around accidental-like on a breeze. But I ... I think that maybe it's both. Maybe both are happening at the same time. I miss you, Jenny. If there's anything you need, I won't be far away.

Unit 2

Clip 1

Task 1: 1. fashion mags 2. the whole kit and caboodle 3. couldn't be better 4. policy

5. directory assistance 6. uninsurable 7. prospect 8. cutbacks

Task 2: a) F b) F

Clip 2

Task 1: 1. insane 2. hugged a perfect stranger 3. forced him onto a bus

4. cleaned up the trash downtown 5. You sailing off into that storm

Task 2: a) He thought his dad died because of rescuing him.

b) No. She just tried to persuade Truman to believe his father was dead.

Clip 3

Task 1: a) T b) F c) F d) F

Task 2: a) Because the director didn't allow her to do so.

b) Maybe.

Clip 4

Task 1: 1. Early bird gathers no moss 2. Rolling stone catches the worm 3. spontaneous

4. gamble 5. throw up 6. Blocked at every turn 7. You're not right in the head

8. I'm sure they are exaggerating 9. eat into our savings 10. a leak at the plant

Task 2: a) Because the man should not have known his name. They never met before.

Clip 5

Task 1: a) It's a great building in the world, just like the giant studio.

b) Truman's father burst into the studio. Amnesia.

c) They are concerned about Truman.

d) Everything on the show is for sale, from the actors' wardrobe, food products, to the very homes they live in.

Task 2: (Omitted)

Clip 6

Task 1: (Omitted)

Clip 7

Task 1: (Omitted)

Unit 3

Clip 1

Task 1: 1. What do you do? 2. And how do you do it? 3. hang on to my car

4. Feed the meter 5. rent is due next week 6. pulling double shifts

Task 2: a) He wants to know the secret of the man's success.

b) She doesn't believe in Chris.

Clip 2

Task 1: a) F b) T c) T

Task 2: a) He wants to get a job opportunity.

b) He doesn't want to, but he has no money.

Clip 3

Task 1: 1. Payable to the City of San Francisco 2. the full amount

3. parking ticket 4. 10:15 5. Social Services pick him up

Task 2: a) The rent is cheap there.

b) Chris permitted to paint the house.

c) Failing to pay the parking ticket.

Clip 4

Task 1: 1. trying to come up with a story 2. demonstrate qualities

3. failure to pay parking tickets 4. you're pretty determined 5. One too many

6. Jacket and tie 7. I bet you what 8. must've had on some really nice pants.

Task 2: (Omitted)

Clip 5

Task 1: 1. call sheets with the phone numbers 2. in the financial district

3. cold-calling potential 4. familiarize them with our packages.

5. match their needs and goals 6. In essence

7. turn this into this. 800,000 in commission dollars

Clip 6

Task 1: a) He succeeds in getting a job in the company.

b) He wants someone to share his happiness.

Task 2: (Omitted)

Unit 4

Clip 1

Task 1: 1. convict crew 2. courtesy 3. managed 4. lords of all creation 5. feel normal

Task 2: a) Andy helps the captain of the guards. He wins beers for his inmates. The beer makes the men feel from their hopeless prison environment.

b) No, he is different from others. He is the one who considers others' empathy, cherishes friendship and has a super brain.

Clip 2

Task 1: a) F b)T

Task 2: a) He does not adjust to the life outside Shawshank. And he wants to commit crime so that he can go "home".

b) First, you hate the word "institutionalized". Then you get used to it. Enough time passes. You get used to it so you depend on it. That is "institutionalized".

Clip 3

Task 1: 1. channel it. Filter it. Funnel it 2. wearing a number himself

3. phantom, and appartition

Task 2: (Omitted)

Clip 4

Task 1: a) T b) F c) F

Task 2: (Omitted)

Clip 5

Task 1: a) It takes less than 20 years to make his plan successful.

b) Andy's strong determination, courage and desire for freedom.

Task 2: (Omitted)

Clip 6

Task 1: 1. who committed that terrible crime 2. stamp your form

Task 2: a) 我没有一天不后悔。

b) 改过自新？狗屁不通的词。

Clip 7

Task 1: I find I'm so excited. I can barely sit still or hold a thought in my head. I think it's the excitement only a free man can feel. A free man at the start of a long journey whose conclusion is uncertain. I hope I can make it across the border. I hope to see my friend, and shake his hand. I hope the Pacific is as blue as it has been in my dreams. I hope.

Unit 5

Clip 1

Task 1: 1. Fight and you may die. Run and you may live. 2. would you be willing to trade all the days

Task 2: (Omitted)

Clip 2

Task 1: 1. you withdraw your attack 2. Slaves are made in such ways

3. he had them hanged 4. will not be ruled

Task 2: (Omitted)

Clip 3

Task 1: a) T b) F

Task 2: a) He feels remorseful, guilty, resentful for what he has done.

b) He will not stand on the wrong side and awaken himself to fight for freedom.

Clip 4

Task 1: 1. might be taken hostage 2. she were to be killed

3. Because of the way you are looking at me now

Clip 5

Task 1: (Omitted)

Task 2: (Omitted)

Clip 6

Task 1: 1. treason 2. allegiance 3. purified 4. purification

Clip 7

Task 1: a) 每个人都会死，但不是每个人都真正活过。

b) 如果我不省人事，或大声哀号，那么正中长腿下怀。

Clip 8

Task 1: Your blood dies with you. A child who is not of your line grows in my belly. Your son will not sit long on the throne, I swear it.

Unit 6

Clip 1

Task 1: a) T b) T c) F

Task 2: a) The smug students flauntered their exhaustive knowledge of the text.

b) Her first day of class is more like a baptism by fire. But she does not concede and lose confidence.

Clip 2

Task 1: (Omitted)

Task 2: a) She switches to teach modern art.

b) yes, it makes a little difference. Girls starts to think art course from a new angle, which can help them reexamine themselves.

Task 3: (Omitted)

Clip 3

Task 1: 1. calls 2. unorthodox 3. traditionalists 4. discussion 5. formal review

Task 2: a) No. she thinks Katherine is aggressive and disobeys the teaching syllabus.

b) Teach a little less modern art or she will be dismissed.

Clip 4

Task 1: (Omitted)

Task 2: a) B b) A

Task 3: a) Joan should ask Betty for advice. But she has applied to law school and would get in.

Clip 5

Task 1: 1. Attendance 2. stepping foot 3. disregard 4. subversive 5. disrespect 6. fail 7. consequences 8. threatening

Task 2: a) Betty shows apathy, vicious, blunt which embodies she has lost the freedom of soul, stubborn to the outworn rules and ideas.

b) She is a responsible, serious, passionate, and inspiring teacher.

Clip 6

Task 1: a) 不会比放弃家庭、放弃抚养孩子更后悔。我知道我在做什么，这不会让我变得更愚笨。这对你来说一定很可怕。

b) 对你来说，做家庭主妇就是出卖了自己的灵魂。她们肤浅、愚蠢、没有趣味。

Task 2: a) F b) T c) T

Clip 7

Task 1: a) F b) F

Task 2: a) She desires love which is based on honesty.

b) In Bill's eyes, Katherine is intelligent, smart, determined, independent, the one with ideas. So Bill has no confidence to catch her attention.

Clip 8

Task 1: a) She has filed for divorce and ended a marriage without love.

b) She will move to Greenwich Village and apply for law school.

Unit 7

Clip 1

Task 1: (1) on earth; (2) by blood; (3) my expectation in life is to be invisible; (4) I never expected this to happen; (5) languages, history, art, political science; (6) rewind and freeze

Task 2: a) Her father was the prince of Genovia. Since her father died, she is the natural heir to the throne of Genovia. She is royal by blood.

b) She never leads anybody at Brownies, not at Camp Fire Girls, and her expectation in life is to be invisible, and she's good at it. What's more, she doesn't want to be a princess!

Clip 2

Task 1: a) F b) F

Task 2: a) Because she wants to make Gupta out and speaks to Mia alone.

b) Helen thinks that Mia doesn't have to do this. She can get out of this whole thing right now.

Clip 3

Task 1: (1) I'm beginning to feel that corn dog; (2) blaze on up; (3) put me on hold; (4) public property; (5) last but not least; (6) diplomatic immunity; (7) function peacefully; (8) the letter of the law; (9) two such fine, honorable gentlemen serving; (10) we're not all that.

Task 2: 略

Clip 4

Task 1: a) F b) T c) F

Task 2: 言之有理即可。

Clip 5

My dearest daughter, today is your sixteenth birthday. Congratulations. I present you with this diary to fill the pages with your special thoughts, special thoughts of your wonderful life. It is a custom in my family to pass on a piece of wisdom when one reaches this age. I pass it on to you as my father passed it on to me. Amelia, courage is not the absence of fear ... but rather the judgement that something else is more important than fear. The brave may not live forever, but the cautious do not live at all. From now on, you'll be traveling the road between who you think you are, and who you can be. The key is to allow yourself to make the journey. I also want you to know. I loved your mother very much. And still think of her often. Happy birthday, my Mia. All my love, your father.

Clip 6

Task 1: a) Mia gets the courage from her father's letter and her mother helped her by telling Mia that it was OK and by supporting Mia like she has done for Mia's entire life.

b) If Mia were princess of Genovia then her thoughts and the thoughts of people smarter than Mia would be much better heard and she maybe turned those thoughts into actions.

c) The queen, herself.

Task 2: I used to be very afraid of getting up in front of people and speaking. I would get sweaty palms and my stomach would be so tied up that I wouldn't be able to eat. I would experience so much tension in my neck and shoulders that I would almost always have a headache by the time I had to speak or shortly thereafter. Each time I spoke though, I noticed afterwards that it wasn't that bad. This is a trend I've noticed throughout my life. Things I fear are never as bad in reality as I make them out to be in my mind. So one element of training for fearlessness is to simply push ourselves to do things that we fear so that we have more opportunities to develop the wisdom that the things we fear are always worse in our minds than they are when we actually experience them.

Unit 8

Clip 1

Task 1: (1) graduated from; (2) do a good job as your assistant; (3) sent letters out everywhere; (4) heard of me; (5) have no style or sense of fashion; (6) editor in chief of *The Daily Northwestern*; (7) I am not skinny or glamorous and I don't know that much about fashion.

Task 2: (a) She came to New York to be a journalist, and sent letters out everywhere, and finally got a call from Elias Clarke, and met with Sherry up at Human Resources.

(b) Because she's smart, learns fast and works hard.

Clip 2

Task 1: (1) F (2) T

Task 2: (a) She just wants to get a little credit if she does something right.

(b) He is working at the place that published some of the greatest artists of the century. It is not just a magazine. It is a shining beacon of hope.

Clip 3

Task 1: (1) That is a pathetic excuse; (2) you don't really care about this stuff; (3) I don't blame you. (4) sold your soul; (5) I mean, you don't deserve them

Task 2: a) Andrea said that she doesn't really care about fashion, and she just wanna be a journalist.

b) Emily thinks Andrea doesn't deserve the clothes because she eats carbs.

Clip 4

Task 1: a) F b) F

Task 2: Sometimes life forces us to put more weight on one thing than on another. Sometimes this priority shift means you have to forgo one goal in exchange for another; for example, you might have to tone down your professional aspirations in return for a strong relationship. But you shouldn't have to sacrifice one aspect of your life for another. After all, what's the fun of a promotion if you don't have someone to share it with?

The good news is that just because you set priorities, you don't have to sacrifice. It means you have to adjust. If you build a strong foundation for both your romantic and work life, you can prevent disruption when priorities shift. (言之有理即可)

Clip 5

Task 1: a) Miranda introduced Jacqueline to James Holt for another job, which was just so absurdly overpaid.

b) Because Jacqueline was unavailable, and no one that can do what Miranda does. What's more, Miranda shows him a list. The list of designers, photographers, editors, writers, models, all of whom were found by her, nurtured by her and have promised her they will follow her whenever and if ever she chose to leave *Runway*.

c) She can see beyond what people want, and what they need and she can choose for herself.

d) Because this isn't what she wants, and she doesn't wanna live the way Miranda lives.

Task 2: I disagree with what she does. It is not ethical. Not everyone wants to live as she does. Friends and families are more important than money, fame and fortune.(言之有理即可)

Clip 6

(Omitted)

Unit 9

Clip 1

Task 1: (1) what's going on; (2) Perfect timing. (3) have the key ingredient; (4) split up; (5) It's on your blog. (6) We're ranking girls. (7) At any given time; (8) matched up; (9) And all those expectations are expressed this way.

Task 2: a) Because Erica and he split up and what Erica said makes him feel embarrassed. He wants to revenge Erica and girls.

b) He needs the algorithm Eduardo uses to rank chess players to rank girls.

Clip 2

Task 1: a) F b) T

Task 2: a) Harvard.edu is the most prestigious e-mail address in the country, and the whole site's kind of based on the idea that girls want to go with guys who go to Harvard. What's more, the main difference between what we're talking about and MySpace or Friendster, or any of those other social networking sites is exclusivity.

b) They need a gifted programmer who's creative, and they know that Mark has been taking it in the shins. Women's groups are ready to declare a war. This could help rehabilitate his image.

Clip 3

Task 1: (1) Be right back; (2) come up with something; (3) I gotta tell you something that you're not going to believe. (4) got punched; (5) Are you kidding? (6) first of the four-step process; (7) a diversity thing; (8) It's 20 degrees outside. (9) has absolutely nothing to do

Task 2: a) He got punched by the Phoenix.

b) It wasn't because they saw pictures of hot girls. It was because they saw pictures of girls that they knew. People want to go on the Internet and check out their friends.

Clip 4

Task 1: a) F b) F

Clip 5

Task 1: a) F b) T

Task 2: a) That was a good race, and that was a fair race. And Winklevoss'll see them again.

b) They have tried talking to him themselves. They tried writing a letter. They tried the Ad Board, and they tried talking to the president of the university.

Clip 6

Task 1: (1) You set me up. (2) and you made a bad business deal with your own company. (3) on the masthead; (4) Just because I froze the account? (5) we were gonna let you parade around in your ridiculous suits; (6) You planted that story about the chicken! (7) You had me accused of animal cruelty! (8) Because I'm not coming back for 30%; (9) I wouldn't cash it.

Task 2: This episode is so real and something that so many of us struggle with. Early on, when I was just starting my blog and had limited funds, I remember swapping service with friends or hiring friends to do projects for me at a discounted rate.

Unfortunately, this never worked out the way that I planned. Either I felt uncomfortable asking friends to correct/modify work in order to get it up to my standards or, because they felt like they were doing me a favor, projects took forever to complete!

While realizing this isn't exactly what the question was about to me, it's further affirmed that it can be difficult to work with friends if no other reason than you don't want to be "mean"/critical/brutally honest even when the situation might call for it!

Unit 10

Clip 1

Task 1: 1. breathing 2. panting 3. scraping 4. waitressing 5. decent

Task 2: a) Maggie is firm and persistent to her dream, optimistic and proud.

b) Firstly, the leave of Big Willie hurts Frankie a lot. Frankie does not want to pay as much attention to other people as Willie. Secondly, Frankie has never trained a female boxer, and he is down on Maggie, the "old" girl. Last but not the least, it needs much efforts, especially the coach's love and care, to train a boxer to win the final big fight. In order to train a boxer, Frankie does not have a good relationship with his family, so he cannot easily get into it.

Clip 2

Task 1: a) F b) T

Task 2: 1. protect 2. Twist 3. obviously 4. regain 5. knockout mechanism

Clip 3

Task 1: 1. knock 2. round 3. decent 4. sweetening 5. hated 6. took a chance

Task 2: a) Agree: The coach should put the health of the trainer in the first place.

Disagree: First, no matter what the results are, it is a perfect chance to teach Maggie a lesson, which is to know herself very well. Second, this decision can stimulate the potential of Maggie, which is very important for a boxer.

b) It is an open question, anything students say that makes sense is all right.

Clip 4

Task 2: It is an open question. Anything students say that makes sense is all right. For example, I have a magical sentence: Where there is a will, there is a way. When I was preparing for the College Entrance Examination, the heavy study tasks always make me feel breathless. But once I thought of this sentence, I felt relaxed in my deep heart and confident for myself, and also gained motivation to move on.

Clip 5

Task 1: a) F b) T

Task 2: Open question. For example, I feel astonished and distressed when I see the final results. I feel worried about Maggie and hate the Blue Bear. I look forward to the following story.

Clip 6

Task 1: a) It is the topic sentence. On the one hand, it shows the good relationship and deep love between Frankie and Maggie. For Frankie, caring Maggie also makes up for his daughter as a father. On the other hand, the sentence is a clue, which draws attention of the audience and drives the plot.

b) Open question. For example, the hope for Maggie's better health and life, the enthusiasm for his career, the confidence for himself or the love for the whole world.

Task 2: Open question. Anything students say that makes sense is all right.

Agree: There is no regret for Maggie. She has got her own shot and experienced all she want. The mercy killing is the last wish for her, and will make her feel comfortable at the end of her own life.

Disagree: From Jesus's point, life is sacred and no one has the right to put other's life to an end. Life is precious. We have to struggle to live and face all kinds of difficulties directly.

Unit 11

Clip 1

Task1: 1. aren't meant to survive 2. miracle 3. ex-husband 4. prematurely 5. remembrances

Task 2: a) Firstly, if Queenie says Benjamin is abandoned by his parents, other people will dislike him and are not willing to accept him; Secondly, it will close the distance between Benjamin and other people, and people will care more for him.

b) The old people in the house are most homeless or do not receive much love from their children, so they can better understand Benjamin's poor life. They are very kind and careful to Benjamin. The atmosphere in the house is very warm.

Clip 2

Task 1: a) T b) F

Task 2: (Open question, answers to reference) I agree. Most people have the same feeling: we won't cherish people or things until we lose them. When we lose someone we love, we will start to recall the things we are through together. Everything happy or sad, will be a precious experience for us, and thus we will finally know how important they are meant to us.

Clip 3

Task 2: The two sentences are both trying to say that we should be optimistic when facing the future. No matter how bitter the situation we are in right now, it will be the past. What we should do is to be confident of ourselves and be well prepared to the future.

Clip 4

Task 1: a) At the Paris Opera House.

b) Because the girl had broken up with her boyfriend. Maybe they had an argument.

c) Six.

Task 2: No. Because those detailed sentences all reflect the first top sentence, which is the topic sentence of this part: Sometimes we're on a collision course and we just don't know it. Whether it's by accident or by design, there's not a thing we can do about it. It is not a negative saying. It is not telling people to do nothing when facing their fate. It is just the interesting and mysterious part of our fate. Because Benjamin's life is curious, the things he meets are also interesting.

Clip 5

Task 1: a) T b) T

Task 2: To be whoever you want to be. There's no time limit. Start whenever you want. You can change or stay the same. There are no rules to this thing. We can make the best or the worst of it. And I hope you make the best of it. I hope you see things that startle you. I hope you feel things you never felt before. I hope you meet people with a different point of view. I hope you live a life you're proud of. And if you find that you're not, I hope you have the strength to start all over again.

Clip 6

Discussion: a) Daisy was confused, surprised, doubtful, careful and helpless about Benjamin's suffering, but she has to persuade herself to accept this situation.

b) (Open question, answers to reference)

I think he has a happy, unforgettable and worthy life. Although it is very hard for him to start a living, thanks for the kindness and care from other people and his persistence, Benjamin continues to create miracles in his own life and is eager to meet different kinds of people and deals with different kinds of things. He has never stopped to give warmth to other people though he was abandoned by his parents when he was born, and at the same time, he has received enough warmth from other people. His life is a miracle, and he is the master of his own life. If I had a chance, I would like to be "Benjamin".

Unit 12

Clip 1

Task 1: 1. bit 2. violence 3.unacceptable 4. uncharacteristic 5.provoked 6.regard

Task 2: a) In Miss Grunio's opinion, it is normal for children to tease, but it's not normal for them to bite. Clearly it's because of how he's being raised. Especially a dog can never be a suitable parent to a little boy.

b) On the surface, it is because Penny does not believe what Sherman said and calls him a dog. The deeper reason is that Penny insults the family education of Sherman, insults Sherman's loving and respectful father, Mr. Peabody.

Clip 2

Task 1: a) F b) T

Clip 3

Task 1: 1. amazing 2. priceless historical artifact 3. complete 4. hooligan 5. judgment

Task 2: Open question

Clip 4

Task 1: 1. delightful 2. investigation 3. investigating 4. combination 5. constructed

Task 2: a) Miss Grunion works for the bureau of Child Safety and Protection. She is shrewish and has a loud voice. She insists that what she only cares about is the well-being of children, but in fact she only concentrates on all kinds of rules and bureaucrats. She thinks most parents, especially Mr. Peabody, spoil the children and even know nothing about tutoring a child. She is narrow-minded and feels dissatisfactory about Mr. Peabody, a dog that adopts a human boy.

b) Mr. Peabody does not lose his mind, for it is very natural and understandable for a parent when its child is going to be taken away. It is not a weird action but a human performance.

Clip 5

Task 1: (Omitted)

Task 2: Definitely yes. As Sherman says, although Mr. Peabody is a dog, he has done much better than many parents in tutoring children, and better be a qualified human than many human beings. He is considerate to care about the child's daily life and look further about the child's future. He has already been the model parent. So I will back him up.

Clip 6

Task 1: (Students can grasp one scene of the movie and talk about the feelings) For example, Mr. Peabody is considerate about Sherman's daily life, paying attention to his eating nutrition, and also cares about his studying, arranging the learning schedule ahead of time; Mr. Peabody concentrates on Sherman's safety, telling him not to use the WABAC without permission, but also chooses to believe in his ability to deal with things independently. In a word, on the one hand, Mr. Peabody is strict with Sherman in life and studying; on the other hand, Mr. Peabody can also give Sherman much freedom and trust to give his child confidence. That's what we have to learn from Mr. Peabody.

References

张菊芳，许明珠，杨宇威. 2012. 精选当代美国电影赏析. 上海：复旦大学出版社.

李兵绒. 2009. 经典英文电影赏析. 北京：国防工业出版社.

Lynn. A. 2005. 英语电影赏析. 北京：外语教学与研究出版社.

沈渭菊. 2012. 英语电影赏析. 北京：高等教育出版社.

http://en.wikipedia.org/wiki/

http://wenku.baidu.com/

http://movie.douban.com/